THE SLIPPERY ARE

David Green
November 2016 —

ACKNOWLEDGEMENTS
Sidney Blackmore, The Blackmore Vale Magazine,
The Brimstone Press, Du Bin, Carmen Lee, Jerry McDuff,
Joss and Linda Nizan, Reds Wang, Shuzhen Richards,
Vivienne Rudd, Jan Rutter, Brian Watts, David Wiltshire,
Zhang Xin Cheng, Zou Haitao

The Slippery are Very Crafty

Four Years in The People's Republic

David Grierson

Brimstone Press

First published in 2006
by Brimstone Press
PO Box 114
Shaftesbury SP7 8XN

www.brimstonepress.co.uk

Designed by Linda Reed and Associates
Shaftesbury SP7 8NE
Email: lindareedassoc@btconnect.com

Printed by CPI Group (UK) Ltd,
Croydon, CR0 4YY
www.cpibooks.co.uk

ISBN 13: 978-0-9548171-3-8

Contents

马年

THE YEAR OF THE HORSE *ma nian*

羊年

THE YEAR OF THE SHEEP *yang nian*

猴年

THE YEAR OF THE MONKEY *hou nian*

CONTENTS

鸡年

THE YEAR OF THE ROOSTER *ji nian*

Dedication

Keith and Jan Defter enjoying cabin service near Yichang, on the Yangtse, Hubei Province.

Vivienne Rudd being taken for a ride in Tian'anmen Square, Beijing.

Kate Wood, Ali Sedgwick and Von Buksh – The Three Gladys – in Shanghai.

DEDICATION

Left: Janice King and John Pickard roughing it in Chengdu, Sichuan Province.

Below: David and Denise Stone at the First Bend on the Yangtse, Yunnan Province.

Left: John and Elaine Affleck, back in John's family home in Tianjin after more than seventy years.

Below: The Reed Family admiring the view in Lijiang, Yunnan Province.

Left: Mark Blackham on the Great Wall at Huangyaguan, Tianjin.

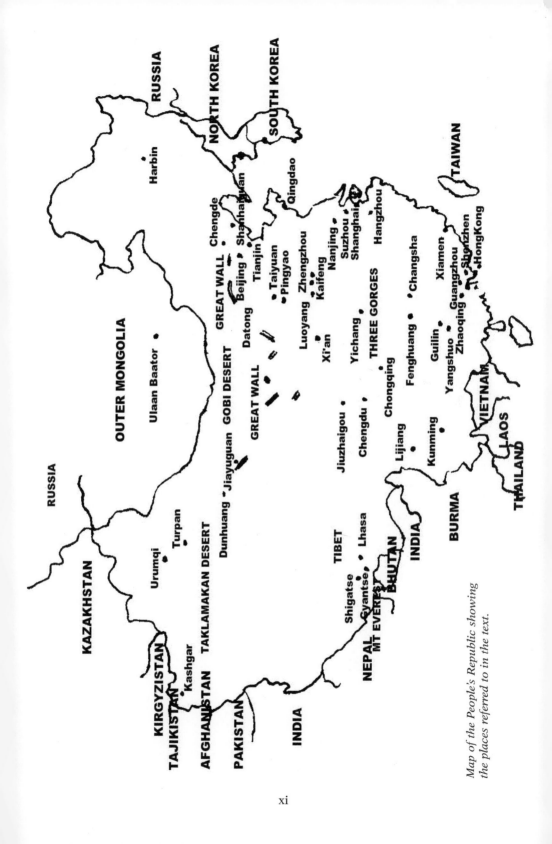

Map of the People's Republic showing
the places referred to in the text.

RUSSIA
NORTH KOREA
SOUTH KOREA
TAIWAN
Harbin
Qingdao
Chengde
Shanhaiguan
GREAT WALL
Beijing
Tianjin
Taiyuan
Pingyao
Zhengzhou
Nanjing
Suzhou
Shanghai
Hangzhou
Kaifeng
Luoyang
Xi'an
Yichang
THREE GORGES
Changsha
Xiamen
Shenzhen
HongKong
Guangzhou
Zhaoqing
Yangshuo
Guilin
Fenghuang
Chongqing
OUTER MONGOLIA
Ulaan Baator
GOBI DESERT
GREAT WALL
Datong
Dunhuang
Jiayuguan
Jiuzhaigou
Chengdu
Lijiang
Kunming
VIETNAM
LAOS
THAILAND
RUSSIA
KAZAKHSTAN
Urumqi
Turpan
TAKLAMAKAN DESERT
KIRGYZISTAN
Kashgar
TAJIKISTAN
AFGHANISTAN
PAKISTAN
TIBET
Shigatse
Gyantse
Lhasa
BHUTAN
NEPAL
MT EVEREST
INDIA
BURMA
INDIA

xi

龙年

THE YEAR OF
THE DRAGON

long nian

CHAPTER 1

First Impressions

September 2000　2000年 九月

I should make it clear at the outset that I didn't really apply for a job at the new Tianjin Rego International School. I was still recovering from an almighty blow to my ego, having been turned down for what I thought was a tailor-made job in Budapest, when I faxed a request for further details of the position as music co-ordinator and, as an afterthought, attached my CV. Further details never did arrive, and instead I was offered an interview a week or so later in Manchester. I re-read the letter. Where was Tianjin? Quite truthfully I had no idea and consulted my atlas. Ah … China! I looked up the date in my diary. 'B and L' it said. Oh well, such is life – I had friends coming to stay and would have to turn the interview down. A pity really. China might have been quite nice. I'd not really thought about it before. I made a phone call, spoke to an answering machine expressing my regrets, and thought little more about it.

However, luck was on my side at least; Brian and Linda, my friends from Leicester, were struck down with flu and cancelled at the last minute. I telephoned Manchester, and, fortunately, spoke to a real person this time. Yes, the interview panel could still see me. I hesitated no longer, packed an overnight bag and headed for the station. One day later, waiting outside an interview room somewhere near Manchester airport, looking at the embryonic prospectus and pictures of the building works going on and reading something about the ethos of the place, I decided that if I liked what the Principal had to say then I would give China a go.

Well, since that weekend just before Easter a lot of water has flowed under the bridge. There was a briefing weekend in the Lake District at which I was promoted from mere music co-ordinator to the dizzy heights of Vice Principal and Head of Upper School; there were basic Chinese lessons from Shuzhen Richards, a friend at home in Dorset; and there was my introduction to John Affleck, born in China, brought up in the British Consulate in Tientsin (as Tianjin was then called) in the 1930s, and who was really keen that I should discover some of the places he remembered as a little boy.

So, with a job, a smattering of Mandarin and a photographic mission, here I am in northern China and raring to go. *Ni hao* – welcome to both my first attempt at a little bit of Chinese, it means 'hello' by the way, and my first stab at writing something newsy since arriving a little over three weeks ago.

To set the scene, Tianjin is a huge industrial city of ten million or so to the south east of Beijing – the third or fourth biggest city in China after Shanghai, Beijing itself and, arguably, Chongqing on the Yangtse River. It seems strange to think I had not so much as heard of the place six months ago, and yet here I am – my new home for the next two years – assuming all goes well of course. Several staff have already gone native and bought bikes although, needless to say, I intend to rely on walking and taxis. When the average taxi ride costs only five *yuan* (about forty-five pence) this is hardly going to break the bank.

So far though, I have generally walked to school, a twenty-minute stroll, which, for the most part, takes me along the busy *Zijinshan Lu*, which runs parallel to what at first appeared to be a waterlogged trench but is, in fact, a disused canal. Tianjin used to be the main port for Beijing up until the early years of the last century, but these days, with the silting up of the *Hai He* River, all commercial shipping stops thirty kilometres away at the port of Tanggu on the Bohai Gulf. The canal is extraordinarily smelly now as you might imagine although I have seen people swimming in it from time to time – no doubt cooling down from the heat and humidity. About half way to school there is a crossroads which, quite honestly, used to terrify me but which I now already treat with a fair degree of confidence. This confidence, possibly misplaced, is built on the assumption that the penalties for knocking down a *lao wai* (or 'old outsider' as Europeans and other westerners are sometimes called) are likely to be draconian. The method is simple – I think of England and sally forth into the middle of the road without altering speed or direction. Everything then has to skirt around me – at least that's the theory.

This walk to school is my main bit of exercise at present although I have been swimming a few times at the Crystal Palace, one of the nearby hotels, which, superficially at least, is quite swish ... with prices to match. The hotel, however, like so much of what I see around me, seems to have been just built and then left to deteriorate – usually rather less than gracefully. There seems to be little sense of maintenance, and everywhere I look or tread I find something that isn't quite working properly or isn't quite as nature intended it to be.

The architecture, though, is striking and Tianjin's skyline quite amazing, with huge modern skyscrapers in various stages of con-struction/disrepair, many of the concrete and steel variety and often in some of the most bizarre shapes imaginable. The Tianjin TV Tower (once the tallest structure in Asia I am told) is clearly visible from my flat, but this is quite ordinary in comparison with some of the weird shapes that loom on the horizon. My favourite bears a remarkable similarity to one of the robots from the old Cadbury's Smash advert of the '80s. Other new buildings though conform so completely to the pictures you see of communist modernity that I suspect they could be found no place else other than China. However, alongside all of these images of wondrous wealth there is a lot of run-down housing and other areas are little short of squalid.

Immediately outside my flat, which consists of kitchen, toilet/bathroom, living room and bedroom (plus small balcony), there is an almost twenty-four hour street market where you can buy a lot of extraordinary things to cook yourself (at ridiculously cheap prices) as well as a number of restaurants – Tianjin is literally burst-ing with places to eat. Deep fried dough twists and Shandong noodles are particular favourites. I had a delicious bowl of stir-fried chicken with peppers and cashew nuts plus a huge portion of steamed rice for just eight *yuan* last night – rather less than seventy-five pence. (I left about a third too – there was simply too much.) I fear my metabolism is already showing itself to be inferior to that of the Chinese – most people I come across seem wonderfully slim, although, to be honest, there are quite a number of porkers amongst the children.

Weekdays, I set my alarm for a quarter to seven and switch on the BBC World Service, which I can generally get, provided I move slowly around my flat. Short wave radio signals evidently don't like sudden movement. But I am usually already awake, often being roused from my slumbers by a curious man with a three-wheeler

Ready, Steady, Go! Gillingham Station, North Dorset. August 2000.

bike, a cart full of packaging material and a voice for all the world like Aladdin's Uncle Abanazar. Clearly the Chinese for 'Any old cardboard?' is a little like 'New lamps for old!' I can hear him as I write and he seems to have brought a friend with him today – or maybe she is a rival trader. In any case it's very noisy but very nice all the same. Tianjin is, in fact, extraordinarily noisy; cars of course, people talking or rather shouting at each other, and the constant 'ting' of bicycle bells. But amidst all of this you will often see a solitary figure engaged in *tai chi* or someone just squatting on the pavement (or the road), possibly deep in thought, who knows, but certainly oblivious to his surroundings.

I managed a partial escape from the noise of the city myself when I paid my first visit to the Friendship Store – a rather upmarket department store, crammed full of staff but with only a light sprinkling of customers. A rather skilful piece of mime on my part was sufficient to tell Shop Assistant Number 1 what I wanted. 'Yes!' they did sell nail scissors and she proudly took me to the locked display case where I saw the perfect pair for eleven *yuan* (about one pound). 'Yes, I would like them.'

Left: Deep fried dough twists – a Tianjin speciality and perfect high cholesterol breakfast.

Below: Noodle restaurant (long since demolished) off Zijin Shan Lu, Tianjin.

Left: Panshan, to the north of Tianjin – my first experience of the China of the picture books.

The order of events then runs roughly as follows: Assistant Number 1 attracts the attention of Assistant i/c Nail Scissors who in turn finds the man (presumably the Floor Manager) who has the key to the display case. (He had about sixty keys on his ring although, to give him his due, he did manage to find the correct one within an acceptable amount of time.) Out come the nail scissors, plus three or more identical pairs, from which I was required to make an informed choice. I finally settled on pair A and proffered my eleven *yuan*. Oh that life was so simple. Assistant Number 1, or was it Number 2, I forget, but anyway one of them fills in a form, in triplicate, and points me to a cash booth a little way down the aisle. I leave the scissors in the safety of three pairs of hands while I take the forms to the aforementioned booth. I pay, the forms are duly stamped, the cashier takes one and gives me two forms back, I present them to the three people waiting at the nail scissors cabinet, they examine them, take one, impale it on a little spike, and then, with no little ceremony, give me my scissors, surreptitiously slipping the third form into the plastic bag. '*Xie xie*' I say. '*Mei guanxi*' they reply in unison.

Away from Tianjin, I have already enjoyed my first day out, when I took the train to the mountains at Panshan about one hundred kilometres to the north of the city. This was like the China you see in the pictures pinned on the walls of takeaway restaurants back home – high peaks dotted with pagodas and temples; a welcome change from Tianjin itself which is flat and sprawling and desperately polluted.

Nevertheless I really love it here – at the moment at any rate, and every day brings some new experience – often to despair over and/or laugh at. Last Saturday for instance I went on another shopping spree, to a huge Carrefour in the city centre. I bought a DVD player and a few other things – amongst them a set of coat hangers. When it came to the check out, the coat hangers were unpriced so were whisked away and put under the counter. No arguments and no questions – I simply wasn't allowed to have them. Amongst the purchases I was allowed to take away though was a tin of 'Licky Dog' shoe polish and a bottle of 'spanking' as opposed to 'sparkling' wine. I intend starting a collection of such *objects d'art*.

So far I am enjoying all aspects of my work, which is far less stressful than it was back in England. Classes are small, and despite the language difficulties, the vast majority of children are making good progress and really keen to learn. The time too, really flies by.

And whilst our official working day is significantly longer than I am used to (8.00 a.m. – 5.00 p.m.), thereafter it is expected that we finish. How unlike England, when for many teachers, myself included I hasten to add, the day would barely be half way through.

But that's all for now. Apologies that it is a circular letter, but at the moment I don't have the internet at home and rely on short bursts of activity in my classroom and at the local cyber café which is just around the corner.

CHAPTER 2

A Great Leap Forward

October 2000　2000年 十月

The writing of this particular letter is a momentous occasion for me. At long last I've given in to public pressure and invested in a computer of my own. So, at this very moment I'm sitting at my desk in my flat and writing to you. I hope you appreciate this – a small step for mankind maybe, but giant leap forward for me.

Buying the computer was, in itself, both an education and an adventure. I'd listened to lots of advice both in UK and here in China about the wisdom of buying at home or abroad, whether to go for a laptop or 'proper' job, and the sense (or lack of it) of going for a PC as opposed to an AppleMac. Well, in the end I've bought a proper Chinese PC, and, so far, everything is OK. Long may it continue as the instruction books are entirely in Chinese. 'But how can this be possibly classed as an adventure?' I hear you ask. The answer is simple – buying a computer over here is a bit like buying a bespoke suit – it is made to measure. None of your 'off the peg' jobs for me.

Initially I took Barbara, our Head of ICT ('Information-and-Communications-Technology' to the uninitiated) together with our Chinese lab technician along to look at various gadgets and bits, and last week, XiaoWang (Little Wang – the technician) and I went again and agreed precisely what I wanted – a bit of this, a bit of that, you know the sort of thing. The price was settled – after a lot of hard bargaining, but, strangely, without any software. Not to worry – Little Wang knew where to get these things at bargain prices. Sure enough, no sooner had we got out of the computer shop than we were approached by a series of shifty oriental men in long coats anxious to sell us this, that and t'other. (My computer doesn't like this last word – it suggests 'toothier' as an alternative.) We followed this man through a series of dark alleys and up six flights of stairs to his flat. Inside, his wife was knitting. She got up and showed us into the back room where there were dozen of plastic crates containing pirated computer software. Programmes that, I am told, would cost fifty pounds or more in UK were all available for eight *yuan* – approximately seventy-five pence each. So I bought what I was told I needed and a good bit more besides for a little over three pounds fifty.

Little Wang and I went back last weekend, and four hours later left the shop – the staff having built the computer from its various components and installed the software in front of our very eyes. All rather different from 'Dixons' I think. With luck it will help me keep in touch with friends at home rather more easily. Rather less easily though, I have recently discovered that you can rarely pay with plastic over here, and with only three international ATMs in the whole city (at least I've only found three) getting the money was a bit of an ordeal to say the least. The machines, which only allow you to take three thousand *yuan* out at a time, are spread over the city and are, more often than not, out of order. Hardly twenty-first century maybe, but, I am coming to realise, very Chinese all the same.

Last weekend I visited the Great Wall for the first time, at the place where it eventually reaches the Yellow Sea – Shanhaiguan, situated on the Bohai Gulf. I had a wonderful weekend, having travelled by train to the nearest station – Qinhuangdao, caught a local bus to Shanhaiguan Bus Depot and thereafter walked or took taxis. When the likes of President Nixon can come up with such gems as: 'This sure is a great wall!' it hardly needs me to tell you that it really is stunning. In particular, the section to the north of Shanhaiguan itself where I was able to take a cable car up before taking my life in my hands and scrambling back down a great section of unrestored 'Wild Wall', as it is known, took my breath away – figuratively and literally. Possibly even more memorable though, there was, at the base of Mount Jiaoshan, a most dazzling lake that must rank as just about *the* most beautiful thing I've seen so far – a definite port of call next year when the visitors start arriving.

Not all was plain sailing though, and finding a place for the night was tricky to say the least. MuRong, our School secretary, knew Shanhaiguan well and suggested a particular hotel the details of which I gave to my taxi driver. He took me there and, fortunately, went in with me as I had not got enough change for the fare. As the

*The demon barber of
Zijin Shan Lu, Tianjin*

*Left: Enjoying a beer
and kebab in one of
Tianjin's many street
cafes.*

*Below: One of the
many busy bicycle
lanes in Tianjin.*

A view from Mount Jiaoshan near Shanhaiguan where the Great Wall meets the sea, Hebei Province.

receptionists/cashiers/doormen ... the lot set about changing my fifty *yuan* note (four pounds fifty pence or so) another group of well wishers watched as I was registered for an overnight stay. 'Could I have your passport please Mr. Grierson?' 'Uhh, no! The police have it in Tianjin where they are processing it in order to give me a work permit and residents card.' To cut a long story short, they wouldn't allow me to stay, so the taxi driver took me to hotel number two. Much, much nicer, but the same story. 'We will get in trouble with the police,' they said, and they meant it. Well! I couldn't believe they would allow one of HM's subjects to wander the streets, but despite my protestations (and those of the Chinese taxi driver) they wouldn't let me stay, and 'No' they didn't think any hotel in the town would have me. The taxi driver then took over, demanded the equivalent of the Chinese Yellow Pages (highly appropriate I thought) and proceeded to make a series of phone calls, eventually tracking down a place that would put me up. He took me there, watched me as I completed the necessary registration forms and bid me goodnight. I wonder whether a taxi driver back home would show the same care and concern for a stranger there? I doubt it somehow.

The Shanhaiguan Majestic sort of lived up to its name in that it was big, but in reality it had little else going for it. I was in Room 508, yet I don't think there were any other residents there at all. Certainly no one else ate in the restaurant which could easily have accommodated a hundred or more and had a staff to match. Needless to say I felt rather self-conscious. The hotel brochure was wonderful though with instructions along the lines of...

'Insert the keyplate into the electrified hole' (I wouldn't), 'Visit the banquet hall – at the frist floor side building filted with sound facilities and unsteady stage' (I didn't) and a threat 'Our hotel has the right to fine or refuse to receive those who break rules and regulations AND CAN'T LISTEN INSPITE OF TALKING AROUND.' Being a schoolteacher I particularly liked the hint of reprimand in those capitals.

There was a knock on my door at 8.30 the following morning. Was I to be evicted, *sans* passport, and locked up for failing to set foot on the unsteady stage? I needn't have worried. It was the taxi driver. Had I had a good night? Did I want a taxi for the day? Yes I did.

CHAPTER 3

Good News from a Far Country

November 2000   2000年 十一月

Not quite a letter from Tianjin this time, as I've just come back from a few days away in Qingdao – on the coast a little way down from Tianjin – a little way by Chinese standards that is. If you're looking for it on a map (i.e. if you're one of the 'want-to-know' sorts – as I know you are) you may find it spelt Tsingtao like the beer – it's still the same place. I say 'a little way down', but I forget China is such a big place. It took just under two hours by air, and I came back on the train, which was an eleven hour journey. That should give you some idea of the scale of the map.

Tianjin airport is quite a reasonable place actually – lots of internal flights of course, plus a couple of short hauls to Japan, Korea (North and South) and one weekly jaunt to Moscow. Getting a ticket is also much easier than buying a train ticket, would you believe. I started trying to make my Qingdao arrangements about a week before I left and originally wanted to go by rail. I was told that there were two or three trains a day from Tianjin so I initially tried for a 'soft class' sleeper. However I couldn't get a ticket. To go soft class to Qingdao, I would have to go back up the line to Beijing in order to be able to reserve the berth – presumably they don't want to disturb passengers at intermediate stops. Not totally unreasonable, I suppose, but a bit irritating for me none the less. So I tried for a soft class seat – but no, they had none on that service. Next, I tried for a hard class sleeper – and here I was told 'maybe' – a word that seems to be given as a response to almost any mildly troublesome question. When could they let me know? Maybe tomorrow. Well tomorrow never did come and in the end I decided to fly. I made the decision late on Saturday afternoon and at crack of dawn on the Sunday morning a small bespectacled gentleman with an airline ticket came round to my flat. I paid the fare of about fifty pounds in cash (it's all cash here as I have mentioned before) and duly arrived at the airport on the Monday morning. It was as easy as that. Three cheers for private enterprise.

I shared the taxi to the airport with Jeanne, a friend from school, who was flying to Shanghai and whose flight left around midday. I knew I was going to be early for my flight, which wasn't until 2.15 p.m., but at the time it seemed sensible to share the taxi. However, my flight was delayed by well over two hours and so I had a five hour wait. Hardly the best way to start to the holidays. Now, Tianjin airport might be 'quite reasonable' as I said before, but five hours without a coffee shop, foreign language book shop, bar, or indeed book to read (I had only brought my travel books and these had already been checked in) is a long, long time. But two good things did come out of it: number one, I bought a book called 'Photographs of Old Tianjin' at the airport nicknack shop which was fascinating. I can't read any of the text but as the photos are almost entirely reproduced from old postcards there are quite a number of English and German captions while many of the messages on the back have been copied too and are quite legible. I spent the entire five hours pouring over the pictures and now, I believe, probably know more about the place than the average citizen.

The other good thing to come out of the wait was the fact that I arrived in Qingdao at night. Qingdao airport is small, about twenty-five kilometres away from the city centre, and as I didn't know how I was going to get to the town itself, I asked a young man (who looked as though he might speak some English) if there was a bus service. Fortunately he did speak a little, 'Yes' there was a bus, but, as he was going to Qingdao as well, I could, if I wished, share his taxi, which his firm was paying for anyway. Great, I'd fallen on my feet. 'What about my hotel? Where was I staying?' Well, as I had expected to arrive in daylight I was hoping to wander around and choose something I liked the look of. As it was going to be 7.00 p.m. or so before arriving in the town, this was a bit more problematical. *'Mei guanxi'* the young man said. 'No problem. I know a good hotel!' Which he did. He booked me in for three nights, negotiated a 15%

discount and got breakfast included as well. By 7.15 p.m. I was already in a local taxi being taken down to the sea front. My life seems to be a series of encounters with good Samaritans – long may it continue.

One of the first things I did was read the hotel brochure of course. It kept me chuckling for so long that I actually took a copy back with me. The HiSense Hotel is new. 'It just like a new brilliant star in the sky' it proclaims boldly. (I could hear Chinese voices in my head when I read that.) But they were right, because 'you can enjoy the sea weaves of the Yellow sea and the night view of the city from your rom.' I did.

Monday night was very warm and I was able to wander down the promenade in just a T-shirt. I strolled along the pier and had my photo taken and then I drifted down to the pavilion at the end that I thought had a familiar look about it. It is, in fact, the logo that you see on the Tsingtao beer cans and bottles in UK. So, yes, I did recognise it and now I've been there, I shall, henceforth, drink my beer with a knowing air.

On Tuesday morning, my first job after breakfast, (which wasn't really what I fancied – give me Marmite any day) was to go down to the station to get my train ticket back. I really wanted to try the long distance trains. Well, there was no English anywhere, neither was there any *pinyin* (which is the 'Romanised' Chinese writing) either of which would have made life that bit easier. However, I did recognise the Chinese characters for Tianjin and was very proud of myself when I deciphered that there was a train (route 2540) at 21.26 bound for some unknown destination, maybe, but which stopped at Tianjin at 07.58. I was going to get my sleeper.

Or so I thought. Perversely, I am sure that, had I been in the company of a Chinese person, I would have failed, and that it was only my dogged determination to get a berth on the train that enabled me to succeed. I had looked up the words and phrases for 'soft class', 'berth' and 'seat', and wrote down the times, the train number and the rest. All was clear to them, I know it was, but it still took thirty minutes hard bargaining to end up with my ticket and reservation which cost me somewhere between twenty and twenty-five pounds – about half the price of the plane as I had expected. I'm not put off trains, but travelling by air is going to be a lot easier in future I feel.

Having succeeded in my mission it was time to celebrate. It was coffee time, and as luck would have it, there is a McDonalds and a KFC just by the station. Although I rarely go into either in the UK, in a foreign country they are very welcome sights. A cup of coffee which could be described as repellent in England is definitely on the plus side of OK in China, and the deep fried teabag they called a pineapple fritter was like manna from heaven. I celebrated my ticket success in great style and ordered an extra dollop of ice-cream.

Qingdao is a very strange mix of old Chinese, new modernist Chinese and, would you believe, German architecture. Qingdao Station looks for all the world like a cross between a *bahnhof* and a *schloss*, and there are many other buildings in the town with the same appearance. In fact, I was wandering through some streets on Tuesday afternoon, looking at some of the villas, and thinking how like Stuttgart is was (what it is to be a seasoned traveller) only to discover, the following day, that most of the furniture in one of the National-Trusty-sort of buildings had all its furniture made in Stuttgart in the early 1900s! Perhaps I am more perceptive than I give myself credit for. Incidentally, displayed in the same building was Chairman Mao's bed – but this was *not* made in Germany – oh no, this was the product of 'The Qingdao Number One Wood Working Factory'. Well, what did you expect? The reasons why the Germans had such a foothold in Qingdao in the first part of the twentieth century are long and complicated, but the legacies of the buildings and Tsingtao beer (which is brewed from local spring water the German way) remain to make the whole place a real delight, and yet another point of call on the visitor circuit.

One of the highlights of Wednesday was the Naval Museum where I went into my very first submarine (decommissioned four or five years ago) and into an American aircraft shot down by the Chinese forces for spying. Having recently seen the film 'Memphis Belle' I could really sense it all, (a bit like crossing a ley line) and was particularly pleased I was going to return to Tianjin by train. I also enjoyed the Catholic Church, which had recently been restored following the abuses of the Cultural Revolution, and which, along with the Christian Church are both thriving in Qingdao. I particularly liked the distinction the Chinese drew between Catholics and Christians. Both had a terrific atmosphere about them, the German-Protestant ethic of the latter being reinforced by such notices as

Qingdao, Shandong Province, with its mixture of modern Chinese and twentieth century European architecture. (Connoisseurs may recognise the pavilion in the bay as the Tsingtao beer logo.)

'Keep Clean'. I wasn't tempted by the 'Marine Products Museum' however, which I think was an aquarium. You see enough of those in the restaurants.

I spent Thursday in the Laoshan Mountains having booked a trip there with my hotel. It turned out, initially, that I was the only passenger, with a guide who spoke not one word of English. After about twenty-five minutes driving around the suburbs of Qingdao, I was surprised to see that we were back at the hotel and I wondered, as well I might, if I had got the right tour or if I'd taken a highlights-of-the-town tour by mistake. I needn't have worried. (In fact it seems you need never worry in China. Maybe they are just not worriers by nature.) My guide simply went into the hotel and five minutes later returned with one of the receptionists who had been excused her duties for the day and who was to act as my personal interpreter.

Five minutes later we had stopped on the seafront. 'Where are we?' I asked. 'The Pearl' she replied. 'What is there?' 'I do not know.

I have never been before'. It turned out to be one of those places that make jewellery but at least there was a soft-sell approach about it. *Wo bu yao* is perhaps the most useful phrase in Chinese. 'I don't want it'. The Chinese love to hear me say it and frequently encourage repetition. I don't know why. The jewellery was quite nice I suppose, but what really took my fancy was a mannequin in a dusty glass case, slumped on her right shoulder, and with one of her hands lying ghoulishly on the ground in front of her. Alas, the lady was not for buying.

When we returned to the bus, a few other passengers joined us, although I still had my personal interpreter who admitted she knew nothing but who was able to make a few pithy comments from time to time. Her Western name was 'Hedy' after, I suppose Hedy Lamarr. She used to call herself 'Rose' she told me, but having seen 'Titanic' decided to change her name. I nodded as though I understood what she was talking about. Perhaps if someone out there has seen the film they can enlighten me? One of the people on the bus was a very very Chinese girl with an enigmatic logo on her T-shirt. 'Town Step City Try' it said, bold as brass. She also had a very, very loud voice, but it wasn't until she adjusted her microphone level and turned on the reverb that I realised that she was the new tour guide and was telling the passengers about the trip ahead. She had no need for her microphone though with or without the reverberation. She would wax lyrical for two or three minutes or so and then my interpreter would do her bit, point at something and say 'Very pretty' or 'Interesting' and I would nod in total agreement.

Laoshan is only about twenty kilometres from Qingdao and truly spectacular. Autumn colours, little rivers and bridges, waterfalls, and hundreds of Chinese tourists – one particular group of whom all wore identical yellow caps, presumably to distinguish them from the hordes of other tourists. I told my interpreter that I expected they were an outing of workers from the 'Qingdao Number One Yellow Cap Factory', which she found mildly amusing. I did too, I might add. The drive along the cliff tops there and back was quite awe inspiring, and I loved the little boats bobbing about in the water. I wondered what was strange about them and it was only after several minutes that I cottoned onto the fact that they were all in shades of brown – i.e. natural (or presumably tarred/creosoted) wood. I hope my photos come out well – they had a tremendous charm about them.

Thursday evening arrived all too soon; I caught my train back and travelled in my soft class sleeper very comfortably indeed. It was certainly worth the battle. The soundness of my sleep was perhaps a bit surprising since I had had an unfortunate experience a little while before. 'The Saga of the Severed Scrotum' was mildly unpleasant to say the least. To cut a long story short, I was having a quick shower in my hotel room before catching the train, and nicked myself with a bit of jagged fingernail (not deliberately I hasten to add). I thought nothing of it until I stepped out of the shower and saw all the blood swirling round the plughole. It was just like 'Psycho'. I was really frightened, obviously thinking I might have done myself a lot of damage. I gingerly investigated (very gingerly actually, as I didn't want to pull myself apart) and tried to staunch the flow with my towel which, after a bit of dabbing became very bloody indeed. I had some Kleenex with me so I patched myself up with some wadding (I didn't fancy Elastoplasts) and put on my swimming trunks to hold myself together. (Do you know that bit from 'Catch 22' when they unzip his bomber jacket? – well it was just like that, except in reverse of course) I was OK, but when I came to check out of the hotel, the staff had obviously checked my room, noticed the bloody towel and told me I must pay for the cleaning of same. 'Don't worry,' I said. 'It's OK, and I'm OK.' And quick as a flash I had the good sense to say: 'I had a bit of a nose bleed.'

CHAPTER 4

'Ristmas Merrych' to One and All

December 2000   2000年 十二月

Herewith, my anxiously awaited Christmas newsletter. I thought I'd send it a bit early as I know from personal experience just how long Christmas circulars take to read and just how little time and inclination people seem to have to settle down to read them. I hope this one is worth the effort.

A recent e-mail from a friend in Dorset said how exciting and foreign my life in China seemed to be. Although this is hardly surprising, as I become more acclimatised and my every day existence takes on something more akin to a routine, I am beginning to find many aspects of daily living totally without any form of surprise at all. As this is probably a bit of a pity, on a recent away-day to Beijing, I jotted down absolutely everything I could think of in connection with my weekday life that could be remotely described as 'exciting and foreign'. Here goes.

First and foremost, getting up, having my breakfast, reading the e-mails and setting off to school has been got down to a fairly fine art. Although the vagaries of China Telecom make logging onto the internet something less than a dead cert., I can usually manage to read the 'post' in between getting washed, shaved, dressed etc. Watching that little lozenge at the bottom of the screen can be a hellishly tedious job though, so it's sensible to have a few early morning chores lined up to help pass the time.

My walk to school takes about twenty minutes and, yes, I still walk almost every morning, although, I have to confess, taxis home at five o'clock and at about forty-five pence a go are sometimes too much of a temptation. I leave at about twenty-five to eight, complete, these crisp, bright mornings, with my extraordinarily dashing Afghan mujahedin rebel's hat (bought in a street market in Ipswich) and set off past the scruffy pavement cafes which have already been doing a brisk business for some time. Flat pancakey things, deep-fried dough twists, naan bread (Chinese style) or bowls of noodles seem to be the local specialities, but as I've already had an 'English breakfast' in my apartment I generally give them a miss. I don't mean a fry-up of course; neither do I mean toast and marmalade, or cereals and coffee for that matter. In fact, on second thoughts it's not really an English breakfast at all. Two cups of tea, bread and Marmite (stocks are running low now) and, maybe if I'm feeling extravagant, a banana with a splash as opposed to a dollop of yoghurt on it. Yoghurt comes thin in the far east, but is delicious and sets me up for the morning.

My walk takes me past a barbers – already doing a brisk business – and a couple of bicycle repair stands (hardly shops or even stalls for that matter) which are always busy with customers getting punctures or chains fixed (jobs for the specialist). Others can be seen pumping up their tyres, for which there are ancient polythene bags attached to nearby trees for people to leave payment. A very honest race the Chinese. Almost everyone rides bikes, mostly of the old sit-up-and-beg sort, and I am told that China is now the only place where these 'Flying Pigeons' as they are called are still made. Children being taken by bike by their parents or grandparents to school, (one child per family of course) regularly turn and stare (perhaps it's the hat), a few wave and you get the occasional 'Hello' which makes me feel a bit of a Tianjin celebrity. In fact, it is the very absence of these reactions in Beijing that make you realise you are a total nobody most of the time. Give me Tianjin any day.

There are usually a dozen or so people doing *tai chi* (or *tai ji* in 'proper' pinyin) on the way, which, together with a factory hoarding proclaiming 'China North Industries Corporation' helps me remember that despite the familiarity of it all, I am in a far-off land. One man I see every morning, rooted to the spot, is focussing all his attention on a nondescript tree. Another, a lady probably in her mid sixties, stands more or less still yet keeps a tennis ball (or sometimes a shuttlecock) in the air with her feet, juggling it from one foot to the other with incredible skill. (I'm not sure whether you can use the word dextrous for feet, but if you can, she is.) A third person simply walks backwards along the school drive, but as he has less grace than the other two, he could be a novice or perhaps simply recovering from the excesses of the night before. I don't suppose I ever will know for sure.

As you may know, China is undertaking a massive census of its entire population involving five million data collectors alone. Although one reads that boys out number the girls in China, I see no evidence of this in the cities. Matters might be very different in the countryside though and one shudders to think why.I have heard on the BBC World Service that the Chinese government is worried about people telling the truth to the census officers and it has promised a degree of clemency to families found breaking the one child per family law. I'm not too sure how much comfort to take from this assurance though. Others I have spoken to are more concerned about the longer-term social consequences of an entire generation growing up without brothers or sisters.

With the onset of winter and the inevitable colds, the spitting is getting worse by the day. The national hobby of 'hoicking' and 'gobbing' is almost as hilarious as it is revolting, and efforts by the Chinese government to outlaw the practice seem to have had little effect here. Even the most refined looking adults will turn away and spit mid-sentence if the mood takes them. If mere coughs and sneezes spread diseases, then it is hardly surprising that Asian flu originates in this part of the world. As some sort of health precaution, many Chinese, children and adults, wear lint face masks in the flu season, but whether these are to keep the germs in or out I'm not too sure. In addition, many of the ladies cover their entire faces with pieces of net or perhaps a thin scarf giving them an air of the exotic totally at odds with their bikes. We had flu jabs at School the other day but I chickened out. Dare I say it, I've never had flu in my life so I'm hoping I have an in-built immunity to the thing. We shall see.

The children I teach are a delight although I still find the youngest ones a significant challenge. Working with Year 2 and above is fine – I teach up to Year 11 – but teachers in Reception and Year 1 are of a different breed. In my afternoon lessons I often get a couple of little ones who fall asleep, and if they're awake but just not interested, they don't even bother to feign concentration. At least the older children will generally pretend things are absorbing. I do a lunch duty three times a week, which is generally a lot of fun – not a word I would ever have thought of using in connection with school duties before. The Year 7s and below are so keen to talk to you, and the real tinies just come up and hug you. I love it. The older ones are equally pleasant although I must confess that, as Head of the Secondary School, I have a bit of bother with two Year 10 boys for whom uniform is something of an anathema. But, goodness me, if this is the only thing that I causing me any stress then things can't be too bad.

There are sixteen nationalities represented at the school, and the pupils' names take some getting used to. As well as Ting Wei (boy), we have the delightfully named Wei Ting (girl) – both Taiwanese I believe. We also have a Korean girl called Eun (pronounced like the French 'un'). The first time I spoke to her she was with a couple of Korean friends who had adopted English names. 'What are you all called?' I asked. 'Christie!' said one girl, 'Tommy!' said the boy. I looked at number three. 'Eun!' she said. So, of course I repeated the question but a little more slowly this time. 'Eun!' she said, a second time. 'Talk about dense' I thought rather uncharitably/unprofessionally. 'No!' I said, with a touch of exasperation in my voice, 'Here is Christie, here is Tommy, I am Mr. Grierson, and you are …?' (I waited expectantly) 'Eun!' she exclaimed for a third time. 'Never mind,' I replied, 'we can talk later'. I wandered off making a mental note to avoid the girl at all costs in future.

We have eight thirty-five minute lessons a day – usually doubles in the senior school – considerably shorter periods of time than I am used to, and even after a term, I am still planning far too much. But, something really good is happening in my classes that I have long felt ought to be the case, and that is, the pupils are, by and large, working harder than I am. I maybe under some illusion here, but I genuinely do think this to be true, and long may it continue. On the down side, I am only teaching music at the moment and am greatly missing the variety that drama injected into my life. A-level work, too, won't begin until next year, so the intellectual challenge of that is also absent. I am fairly confident that A-level music will run next year, and I intend doing my utmost to get drama on to the timetable. Having been rapidly promoted from music co-ordinator (the job I initially applied for) to Vice Principal (my title in our new glossy school prospectus) I hope to have a bit of clout here.

For my own personal challenges, I am pleased with the progress I have made with computers. Although I am far from advanced, I send e-mails round the world and do a host of other things that I had previously thought were the prerogative of a nerdish fringe. Cooking with a wok has been a non-starter though – I eat out too much. Similarly my knowledge of Chinese music and theatre is no further advanced than it was six months ago, although a few days back I did entertain a crowd of shoppers in one of the antique markets by playing 'I'm Dreaming of a White Christmas' on a sort of two-stringed fiddle with integral bow known as an *erhu*. However, I am most disappointed that my Chinese studies have not progressed although I am determined to improve in the New Year. This afternoon I am setting out to buy 'Chinese for Children' Books 1, 2 and 3 (the course book we use at School) from the local book shop – that is if I can find any copies beneath the mounds of 'Hali Bote' recently published over here – on green paper for some reason. Practise saying 'Hali Bote' in a variety of ways and you might just work out what I am talking about. (The answer is 'Harry Potter' of course.).

The contents of the shops never cease to amaze me, and this morning I actually found three shrink-wrapped currant scones and some cans of Schweppes ginger ale. Needless to say I bought the former and quite a few of the latter, although, in the taxi coming home, I wondered about the wisdom of doing this. Hitherto, I had maintained that the only reason I poured myself such large whiskies was to deaden the repellent taste of Chinese ginger ale. The scones too were pretty dry, but beggars can't be choosers and scones have never really been a speciality of mine either.

Going to Beijing, about a hundred kilometres away, is exciting, and I have been three times now (including both last weekend and the one before). The fast double-decker trains from Tianjin take just over one hour and are very comfortable. I also have the luxury of being able to buy my tickets from the foreigners' ticket office, which, in Tianjin, not only has lots of well stocked fish tanks to keep you amused, but also a grand piano in the middle. Perhaps I will play my way to Beijing one day.

The main tourist sights are tremendous although, as yet, I have avoided the temptation of seeing Chairman Mao – his body is raised from its freezer each morning and descends after the last of the morning pilgrims. Perhaps next time I say to myself. Most of the

The fountain in the grounds of the Old Summer Palace, Beijing destroyed on the orders of Lord Elgin.

major attractions are within walking distance of each other and of the railway station, as is O'Reilly's Bar – a real home from home and a must for any western visitor. I had the pleasure of showing a group of Chinese friends where it was the other day, which, for a foreigner, was quite a novel experience to say the least. I also took considerable pleasure in trying to expound on the inestimable delights of 'Chinglish', for right next door to O'Reilly's is possibly Beijing's best known example. Whereas we in the UK might have to make do with, perhaps, 'slippery slope', here in the People's Republic one is urged to take care as 'the slippery are very crafty.' Much more evocative, I'm sure you will agree.

Some idea of the scale and grandeur of Tian'anmen Square and the Forbidden City (or the Palace Museum as the Chinese call it) is captured in the film 'The Last Emperor' which I watched with renewed interest after my visit – I must confess that I was rather surprised you could get copies out here. However, my two favourite places, so far at least, are a fair way out of the city centre and involve the metro and a taxi. These are the Old Summer Palace, destroyed by Lord Elgin – grandson of 'he-of-the-marbles' – in the 1860s (they must have been a jolly lot those Elgins) and the Summer Palace itself, laid out in the 18th century, partially wrecked by the French in 1900 but rebuilt soon after and restored in the mid '50s. What you see today is the result of funds misappropriated by the Empress Dowager Cixi, intended for the navy but spent instead on a lavish set of pavilions and parks. The *piece de resistance* to my mind is a

One of the stone lions guarding the entrance to the Summer Palace, Beijing.

Left: The Long Corridor which runs alongside the man-made Kumming Lake at the Summer Palace, Beijing.

Below: Dowager Cixi's extravagant marble boat on Kumming Lake, Beijing.

wonderfully hideous marble boat berthed in Kumming Lake. Cixi would get my vote any day.

Elsewhere in Beijing, as in Tianjin, eastern markets vie with large department stores for your custom. As a foreigner I will generally go to the markets first but often have to resort to the *proper* shops to avoid the hassle of bartering. Depending upon which market you go to, you can buy absolutely anything you could possibly imagine and probably a great deal more besides. 'DVD' or 'VCD' are the constant cries of the vendors in *Sanlitun Lu* – a particularly touristy street in Beijing, although last weekend I heard 'CD5!' shouted for the first time. 'What is this?' I thought – 'another technological advance?' No! CD5 was simply the price of the pirated CDs on sale – five *yuan* – rather less than forty-five pence apiece. I did most of my Christmas shopping in the markets and really loved it. *Chinoiserie* all round this year. I was probably ripped off right, left and centre but felt I had done what was expected of me, and deep down feel rather proud of my achievements.

There is an awful lot of junk in the shops as well as in the markets though, and quite a lot of the new stuff we have at School is disintegrating fast. I'm on my third stapling machine already (they really are little more than toys) and my hole punch requires a Ph.D. in mechanics to operate correctly and even then the holes do not align correctly with the rings in the ring binders. Glue doesn't seem to be a particular speciality of the Chinese either and the letters on the School's ornate name plaque are forever falling off. Each morning I'm reminded of 'Fawlty Towers' and wonder what further letter(s) might have bitten the dust overnight. My Christmas party game this year will be to offer prizes for the best anagrams to be got out of 'Tianjin Rego International School'. All readers are invited to submit their entries.* Added to this, $50,000 worth of school resources is currently held up in Beijing. The story goes that in order to hasten things through customs, the shippers (from UK) claimed that the contents of all the crates and cartons were books. Some bright spark in Beijing customs opened crate number one to discover three state of the art electronic keyboards destined for my music room. As a result, everything was impounded. Oh dear – big fines I fear.

The School itself is run not by the Board of Directors or the Principal, or indeed even we Vice Principals but, as ever, by the office staff – hugely over-worked and desperately underpaid as indeed they are in UK. MuRong, the Principal's Secretary is a delight, keeps us all in order and still manages to smile when the Principal calls her 'Maroo' as he always does. (Poor Martin is clearly even less of a linguist than I am.) She is assisted by four or five other admin. staff, while the teachers in the primary department mostly have Chinese classroom assistants. (We in the senior school have to cope on our own). But there are also a lot of other people on the payroll who don't really seem to have any perceptible job at all. One has taken to feeding pigeons and tending the goldfish simply to pass the time, two or three others put out tables at lunchtimes, while Mr. Lee was inherited with the building – I joke not.

MuRong took me out to lunch yesterday to a small café she and many of the other Chinese staff frequent. 'I am lucky' she told me, 'the food is not always as nice as this.' Well, if I was having my lunch on a lucky day, I dare not think what I would have got had I been unlucky. Pigs' trotters are not my idea of good fortune – by any stretch of the imagination. The French (and the Chinese too for that matter) are welcome to them from now on. Mind you, the French don't have to try and manage them with chopsticks.

I'm busy working on two Christmas concerts and an end of term carol service at the moment. I've got almost all the pupils and a majority of the staff involved which is very reassuring. As my contract is for two years I'm indulging myself and including half my favourite Christmas bits in the programme, leaving the remaining 50% for next year. What is also very nice is that there is little evidence of Christmas outside School. I've seen only one Christmas tree in Tianjin and although there are a few decorations in the markets there is virtually nothing at all in the shops. Whilst I usually maintain that the run up to Christmas in the UK is enough to turn any sane person to Mecca, I feel very different about it this year – quite excited in fact.

So, with the second window of my advent calendar now opened (a Christmas tree yesterday and a robin today) I will pour myself a large whisky (with Schweppes ginger ale) and, along with the local Korean restaurant wish you all 'RISTMAS MERRYCH'.

* Best anagrams so far: JOIN THE COLONIAL RESIGNATION RANT and JOG OR HASTEN ORIENTAL INCLINATION.

蛇年

THE YEAR OF
THE SNAKE

she nian

CHAPTER 5

Ring out the Old, Ring in the New

January 2001   2001年 一月

I confess to being confused about new centuries and new millennia and things like that. Did they coincide? Was it 2000 or 2001 or perhaps even both? Whatever the answers, I think that I might have been lucky enough to have experienced my third in little over twelve months. What for most of you may simply have been Wednesday 24th January 2001 possibly a rather ordinary day – raining maybe, a touch of sleet perhaps – was for the Chinese, and lucky me as well, the start of another New Year (the Year of the Snake) and of a new century too. In celebration, volleys of firecrackers are being set off almost continuously as I write, as indeed they have been for several days now, the streets are littered with their pink, papery debris, while the air is thick with the smell of an English bonfire night. My copy of the 'Rough Guide' states that fireworks are banned in cities and that enterprising stall holders sell cassette tapes of explosions as a replacement. Well that may well be the official line on things, but here in Tianjin we have the real thing – I promise you. And for fifteen days too – from crack of dawn until well into the night.

The Chinese New Year, aka the Spring Festival, is China's biggest holiday, and the preparations are easily on a par with the commercial excitement that leads up to Christmas in the UK. Doorways are decorated with 'couplets' – mine is gold on red (red is *the* colour) – to encourage good luck to come into your home – while windows are decorated with red paper hangings, like the stencils I used as a little boy for colouring in. Instead of Santas everywhere, there are brightly coloured images of two chubby children dressed in traditional

33

costume representing something quite significant I am sure, although no-one I asked seemed too sure precisely what that might be. But sadly, I've not seen one single Chinese dragon dance, and although I read that the firecrackers are set off to scare ghosts away, the Chinese I spoke to didn't seem to know that either. More curious and quite touching were the dozens of little fires of imitation paper money that were burning in the streets – particularly on New Year's Eve – tended by small groups of men (mostly) squatting around them and gazing into the flames. Such fires are lit in remembrance of loved ones.

I celebrated the Spring Festival in Harbin, capital of China's northernmost province of Heilongjiang, and part of what used to be known as Manchuria. What an evocative name – quite on a par with Bohemia, Illyria and other such antique lands. Harbin is beyond cold. Despite daytime temperatures of minus twenty-five degrees Celsius (it had reached a record low of minus thirty-six the previous week so I think I was just a bit lucky there) Harbin must still be one of *the* places to go at this time of year. The big draw is its Ice Festival. There are carved ice figures, snow buildings and sculptures of every conceivable kind at every turn. The Songhua River (solid ice at this time of year) is the home of a vast wonderland of ice pavilions, grottos and statuary – much of it floodlit at night, where we wandered quite amazed until the need for warmth lured us back to our hotel. Despite my thick green quilted coat (genuine Chinese army surplus) complete with genuine fur collar I'm ashamed to say, woolly balaclava, mujahedin hat, vast gloves, two layers of thermal underwear, quilted trousers, numerous pairs of socks and extra-thick soled boots, three hours was the most I could stand at a stretch. But it was wonderful. The main ice park is supplemented by two further parks – one of which – on Sun Island – was, if anything, even more stunning. The thickness of the ice can support a fully laden truck, so the mere three passengers + driver in the horse drawn carriage we took to get there was as nothing. Whereas the river park sported the Potala Palace, a dinosaur cavern, Marble Arch (I think), a terracotta warrior or two, Abu Simbel and something that could have been the Millennium Dome, the sculptures on Sun Island were generally more abstract and undoubtedly symbolic (although, unfortunately, their titles meant nothing to me). I went on a sledge pulled by a husky around some of them including an array of iced cogwheels and a vast planet earth supported by four giant human beings with western,

Left: 'Century Pavilion' – snow sculpture at Harbin's Ice Festival, Heilongjiang Province.

Below: The frozen Songhua River in Harbin, Heilongjiang Province.

Asian and African faces. 'Awesome!' as my American friends would say. Yet all for three months or so, because, come the warmer weather, everything will be carted off and thrown into the river. Next year, new designs will emerge and fresh blocks of ice hacked out ready for the sculptors to begin their work again. Nothing seems built to last in China.

Harbin itself is an interesting place, and owes its importance to the fact that the Trans-Siberian railway to Vladivostok passes through this corner or China. Consequently there are many vestiges of early twentieth century Russian grandeur to be seen, although much of it is decayed, and even more has been pulled down and replaced with unimaginative and unlovely low-cost housing. One glory that remains however is St Sofia's Cathedral (which we'd seen the previous day but built of ice). Although no longer used as a place of worship, it has been restored in a spirited Chinesey way and now houses an exhibition of 'twinkling moments' from Harbin's glory days. Although, once more, the official captions were meaningless to me, a number of photographs were enlargements of old postcards on which the odd bit of English or German could still be deciphered. Life certainly looked pretty comfortable for the well to do westerner in those days. Lots of wealthy, smiling European faces (one assumes Russian), but not many Chinese. Despite a recent make-over that includes neon strip lights along the edges of all the outside walls (onion domes included), coloured light bulbs mounted in much of the beautiful William Morris-ish interior (or whoever his Russian counterpart was) and almost continuous background muzak (the Chinese are obsessed with the alto sax) I loved the place.

I actually saw the New Year in from the comfort of the Rongfu Conifer Hotel – highly recommended if ever you get that far north – where we were wished 'Happy and Lucks', invited to watch a firework display and to eat some traditional *jiaozi* (dumplings) in the comfort of the revolving restaurant. All I can say is that it is a pity that it was not double-glazed. Thirty-six floors up, it gets mighty cold outside and we could see nothing through the hard frost on the glass that was clearly a permanent feature over the winter months. Still, the stammering of the firecrackers sounded good, and maybe we would have lost that had the windows been better done. Another strange feature of the hotel was its pedestrian access – or rather the lack of it. We flew to Harbin direct from Tianjin airport – 'we take your bags and send them to all directions' – and took a taxi to the hotel. Admittedly the driver had a little difficulty getting up the icy ramp to the main entrance, but that was as nothing compared to the physical and psychological challenges we intrepid travellers faced later on. As well as sliding perilously on the ice, walking into the city centre involved crossing a very busy and extraordinarily complicated two way roundabout, bending double to scramble under a flyover and climbing two (or was it three) barricades – and that was just to get us the first two hundred yards. I wonder what the architect and town planner are doing now? Perhaps they are involved in the Harbin's present scheme, which appears to be to give as many of the grand old buildings as possible a touch of modernity by cheerfully facing them with white ceramic tiles. One thing really fascinated me whilst struggling to cross the roads though – something I could well have missed had the journey been less arduous – and that was the compacted snow on either side. Like rings in trees or rock strata, you could see, as clearly as anything, the three or four major snow falls of the winter, separated by tarry quarter-inch thick layers of urban grime. They looked for all the world like giant, mis-shapen liquorice allsorts.

Harbin will live in my memory for many reasons: a surprisingly talented Spice Girls look-alike group (with the added bonus of Mrs. Spice – Old Spice perhaps – on the Yamaha keyboard); blocks of ice-cream for sale – stacked one on top of the other in the streets (no need for freezers here); the 25% reduction on air fares given to teachers and students during public holidays (now there's a good idea); the magical walk along the river on the first afternoon … the list goes on. But it all added up to a truly memorable few days that should keep Barbara, Rob and me going for the second half of term. We have an eleven-week stint ahead of us, and the prospect of imminent IGCSE examinations for our Year 11 students who have, of necessity, had two-year courses crammed into a single year. Tianjin Rego International School was, of course, a brand new school when it opened in September last year.

Although the Harbin experience was by air, most of the travelling I have done to date has been by train. Alas, the views have been a far cry from those idyllic wall hangings you see in Chinese restaurants in the UK (and over here as well, come to think of it). In fact, most of the countryside I have seen so far has been decidedly scruffy, and rural life looks very, very hard. (You somehow cannot imagine an oriental version of Country Life magazine, should there ever be such a thing, gracing a Chinese dentist's waiting room.) As a consequence, it is easy to see why the rural population is flocking to the cities. You find yourself looking out from the train windows on acres of derelict buildings and mounds of rubble that could have been army compounds or perhaps factories, and wonder what on earth they were and what they could possibly be used for now. Both men and women labour in the fields, there is little sign of mechanisation, and to say that it looks like back-breaking work is an understatement. Much of the land has been turned into lakes for fish farming, but the icy water, far from sparkling in the winter sunshine, looks decidedly unpleasant. The strip of ground between the railway track and the fields is often dotted with little mounds sometimes capped with flat stones which mark family graves, while the banks of the lakes and ditches are dotted with small shacks that could be workmen's huts or perhaps stores for tools but which are probably homes. It all looks so depressing and in need of a bit of TLC.

Watching Chinese travellers on a train or bus is far from depressing though. They eat non-stop and, as a foreigner, you get offered anything that's going too. Although I find myself longing for the archetypal British Rail pork pie (long gone I know), I am frequently to be found furtively nibbling sunflower seeds, steamed dumplings, deep fried dough twists or the very dull, dry cake that disintegrates on sight and which seems to be the favourite fare of the travelling fraternity. Pot noodles too are eaten by the case load although, to date, I've found enough excuses to be able to leave them well alone. Most importantly, you are not properly prepared for China Railways unless you have your jam jar of green tea for the stewardess to top up from her everlasting kettle of hot water. Oh for MaxPax instant coffee.

Before leaving for China last summer, I had the good fortune to meet up with John and Elaine Affleck from Castle Cary in Somerset. John had spent much of his childhood in Tianjin, and his reminiscences prompted me to go looking for certain buildings and places that he remembered from his youth. One of these was Gordon Hall in Victoria Road, which used to house the British Administrative Offices before the Second World War. I was intrigued – it all sounded terribly 'stiff-upper-lip'. John had shown me an old photograph of the building and we ascertained roughly where it should be – if indeed it was still standing. Although many traces of the former British Concession Area have long since disappeared, including all street names of course, Gordon Hall itself remains, as well as the little park opposite (originally called Victoria Park – but now minus its English name as well as its monument to Victoria). Although things were not quite as they were in the original photograph, they were recognisable all the same. And whilst the gothicky turrets and castellations are all gone, if you look closely you can still make out many of the original features of the building. A photograph was most definitely called for, and I went to take my camera out of its case. Needless to say things did not turn out quite as easily as I had expected and I was very smartly moved on by the uniformed (and armed) sentry on guard. The building today is the home of some local government department or other and photos are forbidden.

However, for the sake of the Afflecks I was not to be thwarted. I went to School the next day and asked Freda, one of our Chinese staff, to write me a letter explaining who I was and why I would very much like to photograph this old building. Freda is a star. Not only

*The Cadre Club
(formerly the Tientsin
Club) then and now,
Tianjin.*

did she write the letter, but she and her fiancé accompanied me the
following weekend to see what we could do. The uniformed man on
guard, after initially ushering us away, was eventually persuaded to
read the letter which he did two or three times. He then made a telephone call (presumably to a higher authority) and we got what I
assumed was the OK. But no, his phone call merely activated a chain
of bureaucratic command. We were directed to a run-down building
diagonally opposite and Freda's fiancé was ushered upstairs to
explain himself. Ten minutes passed. A phone rang, and Freda was
duly summoned to join her young man, leaving me on my own in a
dingy dungeon of a room containing an old radiator, a broken contraption made of wood (an ancient instrument of torture I wondered), one chair, a spittoon and an aged Chinese official eating
sunflower seeds. Ten minutes passed and then ten more before at last
my friends reappeared. We had been granted permission to take photographs of the outside of the building. Great! The three of us walked
across the road to the sentry on duty who telephoned once again and

after much heated discussion with his superiors acknowledged that a couple of photos were in order – provided they were taken from the other side of the road and did not show the building's name plaque or the guard on duty. I complied and have two hard-won if rather indistinct images to show for our afternoon's work. Chinese bureaucracy (and I think, in particular, Tianjin bureaucracy) needs no help in making itself look ridiculous.

Rather easier to manage was a photograph of the so-called 'Tientsin Club' (Tientsin was the old name for Tianjin). John had given me a picture of the place taken in the '30s with the suggestion that this too might still be there. Well, not only was the building still there, but it still functions as a social club (known as the 'Cadre Club' now) and we actually held our school disco there a couple of weeks ago. My photograph is an almost exact replica of the original – very exciting. Fired to find out more, I have now managed to obtain two photocopies of maps of Tianjin drawn up by the US Government in the 1920s, which will, no doubt, assist me on my future forays into local history. I'm particularly intrigued to know what the 'Dream Sale Nurse Appearance Salon' and the 'Good Girls Night Club' were in their previous incarnations. However, I reckon I already know rather more about Tianjin's recent past than the average locals who seem to lack much of the 'wanting to know' that teachers in the west try their utmost to encourage.

I am now nearly one quarter of the way through my contract, and can already sense that time is beginning to run out. My list of must-sees grows almost daily, while the amount of free time ahead of me diminishes with startling rapidity. The Three Gorges on the Yangtse River, the terracotta warriors at Xi'an, Lhasa, the river scenery of Guilin and Guangxi, Hong Kong of course and Shanghai are all on the list. But will I have time (and money) to go to those other places which my Chinese friends recommend? Who could resist the temptation of seeing the ancient Buddhist art work in the Mogao caves of Dunhuang the far north west of the country, or a chance of whizzing south to the delightful-sounding Xishuangbanna in Yunnan province close to the border with Laos. And what about Chuandixiacun? I can't even find this gem on my map yet I'm told it is one of the most unspoilt villages in the country and only a few hours drive from Tianjin. There's not a moment to lose. 'Happy and Lucks' to everyone.

CHAPTER 6

A Walk Down Jeifang Beilu and Other Adventures

March 2001   2001年 三月

Unless I am very much mistaken, spring is in the air at last. Although we've had some very low temperatures for well over three months now, and most mornings are still chilly, the last couple of weekends have been absolutely brilliant. Beijing in particular is looking almost verdant, many of the brown grass verges having been painted green for the International Olympics Committee's visit here at the end of February. And whilst there is scant suggestion of similar brushwork, or even buds and blossom in down town Tianjin, at least there are no more huddles of men sitting round holes cut in the ice Eskimo-style. The security guards at school are even beginning to take the Sellotape off the doors and windows, which, I am told, is always good sign, although I think I'll wait a while longer before I follow their example. However, I've already cast considerable caution to the wind, firstly by discarding my thermal underwear and secondly by having given a highly acclaimed school assembly on the Setsubun Bean Throwing Festival. For those of you who didn't know, bean throwing is how the Japanese herald the arrival of spring. Just one of the joys of teaching at an international school.

Spring was rather more evident in Shanghai, which being about one thousand kilometres south of Tianjin, was, if not exactly balmy, a glorious place to go for a March weekend. If ever I'd had any doubts about coming to China (which, to tell the truth, I never really did), such uncertainties would have been well and truly dispatched during the course of this all too brief city-break. The Shanghai streets exude that sort of brash vitality that is lacking in Tianjin (vitality is most emphatically not a word I would use about my present home), with *al fresco* ballroom dancing on several street corners, a nice bit of 'private massage with blinds' on offer just opposite my hotel – it took me a little while to work that one out, a great Henry Moore exhibition at the Shanghai Art Museum, dozens of men and women with white coats and stethoscopes offering what I think might have been free medicals ... and crowds and crowds of people simply enjoying shopping or strolling in the spring sunshine.

Some of the dazzling modern architecture of Shanghai could have been lifted straight out of a futuristic film, yet these buildings jostled for space comfortably alongside the faded art deco gentility of such places as the Peace Hotel (formerly the Cathay Hotel) on the waterfront or 'Bund' as it is known. This famous hotel was a place I just had to visit – encapsulating everything that Shanghai stood for during the first few decades of the twentieth century. It was emphatically not, however, 'an enterprise believable in prices and measure' – an accolade proudly awarded to many a commercial concern in this great city. Noel Coward may well have finished 'Private Lives' there, but even that could hardly justify the massive eighty-eight *yuan* (a little over eight pounds) I paid for one cup of coffee and a solitary scoop of strawberry ice cream. To add insult to injury, the management also fobbed me of with a forged ten *yuan* note in my change. Needless to say, my own hotel was considerably less expensive. Although it was a fairly modern edifice, there were a few valiant attempts to recapture the spirit of the twenties with its interior décor. At odds with the general stylishness, however, were the sugary announcements in the lift. On descending to the ground floor, this little bit of hi-tech, simply oozing with microchip charm, would announce 'Lobby' and urge me, with perhaps just a little lack of sincerity, to 'Have a Nice Day'.

As expected, Shanghai was filled with friendly Chinese citizens eager to help me, and advice on what to see, what to miss, where to go and how to get there was generally timely. High on my own personal list of 'musts' was a river trip on the Huangpu (also spelt, just a little unfortunately to my way of thinking, 'Hung Poo'), and a visit to the YuYuan Gardens – the China of the willow pattern plate, a bit of an anachronism in the twenty-first century perhaps, but quite lovely all the same. My camera worked overtime and I must confess to being quite proud of one or two of my photographic efforts.

The atmospheric art deco foyer of the Peace Hotel on the Bund, Shanghai.

Rather less aesthetic maybe, but no less memorable for all that, was the 'Bund Touristic Tunnel' – a short train ride under the Huangpu River – all lasers and fibre optics with a few strains of Jean Michel Jarre thrown in for good measure. Far from unpleasant, it was, rather like the Millennium Dome, the sort of thing well worth doing once in your life.

One last place is worthy of a brief mention, and that was Madame Soong Qingling's former residence where, amongst the long list of regulations, I was exhorted 'not to litter and spit all around'. It was difficult to comply, but I did, and managed to restrain myself for all of forty-five minutes. Madame Soong, who died in the early '80s, was the widow of Sun Yat-Sen and, to this day, is held in great respect. Her house, comfortable but far from ostentatious, was the scene of many a meeting with dignitaries from around the world, and the adjacent gallery displayed many artefacts from her distinguished past. I couldn't help but smile, however, for clearly the Soong family were a canny lot, and hedging their bets when Qingling's sister, Meiling, married Chiang KaiShek, – later to become Sun's arch enemy and the dominant figure on the other side of the revolutionary forces within China during the first half of the twentieth century. It came as a big surprise to see photographs of her there as well – I think I was half expecting her to have been airbrushed out of existence.

Back home in Tianjin, I have, at last, been to a proper professional concert, when the city hosted an ensemble from Salzburg. Now, as you may have gathered from the general tone of previous letters, high culture is emphatically not synonymous with Tianjin. This particular concert was about a month ago now, a sort of New Year's day affair to celebrate the 'Year of the Snake'. It's perhaps difficult to imagine a more civilised and generally cultured place than Salzburg, so what the musicians must have thought of Tianjin I cannot begin to think. For a start, the Peoples Gymnasium where it was held was a throwback to Chairman Mao days – sterile in the extreme, incredibly tatty and far, far too big. As a venue, it would have sat three thousand plus easily, yet we numbered four hundred if that – a motley crew, most of whom talked all the way through – as Chinese audiences do. I don't expect the Austrians knew that. Admittedly the chatter got softer as the music softened but it also grew to a crescendo as the playing swelled. And that was not the end of it. People wandered around the auditorium taking photos or buying packets of sunflower seeds to chew, mobile phones went off right, left and centre, and although there was no spitting, the frequent throat clearing made you wonder what might happen next.

There were five or six of us expats in the audience, and literally moments before the concert was due to begin we were ushered to some rather plusher seats in the auditorium. Very nice, except that this involved edging our way through the orchestra's green room much to their consternation (they were being given a last minute pep talk from their conductor) and our acute embarrassment. The programme itself was a weird medley of things including 'Polka of Fullmine' – one of a number of clearly revolutionary titbits thrown in to suit the locals. There was also a lot of improved Mozart, (Salzburgers really know how to reach the masses) and an unusual version of the 'Hallelujah Chorus' which merged almost imperceptibly with 'When the Saints go Marching In'. Why, I ask, has no-one thought of doing this little gem before? I assure you that it would have been a truly memorable concert even without the music, and for those contemporary music nerds amongst you, the perfect occasion for a performance of John Cage's 4'33".

On a rather different note, since Christmas, I've taken to going to the gym most evenings after school. The body beautiful is my aim for summer 2001, and, who knows, this could well be followed by wall-to-wall teeth and highlights. But with excellent facilities literally next door to the school, I reckoned this was a good opportunity to get into some sort of decent physical shape before being put out to grass. True, I have made a few half-hearted attempts in the past to get rather fitter, but I have always maintained that I was just too busy to make a real go of things. Alas, my skiing machine at home began to gather dust after only a couple of weeks of frenzied use, while the thought of going for a jog or, worse still, joining some sports club or other has always filled me with feelings of extreme nausea. But I really quite enjoy the Tianjin gym (actually, I really enjoy the sauna and spa pools afterwards, the gym's merely OK), and genuinely feel better for my efforts, despite suffering from an acute case of builder's bum at the moment. (I have already lost a couple of spare inches around the middle.)

When I'm not working out, travelling or teaching (I mustn't forget this last activity), I have, of course, taken to trying to suss out the locals. The street markets are great places to do this, and as I have mentioned before, there is a fantastic one just outside our apartment building. Food stalls abound – I often buy myself a stir fry for the equivalent of eighty pence (which is more than enough for two days), or bargain for fruit and the weirdest of vegetables, quite convinced I am being ripped off, but enjoying the process all the same. The trick of bargaining is to see how much the person in front of you is paying, and to base your negotiations on that. Not that there is even the semblance of a queue of course – the Chinese are devotees of the old adage that nature abhors a vacuum, and will always seek to barge in front of you, be it in a shop, or hailing a taxi or riding a 'Flying Pigeon' bike. However, I digress. You will be quoted an extortionate price and, in return, offer a figure way below that paid by the previous customer, make as though to wander off when it is rejected, allow yourself to be called back and then proceed to haggle to some sort of half way point. Time consuming maybe, but much more fun than Somerfield or even Waitrose for that matter, and no-one thinks any the worse of you for driving a hard bargain I am sure. (I put the increased spitting in my vicinity these days to the weather.)

Not everything is fruit and veg though, and just the other day I was especially taken with a genuine Chinese all-in-one, marble-effect telephone/clock/bedside lamp. To tell you the truth, I really had to force myself not to buy it. But, it being a Sunday, I felt charitable and, not wanting to deprive my fellow man of the joy of owning such a treasure, resisted. It was a truly remarkable contraption though, requiring only three batteries, two plugs and one phone line – so neat, so compact, so … hmmm. Actually, I think I might just nip back and buy one now. Or maybe one is not enough.

Opportunities to really get to know the Chinese are difficult to come by, and occasions to visit people in their homes are particularly rare and really to be treasured. Among the very few non-school people I've had the privilege of visiting in Tianjin have been Dr Zhang and his wife. This delightful, educated couple are the in-laws of an old school friend of mine – a small world indeed. The Zhangs are comfortably off by Chinese standards, but do not wear their wealth in the glossy, pretentious way that so many other Chinese appear to have adopted. Twenty-first century communism/socialism, far from equalising Chinese society, seems to have widened or at least retai-lored the gap between the 'haves' and the 'have-nots'. Over here, if you have wealth, you generally have to be seen to have it, (I came across the word 'affluenza' the other day which sums this up very well I think) and if you have it, you hang onto it and expend much energy ensuring that others do not catch up with you.

But back to the Zhangs. My evening with them was, of course, dominated by the meal. Starting off with green leaf tea and intro-ductions, we then sat down to a veritable banquet. I lost count of the courses, which is one of the big problems, and almost ate myself into oblivion. If you have not ordered the food yourself, you have no idea how many courses to expect and just munch on. I've come a cropper on many an occasion, but have learnt that soup is generally the last course on offer (always assuming you get that far), and dessert, if there is such a thing, tends, fortunately, to be slices of fruit. Fruit is also what is generally offered if you nip round to see someone. No Victoria sponges, scones, toasted tea-cakes or other niceties. Instead, a couple of slices of apple or perhaps chunks of melon and a glass of water. Very healthy, but you can't help wishing you were tucking into something exceedingly good from Mr. Kipling's pantry. As a foreigner, if you are out for a proper meal, beer or wine is usually offered, and perhaps if you are truly unlucky, a glass of *bai jiu*. This spirit is quite the most repellent substance imaginable, but you do down it in one, which is just about the only thing it has in its favour. '*Gan bei!*' you gasp. 'Bottoms up!' It's truly awful.

The other Saturday afternoon, it being particularly sunny and spring like, I took an afternoon stroll along *Jiefang Beilu* – one of the more interesting streets in Tianjin. Formerly called Rue de France (the bit that was in the old French concession) and Victoria Road (just how imperialist can you get?), *Jiefang Beilu* now contains a rich mix of interesting buildings which, if not actually preserved, still retain a semblance of their former glories. The former British Consulate is just off this road, alas a consulate no more, but rather the home of some municipal committee or other (of which there are very many), while the former All Saints Church next door is an inaccessible factory. But still, the buildings are still there, and having acquired the wisdom not to ask before taking photographs, have a couple of very amateurish snaps of both, complete with the security guards' washing draped on the trees to dry in the afternoon sun. Nearby, the former Tientsin British Club looks slightly more dignified (i.e. there was no washing out to dry) – and now houses the Standing Committee of the Tianjin People's Congress.

Many of the finest buildings on *Jiefang Beilu* were, and indeed still are, banks, although their ownership has changed – much the same as the poor NatWest as I discovered when doing my Internet banking the other day. Alas the 'Banque Belge pour l'Etranger de l'Extreme-Orient' is no more, the business having been taken over by the extraordinarily dull sounding 'Chinese Construction Bank'. (Even the more prosaic 'Russo-Chinese Bank' has a good deal more resonance to it than the 'Monetary Institute of Tianjin Branch of People's Bank of China' I think.) Other buildings have fared even less well though. Although the 'Astor House Hotel' is still there (former guests included Dr Sun Yat-Sen and President Hoover), the former 'Imperial Hotel', built in the early '20s, is now the 'Knitwear Purchasing and Supply Centre of Tianjin', and while one might rejoice that one of the banks at least has been converted into an Art Museum, this latter doesn't look as though it has opened its doors for many a long year.

The former Gordon Hall and Victoria Park just off Jiefang Beilu, Tianjin. The park remains while almost all traces of the Hall disappeared following the earthquake of 1976.

My hard won photograph of what I had taken to be Gordon Hall was nothing of the sort.

Sticking with architecture for a moment longer, dedicated readers may just remember my lengthy brush with Tianjin bureaucracy when trying to photograph the Gordon Hall, just before Christmas. Imagine my reaction when I received a letter from ex-Tianjiner John Affleck to tell me that my much prized and hard won photograph of what I took to be the former British Administrative Offices was, in fact, nothing of the sort. As he wrote, on comparing his 1930s photo with mine, 'the Gordon Hall does not look like the photograph of the one I have here.' He sent me a copy – his remarks were an understatement if ever there was one – and rather like Victor Meldrew, I was apoplectic. I just didn't believe it and, somewhat deflated, went back to the drawing board. However, after several beers with an extraordinarily resourceful Chinese friend of mine called Summer, I eventually discovered that what I had taken to be Gordon Hall – all pomp and circumstance – was in fact originally the 'Kai Lan Mining Administration Building', surely a natural mistake to make. And the real Gordon Hall? Well, this was apparently destroyed in the devastations of the 1976 earthquake. Despite my friend's assertions, however, I'm not so sure about this last bit of information. True, there was a massive earthquake in the Tianjin region in 1976, and yes, many buildings were destroyed. But, Gordon Hall was a very, very substantial building, and everything else in the vicinity remains intact to this day. I can't help but feel that the Cultural Revolution of 1966 – 1976 might just have had something to do with it, especially as the architecture of the place was more British than British. Sadly, but unsurprisingly, the site is now occupied by yet more dreary municipal offices. Summer sticks to the official line on things by the way.

My school term is a long one and goes on until Good Friday when some good friends arrive from the UK for ten days or so. I'm looking forward to this very much and, of course, am swotting up hard on my Chinese to impress them. Beijing, the Great Wall, the sights of Tianjin and a cruise up the Yangtse on 'MV Sunshina China' are all on the agenda. It should be wonderful. In the meantime, have a good Easter, and do keep in touch. I love opening the 'post' over my Marmite sandwiches and orange juice.

CHAPTER 7

Hairy Legs and Hairy Eggs – Tantalising Tales from Old Tianjin

May 2001   2001年 五月

Life has been particularly good to me these past few weeks. Not only have I survived an eleven week half term ('survived' is the wrong word to use – I really enjoyed it), but my increasing knowledge of how things get done in this strange land has enabled me to live rather more adventurously. I have also begun to get to know some of my Chinese friends rather better and, as a result, feel that I am now closer to actually understanding things rather than being merely being able to describe them. From what was hitherto a position of aloof ignorance, I am now, just very occasionally, beginning to view things in the way a Chinese person might.

These days, and in common with many a middle-aged Chinaman, I frequently retreat into my own little cocoon. I can sit for hours in Mosquito World – one of the scruffy street cafés just down my street – with perhaps half a dozen lamb kebabs or a bowl of boiled peanuts and just watch the world go by. I am rather proud to say that I can do this without the slightest feeling of guilt either, and, believe you me, it's bliss and it's cheap. Furthermore, I have also been observed ignoring the traffic police at busy road junctions – quite regularly too I am told. But, if the Chinese are totally oblivious to their presence, who am I to act any differently? Far be it for me to seek to stand out from the crowd in this respect. Nowadays, I hardly so much as glance at the elegant bicycling ladies sporting surgical masks, shrouded in voluminous net curtaining. I have ceased to wonder how they can possibly blow their noses or suck the 'Fisherman's Friends' to which most appear to be addicted, let alone see more than a couple of inches ahead of them. (Actually they can't.) And my list goes on. I can queue comatosed and uncomplaining at supermarket check-outs only to smile when I discover that what are clearly labelled 'sheets' are, in fact, duvet covers and vice-versa, that a 'made-in-China' pillow case is not designed to match the rest of one's bed linen or that any unpriced goods I might have about my person will, most likely, be confiscated and placed irretrievably under the counter. It no longer strikes me as curious that the 7.00 a.m. bus having presumably already filled up with passengers, should leave twenty minutes early or that an overstaffed hotel reception desk has no apparent system in place for registering a guest. Yes, I am becoming well and truly acclimatised (or do I mean numbed?) and take all of these things in my stride ... more or less.

If I have overwhelming evidence to suggest that your average Chinese citizen is totally oblivious to his or her surroundings most of the time, I have also observed a somewhat incongruous other side to this trait. For the Chinese, as a race, also have a truly great sense of collective responsibility and togetherness – whether it is banqueting in large groups in packed restaurants (even lovers choose to talk sweet nothings in crowded KFCs), or engaging in some gigantic municipal project or other. For example, there is a massive road and canal renovation programme on at the moment throughout all of Tianjin. If the equipment is pretty primitive and generally long past its prime, then this is more than compensated for by the amount of willing labour the government can call upon to do the job. I reckon there must be a force of two thousand or more along the one-mile stretch of canal between my apartment and the school drive alone. Until very recently, there have been countless quilted tents, both on the roadside and on the drained canal bed, in which the workers eat and sleep, so enabling the site to operate twenty-four hours a day, seven day a week. It is, I believe, all part of a grand scheme to channel water from the Yellow River (goodness knows how many miles west of Tianjin) to the parched north east of the country. It will also make my part of town look infinitely more attractive – up until now the canal has been, literally, a steaming open sewer. This amazing collective mentality gets things done in a way that maybe even shames us in the west and my walk to school has never been so much fun. I set myself little puzzles as I look around. 'How many Chinese workers does it take to lop a branch off a tree?' for example. (Last Friday's correct answer was seventeen.)

Judging by their weathered, sunburned faces, the labour force for this project is primarily made up of minority ethnic groups and peasants from the rural west of the country; people who have probably spent a lifetime outdoors and who have migrated to Tianjin in search of short-term work. When the project is over they will no doubt go elsewhere and with luck find themselves something to carry them through the next few weeks or months. Actually, it is a sad fact of life that for most Chinese, both here and elsewhere, (and I include my School here) there is little sense of a permanent job, and even in the professions, people are discarded without a second thought. Just when they are becoming useful and perhaps getting to know a particular system, their 'contracts' are mysteriously terminated. And perhaps this is the key. Just maybe they are close to knowing too much. 'We do things differently in China' is the official line on things, but just maybe they are close to spotting a scam and need to be 'let go' – what a wonderful euphemism – before they become just a little bit too wise. The supposedly traditional Chinese curse: 'May you come to the attention of those in high places' has a chilling resonance I feel.

Knowing this, it seems particularly strange that most Chinese should still show little evidence of discontent and instead often display an almost sycophantic deference towards those with money or in positions of authority. For the most part, the Chinese I know are, outwardly at least, happy with their lot and, for the vast majority, the notion of 'aspiration', however humble, seemingly doesn't exist. But if this sounds too depressing, let me add that one of the pleasures of living in China is that it never ceases to surprise, and just when I begin to think I've got a fairly rounded idea of things, then another secret is revealed which upsets everything. Next time I write I might have something very different to say.

I didn't get to a church service at all over the Easter period, although I did manage to visit Tianjin's two cathedrals – the Christian Church and the Catholic Church as they are called. A great distinction don't you think? The former, Xikai Church, built in 1916, is generally open and used for occasional services on Sundays too. I had visited it several times before, enjoying its bizarre green domes, stripey cream and red brickwork and bright yellow emulsioned interior – although

Playing the harmonium inside Wanghailou Cathedral, Tianjin.

this time much of the inside was covered with dark purple cloth. The second cathedral had always been closed though, and, in fact, is now more commonly referred to as the Seaview Tower rather than Wanghailou Cathedral. An austere looking mid 19th century building on the banks of the river, it has an almost sinister appearance, and I wondered whether I would ever get to have a look around inside. But, with a revitalised sense of adventure and the additional incentive of it being Holy Week, I decided to almost force an entry if I needed to. But it wasn't necessary, and on my arrival I was promptly welcomed by the elderly Chinese caretaker. He opened the doors and we had the place to ourselves for twenty minutes before he invited me back to his little shed for a cup of green tea. Although he spoke not one word of English and I struggle when it comes to saying anything remotely worthwhile in Chinese, the two of us got on famously. I don't think he'd ever had an English visitor before, and the occasion was clearly a very special one for both of us.

The 'main event' of my school holiday was the arrival of a couple of good friends – former colleagues of mine from Dorset – who were spending ten days with me here in China. As my term was not due to finish until just before Easter, Jan and Keith spent their first two days in the company of my Chinese friend Summer. He introduced them to some of the delights of Tianjin – antique markets, cheap bars, the Guangdong Theatre (more about that next time), the *hutong* or narrow alleys down which many Chinese in Tianjin still live, and yet more cheap bars – before I took them out to the Great Wall at Huangyaguan, one hundred and forty kilometres north of Tianjin, on Good Friday. Alas, even the best made plans can go very

A glimpse of one of Tianjin's maze of hutong.

wrong. Being cautious, we got to the terminus in good time for the 7.00 a.m. bus only to be greeted with *meiyou* – a word that I have come to know only too well. Not one of the dozens of buses parked in the depot was bound for our intended destination. Limited Chinese and a fair bit of mime later, it appears probable that the bus had filled up and left early that day. There was nothing for it but to grab a taxi and attempt to catch the 7.22 train which would take us to Jixian, from where we'd be able to get a lift for the last leg of the journey – about thirty kilometres. We were in luck, and although the train was slow – it took over three hours – it was cheap (about seventy pence each), and we had the added luxury of cups of warm bean milk to drink and being able to doze from time to time.

On my previous visit to Huangyaguan, four of us had caught a bus which drops you literally right next the Great Wall. I was disappointed that Jan and Keith were not to have this experience. There's

54

Above: Riding up to the Great Wall at Huangyaguan, Tianjin.

Left: The view from the top.

something intrinsically exciting about travelling on a bus where the driver and conductor get paid according to the number of passengers they can cram on board. On this occasion, one traffic cop was quickly bribed with a ready packet of cigarettes while his mate did the head count, pretending not to notice the old guy who suddenly crouched down in the aisle, so that our journey was able to stick to schedule. On this occasion too, we took horses up to some of the more exposed sections of the Wall, which, although enormously exciting, was, in retrospect, a foolish thing to have done and I am mighty relieved not to be writing my auto-obituary here. Needless to say we had no safety helmets, the horses were old and tired and the tracks up and back were exceedingly steep and unstable. 'Game over!' Martin, one of the party, called out on one particularly hairy bit of path. Charlotte, Summer and I laughed, but I suspect I was not the only one feeling just a little bit queasy inside and regretting I was bobbing up and down in the saddle quite so vigorously.

The weather on both occasions was glorious – clear blue skies, warm sun and the gentlest of breezes which prevented us from getting hot and sticky. I had told Jan and Keith that we could expect to have most of the Wall to ourselves as there is no public transport from Beijing to this particular stretch and Tianjin is hardly a tourist hot-spot. I couldn't have been more wrong. When we arrived (at about 11.30 a.m.) there must have been fifty giant coaches in the carpark while the Wall itself was literally heaving with school children. Evidently all of Tianjin municipality's youngsters were having an away-day. But it didn't matter – the Wall is pretty long after all. The three of us were the focus of a lot of celebrity attention at first. Keith in particular, who at over six foot, bearded and with hairy legs was not likely to be mistaken for a Chinese, was a constant source of fascination and amusement. But as we climbed, the Wall getting rougher and the sun growing stronger, we left the children far behind us. It wasn't long before we had the whole place to ourselves as I had predicted. The experience was everything we could have wished for.

Before catching the bus home, we spent a couple of hours in Jixian in order to have something to eat as well as to visit the famous Dule Temple. This is a giant multi-storied wooden pavilion – the oldest and largest such structure in China – containing beautiful Buddhist frescoes and an absolutely gigantic terracotta figure of Guanyin – Goddess of Mercy – sixteen metres high, with not one but eleven heads. Outside again and suitably impressed, we bought some delicious wedges of fresh pineapple and found a shady spot to sit and reflect. Horror of horrors when we discovered we had positioned ourselves next to a street vendor selling 'hairy eggs'. (I now warn those of a nervous disposition or about to eat not to read the remainder of this paragraph.) Hairy eggs are nothing less than chicken embryos at various stages of development, boiled in their shells and then peeled. The fact that you can no doubt see exactly what it is you are eating makes this delicacy all the more repellent. Even Summer who probably has an account with the 'Caos Family Donkey Meat Shop' in Tianjin, who admits to a penchant for fish lips and who regularly chews on chicken feet has never quite been able to summon up the strength to eat one of these little abominations.

The highlight of our Easter holiday was undoubtedly the five-day cruise on the Yangtse – the China of the picture books. Flying into Yichang, I saw paddy fields, terraced hillsides, water buffalo and coolie hats for the first time. I also saw a pig (dead I fear) strapped onto the back of a pushbike – another first, but not one I was expecting. Similarly unexpectedly, we discovered that we had arrived eight hours early (but that's another story), and so had the ship to ourselves. My impression of the general sumptuousness of the five-star 'Sunshine China' was only marginally tinged with disappointment – alas, the 'Sunshina China' of our reservation form was merely a typing error. (It's a good name though.) After a light lunch (five or was it six courses?) and a short burst on the grand piano in the on-board cocktail bar, we settled down to have the first of what was to be several naps in the sun. I dozed, content in the knowledge that all the furniture and daily necessities in my cabin were perfect ('if you have any better ideas, please contact housekeeping') and quite touched that the attentive crew had my best interests at heart ('because of the drain inconvenience on the floor of the bathroom we feel very sorry for you'). Lazy days.

The lasting impression I have of the Yangtse is not of its size (one is, after all, expecting something pretty big) but of the sheer volume of river traffic that uses it. This, together with the smell of the damp woodland that first morning will linger in my memory. Ferries, hydrofoils, small fishing boats, container ships, convoys of coal barges, others carrying livestock or piled high with fruit and veg, all emerged from and then disappeared into the morning haze that blurred the distinction between water and sky. Rivers in China are the primary means of communication and transportation for millions of people, and for those whose livelihoods we were watching this was merely the daily grind. Were they aware of the extraordinary pleasure they were giving us I wonder? Such was the overwhelming experience of it all that the sight of an eagle before breakfast on two consecutive mornings seems hardly worth mentioning.

The Three Gorges Dam, just up from Yichang, is the biggest civil engineering project in the world. Estimated to take seventeen years to construct, the project is now roughly half way through, with final completion scheduled for 2009. Having already diverted the Yangtse (no mean feat – at six thousand four hundred kilometres, it is the third longest river in the world and the drainage basin comprises 20% of China's land mass), the engineers are now in the process of constructing five massive ship locks and a one hundred and thirteen metre ship lift as well as the dam and turbines. The project will eventually generate almost one fifth of China's electricity, improve navigation (making Chongqing the world's first metropolis to be situated on the banks of a major artificial lake) and, most importantly, alleviate the frequent flooding on the lower reaches of the river. The final 'plug', used once already when the river was originally diverted, is now on show like a giant piece of 'Toblerone' awaiting its final resting place. But if none of the above enables you to picture the scene, perhaps the knowledge that the access road to the construction site alone involved the construction of thirty-four bridges and five tunnels or that the whole thing will cost in excess of $20 billion will hit home. Throughout the journey upstream, there are indicators showing precisely how far the water levels are predicted to rise – up to the 135-metre mark by 2003 and then the 175-metre mark (2009). One hopes the Chinese have got their measurements absolutely right as there is an awful lot of building work going on, presumably just above the 175 mark, and the Beijing government, in common with governments everywhere, has a way of being just a bit vague when it comes to statistics. Will it be 1.2 million or nearer two million of the four hundred million people the river supports that will need rehousing for example?

The Three Gorges themselves are stunning and took the best part of two whole days to get through. But, of course, they will be diminished in their majesty with the inexorable march of progress to say nothing of the massive change to the livelihoods of the people who live on and by the river. Farming here is labour intensive, and where the cliffs are not vertical, every scrap of land is cultivated, the green terraces running right down to the water's edge. Those that live there bring their produce to the river's side for the early morning boats – I was up at 5.45 a.m. on the first morning to see the sun rise in Xiling Gorge but the villagers were already hard at work. Cocooned in my five-star existence I was overwhelmed and absorbed, privileged to be glimpsing a way of life that had changed little for generations but which will shortly be lost for ever.

As well touring the dam construction site, a number of other excursions were organised for us, significant among which was boarding a fleet of sampans in various stages of collapse to be hauled up the Shennong Stream – a relatively small but crystal clear tributary of the Yangtse, before letting the current take us back down again (in time for pre-prandials of course). Whereas the practice of 'boat tracking' as it is called is traditional here, for the currents and submerged rocks are treacherous, the Chinese entrepreneurial spirit and the need to conform to western 'niceties' were also very much in evidence. Much to some of the party's disappointment no doubt, twenty-first century boat trackers now wear underpants, unlike the soft-porn postcards they had for sale – brought to us on our sampans by the tracker-in-chief striding manfully through the waters. (Perhaps it was old stock.) But it was still terribly hard work, nothing had changed there – teams of four men calling to each other, Venetian gondolier style, pulling the boat from mid-stream or the bankside and crossing over from right to left as the river's current demanded. There were also the inevitable stalls of trinkets and repro antiques when we reached our destination (to see the rock tombs that had been cut in the cliffs) and again at the end, when we boarded the 'Sunshine China' once more. And if some of these trades-people never missed a trick, why should they? The glimpse of a tiny little child being carried on her mother's back in a wicker rucksack while she was selling us oranges, bottled water and the ubiquitous Coca-Colas was a good tactic and bound to pull in the crowds.

As there were only five native English speakers on the 'Sunshine China' – me, Jan and Keith, and a delightful couple from Australia – the other hundred or more passengers were Germans, Taiwanese and Hong Kong Chinese – we were privileged to have the services of our

Above: Entering the Three Gorges on the Yangtse, Hubei Province.

Right: Strange statuary in Fengdu near Chongqing. Sichuan Province.

Below: The 'ghost city' of Fengdu, shortly to be submerged. Buildings close to the river are gradually being submerged while new apartment blocks are being built on higher ground.

own guide much of the time. Betty was great. Complete with her brightly coloured flag, she posed for photographs and told us all we could possibly wish to know about the Dam with an unerring authority. By way of contrast our guide up the Shennong Stream introduced herself by saying she spoke little English and then proceeded to prove her point by remaining resolutely silent for the entire trip. She didn't even point out the rock tombs which I learned afterwards was, ostensibly, the purpose of the trip in the first place. Charlie the Australian (egged on by his wife and largely for devilment I am sure) tried to engage her in some sort of discussion about the pros and cons of the sampans' front mounted rudders on the journey home, but to no avail. She understood nothing.

Our final excursion ashore was to Fengdu – a 'ghost city' built on Mount Pingdushan close to Chongqing. Miraculously most of this escaped the Cultural Revolution and ancient temples and exotic sculptures of demons and devils greet the visitor today. Traditionally, the Chinese believe that Pingdushan is where they will held accountable on Judgement Day. As visitors, Jan, Keith and I were invited to attempt the three traditional tests to determine our fate in the afterlife – crossing a bridge, crossing a threshold and standing one-legged on a stone whilst focussing and reflecting upon the text of a Chinese proverb. Fortunately we passed all three so there's hope for us yet.

It was cloudy when we arrived at Chongqing, currently China's third or fourth largest city but destined to become the world's largest metropolis. Although there was still a great deal of cultivated land, towns, some quite sizeable, and industry generally had been becoming increasingly evident during the last stages of the journey – quarrying and coal transportation depots being prevalent. Old lime kilns, too, dotted the banks, while ramshackle buildings of indeterminate use abounded. Although we had had an unforgettable time, even after five days afloat we had covered only 10% of the total length of the Yangtse. In Chongqing itself I read a chunk from the 'Rough Guide' to Jan describing the 'Victory Monument' in Jiefang Square which celebrates the communists' liberation of the city from seventy years of colonial and right-wing occupation. I looked up to see that we were surrounded by a crowd of Chinese, totally mesmerised by what we were about. So you see its not just Michael Palin that can pull an audience. I'll miss my celebrity status when I get back home.

CHAPTER 8

Tianjin Calling

July 2001   2001年 七月

I was reading quite a witty little article the other day about the 'u's and 'non-u's of writing an e-mail (should it perhaps be the 'e's and 'non-e's I wonder?) and of the emergence of something called *netiquette*. A bit silly perhaps, but in the list of do's and don'ts, the number one 'do' was to be sure to be brief. Oh dear. I've got a feeling that I'm going to be falling at the first hurdle. Can I sense your right hand moving towards the mouse, itching to press the delete button already? Stay with me please – I suspect that this will be the last letter of the summer term and if I can whet a couple of appetites or raise just a few smiles, then my efforts will have been worthwhile.

As an aside, just as teachers invariably think of autumn, spring and summer terms as a means of dividing up the year (months and dates in particular mean very little to most of us), I am told that your average Chinese thinks of dates rather than days of the week when measuring time. Not that this can ever be used to pin him down though. Oh no! Rarely can anything be done until *mingtian* (tomorrow), and even this oh so vague promise is generally followed by a hushed *keneng* (maybe) as you turn to go. All of this is accompanied by a smile of course.

But enough of this. However one chooses to measure time passing, the cicadas began their chirruping last Wednesday afternoon sometime between 1.00 and 3.00 p.m. (I've no idea what the date was – I am English after all) and by my reckoning that means that summer is well and truly upon us. Air conditioning units have already begun to dribble and drip on unwary passers-by, ladies of all shapes and sizes have taken to wearing hideous little ankle stockings (quite the most unbecoming fashion accessory you would ever wish

62

to see – I try to avert my gaze but I admit I'm completely mesmerised), while many young men wander about with one trouser leg
rolled up to the knee. I've no idea why – can they *all* be free masons?

As I hope will have become obvious to everyone, I'm still thoroughly enjoying my relatively outlandish lifestyle in the far east. The
challenges and responsibilities of being a teacher at a thriving international school give me a real buzz and I genuinely feel quite privileged to be here. I do my job efficiently – actually I do it pretty well
even though I do say so myself – yet still have loads of energy and
enthusiasm to get out-and-about in the evenings and at weekends.
The old TV advert used to advocate that a 'Mars' a day helped you
work, rest and play. Well even if there are no 'Mars' bars (or even
'Aero's) over here and I have to make do with 'Snickers' (which I've
never really taken to since they stopped being called 'Marathon's), I
still work, rest and play with considerable vitality – despite reaching
the grand old age of 51.

Talking of which, I had an amazing birthday party on board a
rather swish boat specially hired for the occasion a couple of weeks
ago. I learned afterwards that it was generally reserved for the party
cadres, so someone was clearly pulling a few strings somewhere. But
what better way of celebrating than a four-hour cruise on the *Hai He*
River here in Tianjin? Tianjin used to be an important port because
of its proximity to Beijing, which of course is inland, and an evening
on the river seemed just the thing to do. Three of us had birthdays
within a few days of each other, so that split the cost of the hire, and
as we all had the same nucleus of friends, the risk of wanting to invite
too many people was greatly diminished. I was 51, my two friends 21
and 31, and, rather neatly, there were 41 passengers on board – both
Chinese and expats of course. It was a perfect evening as we headed
down river into the countryside – passing fishermen and bathers of
all ages and sizes who waved as we sailed past, a couple of cross-river
ferries weighed down with bikes, and several small boats on which
families evidently lived and worked. Then as the sun was about to set
we turned around and headed back into the city, which by then was
lit up – quite spectacularly in places. Hard to believe, but Tianjin
looked almost beautiful. But then cities at night, and from the perspective of a river in particular, are rather like cities from the air –
almost magical in their appearance. Although there are notable
exceptions to the rule, many expats here in Tianjin are, rather sadly,

a fairly long way down the food chain. An American friend of mine rather harshly refers to some of them as 'no brainers' – but, in fact, this is a term that does a fair number of them absolute justice. More than a few of those on short-term contracts with some of the multinational electronics firms in the city make pretty embarrassing ambassadors for Britain, the USA or wherever else they hail from. A number of seamy western bars and clubs have opened up too, and these are largely frequented by young Chinese girls along with overweight and habitually inebriated middle-aged men, desperately in search of an ego (wife and kids back home of course). I leave you to draw your own conclusions, but the expression 'zero to hero' was one I heard for the first time only the other day. One wonders whether the supposedly traditional Chinese curse 'May the gods grant your prayers' might be coming true for some of them.

At the opposite extreme, I've been to the expat church here in Tianjin too. Twice only maybe, but that was twice too often for me. I found the experience shallow in the extreme – 'cosy' and 'smug' are words that spring readily to mind. The sort of service where stale words and trite tunes are interspersed with self-satisfied extempore 'sermonettes'. Have you ever read or seen the film of the Ira Levin's 'The Stepford Wives'? This was the closest I've come to it in real life and it was very, very creepy. On a less opinionated and altogether more uplifting note though, the greatest sense of spiritual awe I've experienced in a long while was during my visit to the Tianjin mosque. With its architecture a bizarre mixture of Indian and Chinese, I went one hot afternoon with two friends of mine and were completed silenced by an overwhelming feeling of presence.

But the expat scene is not all grim. Far from it in fact. China's pending membership of the World Trade Organisation notwithstanding, Tianjin took its most gigantic leap forward ever a few weeks ago when a branch of Starbucks opened in the city centre – the very essence of western civilisation in a cup. Needless to say I intend to become a regular. 'See you next week!' I called out to a friend only last weekend. 'Oh, and have a nice couple of days in Mongolia' I added as a throwaway. Probably not the sort of *adieu* you'd hear very often in Dorset.

Sticking with the plusses of the expat scene for a moment longer, I now run a choir on a Thursday evening, have been on a couple of runs (or rather Sunday afternoon strolls) with the local 'Hash House

Harriers' and, on the strength of a small article I wrote for the 'Tianjin Telegraph' have been asked to arrange walking tours around some of the old concession areas in the city – something I'm quite keen to do later in the year. As I have said before, the architecture and history generally of Tianjin is fascinating. Within the foreign concessions, set up around the turn of the last century, all citizens, be they foreign or Chinese, were governed by the laws of the foreigner and were exempt from the laws of China. Each concession was in effect an independent country – little enclaves of foreign soil with their own government, police force and troops. Well, the foreigners have all but gone, but the extraordinary legacy of building remains, and the more I find out, the more I want to learn. I look forward to running my tours in the autumn.

The Sheraton Hotel, literally next door to the School, provides a real lifeline too. Over the last couple of weeks I calculated that I visited the place for eight quite separate reasons: to post some letters, have a meal, use the ATM (which was actually working for a change), do a bit of exercise in the gym, find out about malaria precautions from the clinic, buy some overpriced western groceries, get my hair cut and have a pint or two of 'Tsingtao' in the bar. And all this within one hundred yards of the school gates – it really is a hard life. Actually, I was in the gym on my own one Saturday morning the other week when an American lady came in and asked if I minded her turning the TV on. 'Not at all' I replied – quite touched by her consideration. 'You see, it's always opera on a Saturday morning' she added. 'Marvellous' I thought, musing over whether it would be Puccini or Verdi, or maybe even Wagner – surely the perfect accompaniment to a gentle work-out – whilst at the same time thinking that perhaps I had misjudged a lot of the westerners in the city. None of it. It wasn't even Rogers and Hammerstein – it was Oprah Winfrey.

Whilst on the subject of opera, one of the most fascinating places I have been to in recent months has been a perfectly preserved traditional Chinese opera house – apparently one of only two left in the entire country. The Guangdong Guildhall Theatre, in the district that is actually known as 'Chinatown' here in Tianjin, only escaped the Cultural Revolution because of its associations with Dr. Sun Yat-Sen who made an important political speech from its platform in the early years of the twentieth century. Despite its cultural significance though, the taxi drivers had no idea where it was, and

Left: The grand birthday party on the Hai He River, Tianjin.

Below: The Guangdong Guildhall Theatre, Chinatown, Tianjin.

when we eventually found the narrow *hutong* or alley down which it was located, street vendors less than one hundred yards away were still unsure of its whereabouts. Unsurprisingly, it was closed the first time I went, but luck was with me on the second occasion, when my resourceful Chinese friend, Summer, not only translated the curator's commentary but also managed to book us a few seats for a 'private' performance of a traditional Peking Opera, being presented the following week.

The auditorium was laid out with tables and chairs, and green tea was charmingly served before and during the show, which in this case was being given by some young students of opera from Beijing. The sound was bizarre in the extreme, the piercing, high pitched singing and speaking being accompanied by a small orchestra consisting of traditional Chinese instruments, percussion predominant. For the uninitiated like myself, the sound was difficult to get into, but visually, (movement, costumes and especially make-up,) it was completely riveting stuff. Although it was a student production, most of the performance was of a very high order indeed. In fact, it was only in the singing that the relative inexperience was apparent – voices occasionally inaudible over the sound of the curious band. Altogether, it was a very special evening, and if, as I suspect, the curator pocketed the five pounds we had each paid for our tickets, so what?

Days out have taken me to Beijing of course, and to Tanggu a couple of times, where the *Hai He* River meets the sea and where I conducted our newly formed choir for our first concert. On one memorable occasion I stayed the night in the Golden Sails Hotel (not recommended) and had just switched the light out when the phone rang. It was room service, and as far as I could gather, massage was on special offer, it being mid week. I thanked the breathy young lady for calling, congratulated her on her English, but said, rather lamely I felt in retrospect, that I was really quite tired and perhaps we could make it another time. Life is nothing if not eventful.

Another trip (a weekend this time) took me to Chengde – the old summer resort of the emperors– and about six hours from Tianjin. With its fantastic mountain scenery and old pagodas, temples and palaces dotted around the place, all in various stages of decay/repair, it was the China of the picture books and definitely worth a return visit. Getting to many of these places is so difficult though. The sole train from Tianjin to Chengde, for example, gets in at 4.00 a.m. (a fat lot of use) while the only fast train from Beijing leaves at 7.10 a.m. – ten minutes before the first express from Tianjin gets in. The only sensible way to do it was to hire a driver – which, in the end, is precisely what we did. I had thought two or three friends might like to come with me and split the cost. In the end there were fourteen of us and a school minibus.

Most recently, my weekends away have taken me to Zhoukoudian – home of Peking Man (before he was spirited away in the late '30s by the Taiwanese, or was it the Japanese or was it the Americans?), some truly fantastic caves nearby, and the small town of Shidu – all to the west of Tianjin. Here the spectacular limestone scenery provides a marked and welcome contrast to the flatness of both Tianjin and Beijing. Bamboo punts and horse-drawn carts were the order of the day, along with cheap beer and delicious food of course. As well as some breathtakingly beautiful mountain walks I also had the hair-raising experience of travelling on a cable railway which descended almost vertically for much of its run. I'm not sure I'll be wanting to repeat that one and was thankful that I had had the foresight to pack a hip flask of whisky in my rucksack. (Purely medicinal of course!)

I am fast coming to another of my transient conclusions about China, and that is that the Chinese are, by and large, not so unlike a nation of children. Delightful children too, most of them, wide-eyed, friendly and an absolute pleasure to be with. But, like so many children, the majority seem more than keen to avoid taking on any form of responsibility if they can help it, and appear happy and content to kowtow to the strict hierarchy of grown-ups who crack the whip where necessary. This, I think, probably owes its origins to Confucianism, and the man himself would undoubtedly be proud of his legacy here in Tianjin at least. But although I speak from a biased European perspective, and more than a few vestiges of English arrogance no doubt remain, there is, as the inevitable result of this pecking order, a sort of immaturity, sometimes even a total lack of common sense, in much of what I see around me.

Like young children the world over, for example, many, maybe even most of the Chinese of my acquaintance seem to love what many of us in the west would probably call tackiness. But why not? There is surely nothing inherently wrong in craving the very brightest colours or the highest platforms possible for the soles of one's shoes, or by being generally beguiled by gizmos of one sort or another. Such things are fun. However, alongside this there is also the childish passion for the quick fix solution and here I am often irritated and sometimes even saddened. 'Why not make things properly in the first place?' I ask myself. Why not use glue that actually sticks, when curiously, Chinese adhesive tape is utterly fantastic? Why not prepare the surface that is to be painted or think ahead when digging up this street or renovating that building? Some poor chap just up the road from my apartment opened a little business selling car batteries just before Easter and no doubt invested what little worldly wealth he had in it. There was much celebration with fire crackers, inflatable red archways (a sure sign that something new lies beyond) and, no doubt, copious amounts of *bai jiu*. Goodness only knows where he is now. The building was actually demolished three weeks later as part of a road widening scheme. Almost everything over here seems to be for the moment and, where possible, for a quick profit. No corner is left uncut and as a result, nothing seems to last. Toys, clothes, musical instruments, buildings, you name it. Repairs too, where they are implemented – which really is very rarely – are generally executed in a completely ham-fisted manner, almost literally with hammer and Sellotape, and could well even hasten the demise of whatever it is that is being attended to.

In their daily living, too, it appears that many Chinese are totally oblivious of their physical surroundings; hence the incredible mess and mounds of junk just about everywhere you look – like a small child's bedroom before he or she is told to clear it up or have their pocket-money stopped. Many too are virtually heedless of their fellow man, as witnessed in the chaotic 'I'm the centre of the universe' sort of cycling (and driving) that is such a feature of my daily journey to school. Think about a child careering around a playground on a tricycle or a teenager on a skate board weaving in and out of both pedestrians and traffic, multiply it by several million, and you might have an inkling of an idea of what Tianjin's roads are like.

On the plus side though, almost all the Chinese I have come across have an incredible charm and a wonderful innocence, a great desire to please (where else could you possibly be told that you can pay for your holiday after you get back?) and take a phenomenal pleasure in corporate activity – this last seen, for example, in the group of old ladies who do their pop-mobility outside my apartment block. They're there at the moment and I've been out twice already just to look at the total self-absorption that simply radiates from their faces.

If an individual Chinese is largely unmindful of his neighbour, then this is possibly a simple reflection of Chinese authority's quite blatant lack of consideration for its individual citizens. For the past couple of weeks, for example, I have been Acting Principal at my School with the extraordinary power to close the place should the big road project going on in its vicinity make the children's journeys dangerous or even impossible. At the moment pupils and teachers alike literally drive, cycle or walk through a one-mile long building site, steering our way through an ever-changing maze of obstacles. The local government has decided the road will be rebuilt – tough on those who need to use it in the meantime.

Little (or big) bribes are also a way of life – one 'secures' (i.e. buys) favours from those who have more *guanxi* than you, and for Tianjin's grown-ups (i.e. those with most *guanxi*) this is exhibited to lesser mortals by flaunting the little trimmings that it affords. Again, very Confucian. In Tianjin, this invariably means posh black car (+ tinted windows if you really reckon you're important), uniformed security guard at the entrance to your apartment block or villa, (the latter often designed like a gigantic 'house-for-one' from a Noddy Book) and a reserved front row seat at all collective gatherings (a personal hate of mine).

Given all this, it is perhaps not so surprising that most Chinese still love the late Chairman Mao in a way that young children hero-worship a TV personality, pop star or a sportsman. (I used to love Valerie Singleton – actually I still do.) Mao, despite presiding over mass murder and cultural devastation, is still the big daddy, the revered cult figure at the very top of the Confucian hierarchy. Even the most critical of my Chinese friends will merely say that his actions were 70% good/30% bad. Yet I am sure I cannot be alone in thinking that his Cultural Revolution (where the collective history of the Chinese and the roots of its civilisation were all but destroyed) is possibly *the* most important factor in the apparent naivety of much of the nation today.

So there you have it. My thoughts for the day are over – at least until next term. I have much travelling ahead of me this summer fol-lowed by another year at school before my contract is finished. By the time I put pen to paper again, we will have analysed our first set of SATs and IGCSE results and China will know whether it has been successful in its bid to host the 2008 Olympics – two quite different things maybe, but definitely cause for some nervous excitement in the weeks and months ahead.

Zai jian for now.

CHAPTER 9

The Great Rickshaw Rip-off

September 2001　　2001年 九月

The long summer holidays over, I am now back at School and earning an honest living once more. Time to commit things to paper, or rather, to my computer hard-drive. So much has happened over the past two months that it's actually quite difficult to know where to begin. I want to tell you where my friends and I have been, of course, but more than that, I want to try and convey something of the impression people and places have made upon me as well. And if I have been getting just a bit blasé about my life in Tianjin, then the opportunity the holiday has given me to sharpen up my perceptions makes it all the more imperative for me to get things written down quickly. For if nothing else, the summer of 2001 has made me realise that China is a country of dizzying strangeness, where, if I can trivialise for a moment, the only common threads would seem to be: (a) an omni-present alto saxophone playing either 'Take My Breath Away' (never my favourite song) or that interminably tacky tune from the 'Titanic' (oh that the ship had gone down sooner), and (b) that wherever you look, someone is out to sell you something. Be it city or countryside, businessman or peasant, market stall or hi-tech shopping precinct, Han Chinese or someone from one of the ethnic minorities – everyone, everywhere has something for sale. Although I just managed to resist the temptation to invest in a month's supply of 'Cocowind Goat Placenta Essence' (made solely from the placentas of black Dongshan goats of course), if you *can* strike a deal, then both parties will surely leave happy – your trader will have made a decent profit while you wander off in the (usually erroneous) belief that you've got a real bargain. There are some bargains to be had of course (I was quite proud of my half-minute's-worth of negotiation

that reduced my Beijing hotel bill from 750 *yuan* to 450, not to mention my little string bag of five pint-sized terracotta warriors for just
under ten pence the lot), but, in general, your average Chinese trader
can just a bit too canny for us westerners. Nevertheless, once you get
into the swing of bartering, it's great fun.

I generally find travelling to be a cheerful business, and this
summer's odyssey went true to form. Wherever we went we were
feted by ever-curious, smiling natives with their familiar cries of
'Hello – where you from?' or, perhaps, 'Hello Postcard!' (rather like
'Hello Sailor!'). Dozens of little children (and their parents) clam-
oured to be photographed with us, by us, on us… One or two braver
souls approached us too. On one occasion they gently squeezed the
arm of one of my friends and exclaimed loudly and, I have to say,
with a degree of hilarity, '*da!*' (It means 'big' by the way.) On another
jaunt I was quizzed in broken English and flamboyant mime about
my companions – the 'three little maids from school'. Who was my
wife and which were my daughters? Ever being one for a quick
and witty retort I exclaimed that my three friends, Von, Ali and
Kate, were all my wives. 'Really?' came the reply, 'you don't look
that potent!' For once, it was I who was lost for words. However,
nothing we went through was quite on a par with the China experience of an American friend of the family some years ago, who,
having surfaced (Mal is a professor of mining engineering by the
way, and had been down some pit or other), underwent a ritual
scrubbing in a large soapy tub, watched by numerous civic dignitaries, their extended families and other worthies. By comparison,
we got off very lightly.

Most days there was at least passing reference to the Olympic
Games, reflecting the current mood of national satisfaction. The
Chinese are, by and large, a patriotic lot, proud to have been selected
as the host nation for 2008, but not offensively so. 'We are happy
because China has been accepted by the world' was something that
was said both to me and to others no doubt as well. Whether it will
have the desired effect of assisting China in its programme of domestic change as its image in the outside world is tested remains to be
seen though. The recent news of the forced repatriation of North
Korean refugees doesn't sound like a terribly good start to me, but
then other nations are not doing too well on the refugee front either
– at least not if the BBC World Service is to believed.

Enough of politics. Xi'an, the home of the Terracotta Warriors, was high on our itinerary, as indeed it is for many travellers to China. According to the 'Lonely Planet' the place once vied with Rome and later Constantinople as the greatest city in the world. Although I fear that Xi'an itself wouldn't get into many people's top ten these days, it is one of the few places in China where the city walls are intact and, incidentally, from which you can get really splendid views of both early morning *tai chi* and al fresco ballroom dancing. The city also boasts the delightfully named 'Big and Small Wild Goose Pagodas' together with an impressive Bell Tower (rung at dawn) and Drum Tower (dusk). Needless to say we each gave both drum and bell three hefty clouts: one for happiness, two for health and three for longevity. Xi'an is also the place where one can settle down to a traditional banquet of seventeen different varieties of *jaozi* or dumpling – each one made by hand – before being whisked off to a traditional Chinese entertainment. 'Hmm!' It was one of those 'all spectacle, no substance' affairs – Chinese kitsch at its most intriguing (what was 'Dong Dancing' going to be? we wondered) and glamorous – for even if the choreography was second rate Busby Berkley, clearly no expense had been spared on the amplification. Suffice to say I loved it.

I loved the Terracotta Warriors too. And whether or not the man who shook my hand and posed for his photograph really was the discoverer of the warriors, it was a memorable experience and good to believe that he might have been. Of course many newspaper column inches have been devoted to one of the greatest archaeological finds of the twentieth century, and as a consequence I am sure I was not alone in being just a little nervous that we might be disappointed. But there was no need to have worried, for the warriors exceeded expectation. Interestingly though, I always had it in my mind that the statues had been found intact, whereas, in reality, an enormous amount of restoration has gone on and is still going on today. Experts even believe that there are further sites in the area just waiting to be discovered and a thorough excavation of the entire complex is expected to take decades.

The following day we found ourselves in Guilin with its fabled river scenery, featured in Chinese restaurants everywhere from Gillingham to John O'Groats. The obligatory half-day boat trip on the Li River took us through a wonderland that is genuinely beyond

Left: Kate poses with a few present warriors from Xi'an, Shaanxi Province.

Below: The fabled Terracotta Army, Xi'an, Shaanxi Province.

superlatives – for the area boasts some twenty thousand limestone peaks, each more beautiful than the last. Our boat's destination was Yangshuo – which at just over two hours by air from Tianjin, is a place I might well return to if ever I should feel the need to get away from it all – a real Shangri-La if ever there was one. The name 'Yangshuo' means 'bright moon' and if I have any regret, it is only that we were not able to spend more time there and actually see it rise – we would only have been a couple of days away from a full moon. As it was, we had previously opted to go back to Guilin itself to visit the Reed Flute Caves (well worth the visit though) and to observe the celebrated cormorant fishing. To quote from the 'Rough

Above: Yangshuo on the Li River, Guanxi Province.

Left: The YuYuan Gardens, Shanghai – the China of the willow-pattern plate.

Guide', 'despite being turned into a tourist activity, people still make their living from this age-old practice throughout central and southern China, raising young birds to dive into the water and swim back to the boat with full beaks.' Ours was a rather bizarre experience. I, for one, had romantic notions of the four of us in a little rowing boat, midstream, in the still of the night, silent witnesses to an ancient and even mystic ritual. In reality we found ourselves with a couple of beers apiece, in a somewhat antiquated and extraordinarily noisy 100+ berth cruise ship in which we rattled around both figuratively and literally, as we had it all to ourselves. But we did see the cormorant fishing, close to as well.

I visited Shanghai for the first time last March, and although I was only there for the weekend, I was pleased at just how much of the place I remembered. The wonderful Peace Hotel on the Bund, which features so prominently in the opening sequences of 'Empire of the Sun', the vibrant shopping streets of Nanjing Lu and the like, and the glorious YuYuan Gardens. This time I was there for six whole days, and had the opportunity of revisiting these places and, of course, doing a lot more besides, significant amongst which was visiting the Shanghai Hyatt Hotel – which forms the upper part of the futuristic Jin Mao Building. With its eighty-nine floors, it is the tallest building in Asia, and home to 'Cloud Nine' – the highest bar in the world. Prices were well on the way to being sky high too, but being of the opinion that the occasional indulgence does no-one any harm, I enjoyed my frozen Margaritas and Manhattan cocktails whilst humming Cole Porter tunes to myself and feeling very 'man-about-town'. With such opulent surroundings and with a view to match, they were worth every *yuan*.

We searched around for a bit of culture while we were in Shanghai too, visiting carpet factories and pearl workshops as well as both the art gallery and museum. Although the former had rather too much 'boy-meets-tractor' stuff for my taste (as well as an indifferent tea shop), the museum was holding a special six month exhibition on the glories of Tibetan art – 'Treasures from Snow Mountains'. The exhibits were extraordinarily beautiful, and beautifully displayed too, although I was left wondering on at least a couple of counts – firstly on how artefacts some 4,000 years old could possibly be quite so well preserved (the altitude perhaps?), and secondly, whether, in the west, one could get away with such blatant, one-sided

View from 'Cloud Nine', Shanghai – the highest bar in the world.

descriptions of the warmth of the relationship between Tibet and the rest of China. I have not yet been to Tibet, but I am drawn to make the obvious parallel between it and, say, the West Bank, which I have visited, and where one race's liberation is, sadly, another's annexation. As a backer of the underdog, I found the exhibition's commentary just a little distasteful. On a lighter note though, I was sorely tempted to attend a concert of choral classics, featuring, amongst other things, the performance of somebody-or-other's 'Anus Dei'. For those of you un-versed in church Latin, the title should have been 'Agnus Dei' or 'Lamb of God'. 'Anus Dei', I fear, means something quite different.

In between seeing one group of friends off and meeting up with another, I spent a couple of days in an apartment belonging to an old school friend of mine and his wife. Stuart and Suzy now live in America, but they have kept their flat on and generously offered it to me. Suzy's mum still lives in Shanghai – conveniently next door too, so I was able to live with all the comforts of a real home, as opposed to a hotel, for a few days. It was lovely. Conversation was limited, of course, but not just because of the mutual language difficulties. In truth, I could barely get a word in, as I was virtually force fed from morning till night. 'Eat-a, eat-a!' she would beseech me, and after I had had my fill, out would come yet another course. I only put on a few pounds that weekend and think myself mighty lucky.

In retrospect, I was also pretty lucky to have found the apartment at all. Suzy had arranged with an English speaking friend of hers to collect me from my hotel and take me there at a pre-arranged time. Unfortunately, our paths crossed and Lincoln was waiting outside my bedroom on the forty-second floor while I, having booked out, was waiting in the foyer. I was beginning to get worried, as two e-mails, a fax, and a transatlantic call later we still hadn't found each other. But, to cut a long story short, a bit of dexterous fingerwork on the keypad of the hotel phone to Lincoln's mobile and the problem was at an end. Never again will I complain so vociferously about mobile phones.

Using Shanghai as our base for a few days, Vivienne and I took trains to Suzhou and Hangzhou where we visited numerous idyllic gardens and enjoyed a short boat trip on the famous West Lake as well – immortalised, like Guilin, in so many paintings. The lake itself was surprisingly deserted, I suspect because the sky's grey wash was heralding the approach of an afternoon rainstorm. However, this had its compensations, as the light brought the glorious scenery into sharp focus and the rain itself, although wet, was far from unpleasant – rather like being under a warm shower, but with your clothes on. I for one can almost go along with Marco Polo when he wrote, 'a voyage on this lake offers more refreshment and pleasure than any other experience on earth'. For refreshment, though, he would have been hard pressed to beat the 'Shelter-from-the-Storm Cafe' as we called it, where it seemed most of the population of Hangzhou were waiting for the rain to stop, and where two bedraggled English tourists, making up 'ancient' Chinese legends (we called them 'Carp Tales') whilst enjoying stir-fried chicken with cashew nuts (and the odd swig of whisky from the hip flask) provided the main entertainment. I have since bought an umbrella – for the first time in my life – and possibly intend publishing the collected tales under a pseudonym.

The peaceful gardens of Suzhou provided a welcome respite from the hustle and bustle of Shanghai too. Adhering to the principle of 'infinite riches in a little room', the gardens aim to produce, for quiet contemplation, that balance, harmony, proportion and variety which the Chinese supposedly seek in life. We visited four real gems: 'The Garden of the Master of the Nets', 'Blue Wave Pavilion', 'Pan Gate' and 'The Humble Administrator's Garden', travelling between the last two in some style (but, it has to be added, no little discomfort) in a sort of pedal rickshaw. Our first rickshaw man (rather frail-looking it has to be said) clearly didn't know what he had let himself in for though, and very soon decided he had got more weight than he had bargained for or indeed could cope with. Having tried unsuccessfully to deliver us to a far nearer garden, (but we stuck to our guns), he eventually struck a deal with a rather tougher colleague who, much hoicking and gobbing later, eventually delivered us to our intended destination.

Later the same week, we had further rickshaw experience, but this time it was in Beijing and it could have turned nasty. Vivienne and I had decided to take a taxi from our hotel to the Forbidden City, and, as for reasons known only to the higher echelons of Chinese bureaucracy, there is no stopping allowed anywhere in the vicinity of Tian'anmen Square, our driver dropped us in a side street some way off. Surprise, surprise, we were immediately pounced upon by two little men with carts attached to the back of their tricycles. Did we want a ride around the Square? Did we? It sounded fun, so we agreed a price of five *yuan* (about forty-five pence). Although I wasn't too sure whether it was five *yuan* each or between us, at that price I wasn't going to argue. Sure enough, we were pedalled down the west side of the square, and turned left towards Qianmen Gate. But half way along this second side, both men did a sudden U-turn, turned a sharp corner and took us down a rather forbidding looking alley. Stopping their little carts, they intimated that this was where the trip ended. Although we were disappointed that the journey was shorter than we had been led to believe, we got out and handed over the cash – and, as we were in buoyant holiday mood, gave them both ten *yuan* – twice the asking price. 'Oh No!' They were going to charge us 240 *yuan*, rather over twenty pounds, each. If ever I was thankful at having a smattering of Chinese it was now. In no way was I going to give them a single *yuan* more. A few short well-chosen phrases and we walked smartly along the alley and made our way as quickly as we could to the crowds in the Square. But they wouldn't leave us alone, following us on their tricycles and then on foot for a good ten or fifteen minutes, shouting and hassling us generally. Eventually we lost them in the crowds but it was an uncomfortable experience at the time – thankfully one of very few from my twelve months of living in China. It hasn't put me off Beijing, but it is the last time I intend travelling by rickshaw.

Although I am disappointed in my continuing failure to become more proficient in spoken Chinese, what little I did know served me well in Beijing that afternoon, so perhaps the great rickshaw rip-off will provide me with the incentive I need to try a bit harder from now on. However, I am getting better. I can now ask a waiter or barman for his attention (hitherto I had only been able to summon a wait-ress), and I can generally make the subtle but necessary differences in the tones that enable me to distinguish between 'cesuo' (toilet) and 'xie xie' (thankyou). Chinese traders too, take a great deal of delight in my mispronunciations. It clearly has a sort of novelty value which possibly adds to the pleasure of their daily living as well as my own. Or do I flatter myself?

One of my guidebooks speaks of travellers becoming 'templed out' when visiting China, and I was anxious not to fall victim of this malady. But North Hill Temple in Hangzhou was well worth the climb – especially as we discovered there was a cable car to take us down again. We had the place almost all to ourselves, and left the hordes of Chinese tourists at the better known 'Lingyin Si' (or 'Temple of Inspired Seclusion'). Not that this wasn't a splendid affair in itself, but it was far from secluded, and its 'fun day out' feel didn't quite suit my mood that day.

But for me, the best temples of all were in Chengde, where I was paying a welcome return visit, and Datong – to the north east and west of Beijing respectively. The Qi Wang Lou Hotel in Chengde is also my idea of a great place to stay and to rest your weary head. Built in Qing Dynasty style, it is just within the walls of the Imperial Summer Villa. Not the most expensive hotel we stayed in – far from it in fact – but, for me, definitely the one with the most atmosphere. I can well do without the four and five-star treatment that serves you up half a dozen deep-fried goldfish after forty-five minutes or more waiting in a cavernous dining room, illuminated by a couple of forty watt light bulbs. Although Chengde itself is a bit of a mess, the hotel and numerous temples more than compensate and, as a consequence, the 'Chengde Experience' will continue to feature

Vivienne settles down in her soft sleeper on board the train from Datong to Beijing.

Templed out at the Qi Wang Lou Hotel, Chengde, Hebei Province. The hotel certainly lived up to 'qi wang' – expectations.

prominently on my visitors' itineraries. Datong, too, is far from beautiful but the nearby Hanging Monastery and, in particular, the Yungang Buddhist Caves made the trip well worth the effort.

Travelling as we did by train from Shanghai and Beijing as well as Tianjin was a very comfortable experience. However, putting yourself so completely in other people's hands when it comes to procuring the actual tickets (in our case the admirable duo of Louie and Alan from China Travel Service in Tianjin,) took some getting used to. But there was no need to have worried, and, as arranged, our onward and return tickets were all waiting to be collected from our various hotels. Whether or not you are hurtling along at the speed of Eurostar or snaking slowly through the mountains, a Chinese express train (and a soft class seat or berth where it is available) is a civilised way of getting about. And if, in addition, you are into loose covers in a big way, then the trains (and soft class waiting rooms of course) will take you to within a few steps of heaven itself. However, such gentility is a world apart from hard seat waiting rooms and other public areas, where vast crowds of people seem to camp out or doss down on any surface where there is a semblance of the horizontal.

*Glorious Chengde, Hebei
Province, as yet relatively
undiscovered.*

On the trains themselves, distraction is provided by the endless
succession of vendors with their maps, magazines, huge kettles or
Thermos flasks of hot water (for green tea), pot noodles, beef jerky
(sounds and looks appalling), sunflower seeds and on one occasion,
perhaps specially for us westerners, cakes. However, I have long
stopped being tempted by these. Imagine, if you will, cheap Swiss
roll sponge (the drier the better), mounds of synthetic cream, and
flavoured/coloured rice crispies or those funny ball bearing things
for decoration, and you will have some idea why I leave them well
alone. A pantomime custard pie tastes better.

Throughout our travels, the scenery varied from the idyllic to the
impoverished, while both inside and out we had the opportunity of
observing the Chinese at close quarters – our fellow passengers
of course, men and women working in the fields, young girls and
old ladies washing their clothes in the rivers and lakes, children
swimming or kite flying and a fair percentage of the population just
sleeping in the shade – surely China's national hobby, and something

In need of some renovation, Chengde, Hebei Province.

at which I'm slowly becoming more proficient. Water buffalo, little herds of goats, giant fishponds, fields of tea, rice, lotus, sunflowers and corn alternated with scruffy little villages and grim, polluted towns, where uniformed station masters stood to attention and saluted as our train passed through, their official spot often painted onto the platform itself. On some of the flashier trains, carriage attendants too positioned themselves in the carriage doorways and saluted in return. A far cry from things back home I think you will agree.

It's hard to believe that my contract is already half over and that I'll be back in the UK looking for a job in the not too distant future. I've got a few ideas in mind of course, but they can go on the back burner for a while yet. My list of 'must sees' grows ever longer, and I'm far from exhausting even what Tianjin has to offer. Coming next time: 'In the Footsteps of PuYi – the last Emperor' and an impending appearance on Tianjin TV. Watch this space!

CHAPTER 10

In the Footsteps of PuYi

November 2001   2001年 十一月

September 11th was widely reported here in China, with the press, TV and radio all giving the day's appalling events full and detailed coverage. Although I had heard that there were a few gatherings of rather less than sombre students elsewhere in the country, those with whom I am in contact were deeply shocked and continued to assure me that, in China at least, western friends were welcome guests.

There is quite a strong Moslem presence in Tianjin, as indeed there is in many other parts of China. However, even in those areas most obviously Moslem, I, for one, have never experienced so much as a hint of animosity. In fact, once the initial shock waves had passed, daily life simply carried on as normal. But thinking about it, there is a surprisingly strong degree of tolerance in China anyway, and provided one does not try and evangelise, (which is strictly pro-hibited), Moslems, Christians, Buddhists, Taoists and Confucianists as well as party members and of those of 'no fixed abode' all co-exist quite peacefully. This pleasing go-with-the-flow mentality permeates most aspects of daily life.

Despite this, however, many Han Chinese, who form far and away the biggest ethnic group, do exhibit a chauvinistic attitude towards those of the minority groups. One hears of crack downs from time to time too, and only last week, I read of a sort of mini purge of Uighurs, a largely Moslem people of Turkic origin, in Xinjiang Province, in far north western China. Xijiang itself is China's largest province – the size of western Europe – and shares its borders with Mongolia, Kazakhstan, Kyrgyzstan, Tajikistan, Pakistan, India and Afghanistan. Whether or not the reported troop movements in the border areas had anything to do with the war in Afghanistan, or were part of a more general campaign against terrorism; a show of strength in case the Moslems in the region might be fractious or simply routine manoeuvres, I have no idea. But as this was the area I visited during the Chinese Moon Festival – a week long National Holiday in October – it is perhaps not too surprising that I was rather vague when describing my travel plans to friends and family back in England. In the end, all that I can say is that I saw no suggestion of trouble, and that my friends and I were greeted with that wide-eyed friendliness that seems to be such a hallmark of ordinary Chinese citizens – whatever their ethnic group or religious persuasion. In fact, a less threatening place is hard to imagine.

Of all the areas I have visited in almost thirty year's worth of school half-term holidays, Turpan is almost certainly the most remote. Our journey to this Old Silk Road oasis was a forty-eight hour trip by twenty carriage express train from Beijing followed by ninety minutes' worth of considerable discomfort in a broken-down bus. We caught the train with less than five minutes to spare and shared our four-berth soft class compartment with an incredibly beautiful dancer from Xi'an. I must say I was rather disappointed when she disembarked the first morning, leaving only her name card as a memento. (Cards, incidentally, are used by people from almost all walks of life and I now have quite a stack of them which, regretfully, I bin from time to time.) Our berths were comfortable – far more so than many of the hotel beds I have tried to sleep in over the last eighteen months – beds so hard that lying down feels as though you are being laid out and thus waking up in the morning comes as a pleasant surprise. But dozing on board the 'T69' and simply letting my mind wander as the train hurtled westwards through the night, with only the occasional jolting of the points to interrupt my dreams, was, for me, one of life's little joys.

The train was clean and well provided for in terms of dining car, western style toilets, air-conditioning, washing facilities and other necessities, and despite the long journey it was absolutely on time. I suppose there were about a dozen stops in all, the train remaining at the stations just long enough to enable us to stretch our legs or buy fruit (huge melons generally), bottles of water, beer and pot-noodles from the dozens of platform vendors. After Xi'an we were the only westerners on the train and thus the objects of considerable fascination, with a steady procession of passers-by wandering along the corridor and peering into our compartment. Another of life's little joys perhaps.

On the first morning we followed the spectacularly muddy Wei River for an appreciable time – a tributary of the Yellow River which it joins just east of Xi'an. This provided the perfect backdrop for light reading, Scrabble and Canasta – a new passion of mine. (It'll be Madeira or port and lemon next I hear you say.) But as we travelled further west and the landscape became more and more desolate, water became increasingly scarce, disappearing altogether once we reached the Gobi Desert and, eventually, Turpan. The Turpan Basin itself is the lowest and hottest spot in China and the second lowest place on the face of the earth after the Dead Sea. Any streams that do flow in this area simply lose themselves and evaporate long before reaching the ocean.

Barbara, an American friend of mine told me that Turpan was one of her favourite places – not just in China but in the whole world – and it was easy to see why. I warmed to it as soon as I had settled down to read the 'Guide to Services' in my hotel room – 'Gold, silver, diamonds and virtue please must be deposited in reception'. Definitely my sort of place I thought, as was 'John's Information Cafe' the vine-covered open-air paradise just opposite, where we ate, booked trips, accessed the internet, and generally chilled out. Although we did without the Uighur traditional dish of glazed roast camel, (I don't actually think John had it on his menu) his breakfasts of honey, yogurt, fresh bread and coffee were probably a more agree-able substitute. And when one could eat to the accompaniment of free live music from the four-piece band rehearsing next door (three drums and a *suona* – a sort of double reed trumpet, requiring the player to breathe in through the nose at the same time as blowing out through his instrument) one quickly realised that it was indeed a privilege to be in this faraway place. Like possibly only a handful of other places in China, Turpan is an easy place to be – in October anyway. But even in the autumn, it was baking hot by ten a.m., and one wondered just how much respite from the searing heat of summer could be provided by the vines and trellises which covered many of the main streets.

Understandably, Turpan is famous for its grapes (and its associ-ated bi-product of course), and the memory of Grape Valley, where one can eat Uighur food and drink Uighur wine (and yes, I did say

The ruined city Jiaohe near Turpan, Xinjiang Province.

they were Moslems) whilst lazing on low carpet-covered platforms stretching one's arms up from time to time to pick bunches of grapes from the roof, is one I vaguely recollect through an alcohol induced haze. Lamb kebabs tend to be the staple fare in these places, but for a change we thought we might ask for chicken. No sooner said than done. The restaurateur shoved his hand through a gap in the wire mesh fence and grabbed a passing hen which, needless to say, protested vigorously. Did we want a whole one or just a portion we were asked? You will be relieved to hear that this bird at least was granted a stay of execution.

Quite by chance, our choice of restaurant was a little up the valley from a museum dedicated to the musical achievements of a certain Wang Luo Bin. Mr. Wang must have been a significant figure in the cultural life of China to warrant such a memorial, but I had never

Gaocheng dancer near Turpan, Xinjiang Province.

heard of him. Being of a musical disposition, I was eager to address this omission and went inside. Wang Luo Bin not only looked like an oriental edition of Roger Whittaker, but he sounded uncannily like one too. Not for me.

Whilst most of the population of Turpan travelled around by donkey cart, we tended to book taxis for the morning or the afternoon. This presented few problems – drivers tout for business twenty-four hours a day, and haggling over the price is always part of the ritual (and fun) of it all. And if most local taxi drivers did seem to be under the 'patronage' of Big Mehmet, this hardly mattered as they did their job efficiently, taking us to a host of wondrous places in the Turpan area. The Flaming Mountains, so called because they have been eroded into fantastic flame shaped forms, camel treks in the desert, and Aydingkol Lake at the very bottom of the Turpan Depression were amongst my particular favourites. Although there

*Kerez irrigation
channel, Turpan,
Xinjiang Province.*

*Busking in the desert,
Xinjiang Province.*

was no water at all in this last spot, there was a sparkling 'lake' of
crystallised salt some two or three hundred yards from where
Mehmet's man dropped us, so we made to walk across to it. The surface of the ground seemed firm enough until it suddenly gave way
and we were up to our thighs in oozing, acrid mud, saturated with
salt. The more we tried to rescue ourselves, the deeper we sank,
much to the hilarity of the taxi driver. Of course we got out eventually, but we were plastered in the stuff. Needless to say, we crept back
to our hotel rooms as surreptitiously as possible.

The ruins of Jiaohe, summarily dismissed in one of my guidebooks
as a place with little left to see, was *the* five-star treat though – indeed,
Martin, one of my friends thought it was the best place he had seen
anywhere in China. We were lucky to have the whole place to ourselves for several hours too, (i.e. before the first of the tourist buses
arrived,) and even then, the majority of these visitors stayed around

the cafeterias and gift shops, or posed for photographs next to the sign that simply said 'Jiaohe' rather than actually explore the place. Jiaohe was a city of fifteen thousand inhabitants, some two thousand years old, and largely carved from the living rock rather than being built up from it. It should have been impregnable, situated as it was on a high plateau at the confluence of two rivers. However, Ghengis Khan did his stuff and wrecked the place in the thirteenth century leaving it in much the same state as it is found in today. Strange how passing time gives ruin and devastation a certain romance though. Jiaohe was nothing if not photogenic, and two reels of film later we reluctantly headed back to 'John's'. But if Ghengis had left the city alone, the Japanese would, no doubt, have destroyed it in the '30s and '40s or the Chinese themselves during the Cultural Revolution. I hardly think it would have been on any traveller's itineraries then.

Moving on from Turpan we next journeyed (by bus) to Urumqi, the capital of Xinjiang Province where we booked into the four-star opulence of the Holiday Inn – and pretty sumptuous it was too. Whereas Turpan is definitely a Uighur area, Urumqi is Han Chinese, and consequently the city itself was not unlike most of the other large towns I have visited in China – Tianjin included. But it was nice to wander around all the same. The Holiday Inn was close to People's Park (we had to pay to get in but I believe it was free for the Chinese), where we spent a very happy three quarters of an hour or so just people watching. So accustomed am I to things Chinese that I no longer even blink at middle aged people walking backwards along the footpaths, line dancing in the squares, or practising their *tai chi* under the trees. Even elderly ladies doing keep fit with gaudy pom-poms in their tightly clenched fists barely merit a second glance. Today, an octogenarian came skipping past. 'All part of life's rich tapestry,' I thought, whilst wondering how long these people stayed here, where they went afterwards, whether their husband or wives knew what they were up to, or indeed whether there were any clandestine liaisons going on. But I never did find out. In the UK you would avoid such people, or just possibly ask them if you could help them in any way or whether there was anyone you could ring. But here it is just life and a great way of spending forty-five minutes whilst waiting for a bus to one's next port of call.

Shut your eyes and imagine Julie Andrews skipping over the mountains in Salzburg and you have the perfect picture of Heaven

Above: Rashit's yurt,
Heaven Lake, Urumqi,
Xinjiang Province.

Left: Taxi for hire,
Xinjiang Province.

Lake. A little bit of oriental Austria no less. But there the similarity ends. Getting off the bus, we were met, not by some *fraulein* or young man in *lederhosen*, but by Rashit – an enterprising Kazakh who offered us a lakeside yurt for the night, to include three meals – cooked by his lady wife no less. Did we want it? At forty *yuan* each (about three pounds fifty it seemed too good an opportunity to miss. The Rashits lived in the yurt next door, and whilst ours would have slept eight or nine quite comfortably, Martin, Charlotte and I had it to ourselves. It was for all the world like being inside an exotic cake.

After our midday meal (stew) we explored the village and went for a scenic and invigorating walk around the lake before heading back to the yurt, Mrs. Rashit's evening meal (stew) and what I suspect was some sort of hallucinogenic tea. A stove was lit and we played Canasta until the light gave out. There were no washing or toilet facilities of course, apart from the lake itself and a few conveniently placed boulders, so being taken short in the night I nipped out only to witness a brilliant night sky with the full moon perfectly reflected in the surface of the lake. Dressed merely in pyjamas, it was pretty cold but I remained there for some time, quite mesmerised by what I could see and could hear – which, of course, was absolutely nothing. Such stillness. But the best was yet to come, for, almost miraculously, it snowed in the night. After breakfast (stew), members of Rashit's family saddled up horses for us and we trekked through the snow-covered mountains towards the bus stop and our journey back to Urumqi. By now the snow was coming down in great lumps and the horses slipped once or twice, but it was a breathtaking experience, both literally and figuratively, and one I am unlikely to forget. And to think that two days before we had been baking in the Turpan Basin.

Our return travel from Urumqi was by air, Beijing a mere three hours away from this enchanted land. Whether I would have actually chosen to watch 'Hit Man in the Land of Buddha' for my in-flight entertainment is doubtful, but there was no other option and it did help me re-acclimatise myself. As the plane came to rest on the tarmac, and I saw the serried ranks of cleaners being given their final instructions, I realised that I had packed even more into my half-term week than normal. But in so doing I had most definitely re-charged my batteries – there is much truth in the old maxim that a change is as good as a rest.

The weeks that followed proved to be very hard. September had already signalled the end of my School's honeymoon period and this on its own was difficult enough. But added to this, the unexpected death of my mother back home in England all but destroyed my charmed existence and brought me back to the real world with con-siderable harshness. I had been back in Tianjin less than ten minutes when my sisters telephoned with the sad news, and less than forty-eight hours later I was back with my family in the UK. I stayed in England for a little over two weeks, but despite the awful strangeness of it all, had a lovely time. An odd choice of word, maybe, but, absolutely the right one – particularly for the funeral itself, where the love that people so evidently had for mum was simply overwhelming. Back in China, colleagues and pupils have been wonderfully supportive too, and I am sure that, for me at least, the worst is over. Although, on occasions, I feel more isolated than I have ever done before, and, inevitably, waves of emotion wash over me from time to time, being so far away has its blessings as well.

I am hopeful, too, that the troubled start to the new term can be relegated to the history books. Orders we thought we had placed with various suppliers we discovered had not been authorised, salaries were late, our new apartments were far from ready, and promises we had been given about a host of other things were denied. I can honestly say that these last few months would have been miserable even without my mother's death. Most of the trouble has been simple heavy handedness on the part of the owners of the School – something which is evident everywhere of course and not just in China. But elsewhere I fear there has been signs of out and out corruption by people grotesquely unfit for positions of authority. On reading an earlier letter of mine, an old school friend, now living in America, remarked that he had detected the cycle of events that overtakes all expats. First the love affair, then the cold realisation that she is not quite the beauty that you thought she was, then the beginning of cynicism and disgust which is usually followed by understanding and tolerance. I hope, by now, to have crossed over to this last stage.

But there have been some special moments too, and back in Tianjin, one of those was undoubtedly when one of my Chinese friends and I set out to find the two houses that had been lived in by PuYi, the last emperor, after his removal from the Forbidden City in Beijing. They were in the old Japanese concession area, and sure enough, after a bit of scouting around, we found them both. The larger of the two, formerly known as *Zhang Garden* was still in fairly good condition and, having been converted into a public library, gave us the rare opportunity of being able to look inside the building. The smaller house, *Jing Garden*, however, had seen better days and had been converted into ten or so residential units. There were vestiges of grand windows behind assorted washing lines and bric-a-brac (do the Chinese ever throw anything away?) with the usual collection of

Jing Garden – one of PuYi's residences in the old Japanese Concession, Tianjin.

Left: Zhang Garden – now a library but formerly one of PuYi's residences, Tianjin.

Below: Seasonal Garden – my second home in Tianjin.

old sheds and dilapidated lean-tos in what was probably originally a formal garden. As we went out from the courtyard and into the street a lady in her late eighties I should say came up to us, and recalled how her husband had moved in the day PuYi was moved out – their paths actually crossing where we were standing at that moment.

A second memorable occasion was when I was showing Vivienne, a friend from England, around the wonderful Guangdong Theatre in Tianjin. I have been several times now and know the place quite well, and on each occasion have been just about the only visitor. This time was to be no exception, apart from the fact that the local TV company was there, filming the place and interviewing the old boy to whom the theatre owes its continued existence. Interviews followed, ably translated by my friend Summer, and I gather the programme has enjoyed at least one public airing.

Although the actual move was far from smooth, my new apartment in *Seasonal Garden* is surprisingly nice – far closer to the city centre but, regrettably, a long way from 'Mosquito World' and the other comfortable, familiar haunts of last year. But as these are being demolished anyway, perhaps it is as well to be away from the destruction and general demise of 'The Street'. In the name of progress, this demolition without consultation goes hand in hand with what I have rather aptly heard called 'bean curd construction'. Certainly there is more than a little evidence of this in my new apartment building where you have to switch off the central heating if you want to use the rinse cycle on your washing machine amongst other eccentricities. My cleaner, too, is a force to be reckoned with – forget the socks, she even irons the dusters. Fearing she has taken the exhortation to 'Keep Cleaning' that is displayed in the lift a little bit too much to heart, the apartment is now littered with bits of paper saying 'Please leave alone' in Chinese.

There are many good things happening in Tianjin as well. The open sewer of a canal that was such a feature of my walk to school last year is now really quite attractive, and although the rickety-rackety bridge that sounded like distant thunder from my previous apartment is no more, the whole canal project is something of which the Tianjin authorities can be proud. I have to confess I am less sure of the artistic merit of cinematic projections into the spray from the fountains which now surround the TV Tower, the electronic bunting that is festooned around virtually every revamped building, or the

*View from the TV
Tower in Tianjin
showing one of the
renovated canals.*

imitation mountain range that encloses one of the hospitals. But
then this is China. We are not in the Home Counties.

There is a strange contradiction in all of this too, and that is while
I can marvel at the tremendous speed with which all this has happened, I can, in the same breath, despair at the almost mind numbing
slowness with which more mundane tasks are tackled. On the surface
of it, Tianjin has been almost literally transformed overnight, and perhaps this is the crucial thing. Tianjin's 'face-lift' is no more than that.

By way of a 'stop press' I feel I should finish by passing on the
news that the BBC World Service and CCTV International
announced last week. China has finally been admitted to the World
Trade Organisation. Not being a business man, I've no idea whether
this is good or bad news for China (or the rest of the world come
to that) but if it can help build any bridges at all then it will be

something to be thankful for. The only local response, so far as have been aware, is that the bookshelf in the Sheraton shop (the best source, indeed the only source of western books, postcards, maps etc in Tianjin) was cleared last weekend apparently on the order of the Public Security Bureau or PSB. Doesn't sound as though the Tianjin authorities are too keen on the local populace broadening its horizons. Funny place, China!

CHAPTER 11

Welcome to Diagon Alley

January 2002   2002年 一月

I spent the other night in my apartment in Tianjin watching a pirated DVD of 'Harry Potter'. A good copy too, apart from the point where someone in the cinema audience, with an extraordinarily large head incidentally, walks in front of the concealed video camera and blocks the view for moment or two. I quite enjoyed it, but was particularly taken with Diagon Alley, that curious street somewhere in central London where witches and wizards buy their essential supplies. I was even more delighted to discover, however, that Diagon Alley is no figment of the imagination, but that it actually exists, and that is here in China. I promise you, Diagon Alley is just off Wangfujing in Beijing – the Oxford Street of the orient – just round the corner from Starbucks and more or less opposite St Joseph's church. Whereas a westerner can go quite unnoticed in Wangfujing, this narrow alley with its happy little huddles of people crowded round steaming cauldrons of food (or maybe they really are witch's brews) is in a different dimension altogether. I felt as though I was the only muggle to have set foot there for a generation or more. This is my sort of China – far removed from urban sophistication; an alternative civilization, co-existing, but almost untouched by the wider world – for the time being at least. The sort of place where you can get your broomstick re-twigged or your spellbook re-bound and have change from five *yuan*. I actually got my watch repaired for around this amount (forty-five pence or so) – literally fifty times cheaper than I was quoted back in UK.

I have a soft spot for nearby St Joseph's too, which looks gloriously out of place amidst Wangfujing's frenzied capitalism. When last I spent any significant time in Beijing, it had been during the

long hot summer. Then, outside St Joseph's, there were skateboard-
ers and young lads roller blading or doing stunts on their designer
bikes. This time however, it was several degrees below freezing and a
huge Christmas tree with garish blue fluorescent lights obstructed
their arena. And whereas, too, on fine summer mornings, the concourse in front of St. Joseph's would generally have been filled with
people maybe doing *tai chi* or simply lying flat out in the sun (to the
accompaniment of their pet caged birds and perhaps a couple of old
boys playing the accordion), this time, the place looked quite dead in
the cold morning light. With the strains of 'When I Grow Too Old To
Dream' emanating from the communion service going on within, I
nipped across to the adjacent McDonald's and grabbed myself a
rather tasty sausage and egg bap.

The vestiges of Christmas can still be seen in Tianjin, which is
strange as it arrived and departed almost unnoticed last year. But
this year, decorations abounded and the Christmas trees in Tianjin
and Beijing will certainly be there until Chinese New Year if not
longer. So, indeed, will the strange and somewhat tatty cross between
the stable in Bethlehem and Santa's grotto that I can see from my
apartment window as I write. And talking about strange crosses, I
am still desperately looking for a very special seasonal artefact spotted by a friend of mine in southern China a couple of years ago. If the
Chinese have an endearing habit of getting things confused, nowhere
can this have been more evident than in a street market somewhere
in Guangdong Province where the stall holder was selling small
Santas nailed to crosses. But just as Mao would have turned in his
grave if he had read my last letter and seen that I had muddled the
October Moon Festival with National Liberation Day, so we must be
careful not to judge the Chinese too harshly if they, unwittingly, get
things just a bit wrong too.

This winter has been particularly mild, with temperatures hover-
ing around zero or even a little way above for most of the time.
Whereas the canals and much of the Hai He River here in Tianjin
were frozen virtually solid last winter, this year there are great
stretches of open water where the ice has had no opportunity to
establish itself. On the lake surrounding the TV Tower however, the
surface at least is frozen over and last weekend the place was swarm-
ing with skaters and the like. You can hire sledges too, and curious
little chairs on skis which you propel by means of poles. My West

Left: Looking down from Tianjin's TV Tower.

Below: Enjoying toffee coated 'tang hu lu' (haws-on-a-stick) in the shadow of the TV Tower.

Country friend John Affleck, who lived in Tianjin in the '30s, remembers these from his youth and will no doubt be delighted to learn that they are still around. Fishermen, too, are in evidence, particularly on my journey to school, squatting on the ice, a round hole cut into the surface Eskimo-style. Uncomfortable maybe, but definitely photogenic.

The cultural highlight of the winter months so far has undoubtedly been the first performance of Handel's 'Messiah' to be given in China since 1949. It was a privilege to have been there and an experience not to have been missed I assure you. It was sung in Chinese of course (although the words 'Hallelujah' and 'Amen' would seem to be universal) and the audience, as well as applauding virtually every single movement (and some of them are no more than five or six bars long) clapped along with the encore of the 'Hallelujah Chorus' during which the soprano soloist (not being required) got out her camera and began to take photographs, before passing it to friends and getting them to take photographs of her with her bouquets. It was an uninhibited, joyous occasion – far more uplifting than merely standing up. And although there was much coming and going in the audience, there was only one mobile phone call that I was aware of so, by Chinese standards, it was very much a reserved affair – befitting the significance of the occasion of course. The chorus were superb by any standard, the soloists quite adequate, but the orchestra a bit creaky – the cellos and basses were out more than once, and, strangely (to western ears used to hearing ultra-authentic renditions), the 'continuo' was played on a piano – which, of course, would not have been invented. But this is nit-picking. I wouldn't have missed it for the world.

Of humbler significance, our School production of 'Joseph and his Amazing Technicolor Dreamcoat' was also a pretty decent affair. I'm not a Lloyd Webber fan – give me Mr. Sondheim any day – but the pupils (and the rest I hasten to add) really loved it. A boy in Year 7 who was playing the drums in the band asked me why we were doing it twice and I explained that we needed to in order to get all the mums and dads in and besides it was a pity to spend so much time rehearsing for a single performance. 'I'd be happy to do it ten times' I said. He thought for a bit and then replied: 'I'd like to do it a hundred times!' It's when you come across enthusiasm like that that you realise that teaching is probably one of the best jobs going. Later, in that same week, the adult choir I run did a concert for the charity 'ActionAid'. The performance was due to be in late October when the Tianjin choir along with hundreds of other choirs throughout the world was scheduled to be singing (sort of) simultaneously. However, the day before the big event, the Public Security Bureau (or PSB) here in Tianjin told us that we were a security risk and could not perform. (I never realised music was so powerful.) Not to be unduly downhearted, we postponed the thing and performed a couple of months later after the miles of red tape had been unravelled. It was worth it too. Tianjin Radio was there and recorded most of the performance (they were all set up and ready to go before they realised that they hadn't brought a tape with them) and two or three of us were interviewed afterwards. 'What is it like singing for charity?' was the first question we were each asked. The concept is quite strange to the Chinese I think.

'*Wo bu dong*' is a phrase I have used to my advantage more than once. It means 'I don't understand' and, of course, as I generally *don't* understand, I can use the phrase without any feeling of deceit. Sometimes, though, albeit rarely, I *do* understand, but choose not to in order to get my own way. Seats on trains for example, or stubbornness when it comes to being told to put your rucksack in a locker when you want to go round the supermarket. But, increasingly, I am finding that the Chinese have stopped trying to understand me – or so it seems. This can be particularly hurtful if I am enjoying what I think might be a 'good Chinese day'. In the mornings, I generally have to tell the taxi driver my school address. Of course, I could cheat and simply give him or her a piece of paper with the directions on; but no, when in Tianjin … Now, sometimes, I just know I am going to get the tones wrong or have a bad accent generally and am fully prepared for endless pronunciations of the same phrases. But on other occasions, I am supremely confident about being understood, only to be humiliated at the first hurdle. It is a good job I generally give myself plenty of time in the mornings.

And talking about understanding, I had a bizarre conversation only last week when I was chatting about *feng shui* in the staff room with another English colleague. We both knew *shui* was water, but, at the time, had no idea about the *feng*, so we asked one of our Chinese staff what it meant. 'Is it Chinese?' she asked. 'Yes', I replied slightly miffed as I thought I was having a 'good Chinese day' and had pronounced it pretty well. 'You know *feng shui*'. She didn't. 'Is it a place? I've not been there...' And so the conversation went on. Eventually, and seemingly endless attempts at pronunciation later, we discovered the word meant 'wind', but it took several minutes of tortuous explanation involving a good deal of mime and a rather wacky drawing on the white board with a marker pen long past its sell-by date. But at the end of the day I'm still convinced she thought both we and the concept were simply barmy.

Generally, though, it's not just that the Chinese don't know, but rather that many of them, possibly even the majority, don't seem to want to know. Few Chinese seem to have that sort of interest in things around them that western teachers try so hard to encourage in their classes. For example, I am a great fan of the 'Kneehigh Theatre Company' who have just performed their version of 'The Red Shoes' in nearby Beijing. I came across the advertisement quite by chance and thought about going. Is there any way in which I could get tickets, I thought, without physically going to Beijing myself a few days in advance? (Plastic transactions over the telephone are completely unheard of by the way.) 'I don't know' comes the reply from one of my Chinese friends and an abrupt end to the conversation. There is no dismissiveness intended. The person I am asking is simply telling the truth. She doesn't know. But, and this is the thing, she doesn't want to know either. She doesn't want to find out. I could, of course, *ask* her if she could find out for me, but the reply will almost always be 'maybe' which, to my mind, is just a face-saving way of say 'no'. This total lack of curiosity seems almost endemic with the result that yet another evening with a DVD is in store. It is comical at times of course, but at other times it is more disturbing. Have the Chinese simply had all curiosity knocked out of them over the years?

On other occasions though, the Chinese cannot be helpful enough. Take my telephone for example. The phone itself has a massive array of twenty-two buttons, some of which have a dual function too. ('Whatever happened to the simple dial?' I ask myself.) With the instruction booklet in Chinese there were bound to be just a few teething problems so a colleague arranged to have it translated. Paragraph one of our new 'Using Guide' is written in 'word soup' – an expression some of us use to describe this wonderfully well-intentioned gibberish. It reads as follows:

'Installation. First you should press setting key 14, the screen displays 'set up 1 – 8', then press 1, the figure that represents month glitter, now you can press 6 press affirmance, key 16, press 15 press affirmance, key 16, press 21, press affirmance, key 16, press 28 press affirmance, key 16, press setting key 21. Now the screen quit the status of setting.'

Paragraph two is shorter but carries on in similar vein:

'When the ring is ringing, or pressing the key for not picking up the receiver, or picking up the receiver, the screen will turn over automatically.'

Puzzled? I was, until I came across paragraph three:

'Connect the telephone wire with the telephone, put the plug into the socket'.

At last, my problems were at an end – I could make a call.

I have friends coming shortly for Chinese New Year which we will be spending with a Chinese family in one of my favourite haunts, Chengde – north of Beijing – before heading off for a few days to slightly warmer climes – Yangshuo, near Guilin. Then at Easter, one of my sister's families and I are planning a trip to the fairly remote south west of the country. Yunnan Province is one of the more exotic parts of China and, true to fashion, we'll be travelling there by train – a spectacular forty hour trip I am led to believe – although we will be flying back. Yunnan is home of the Naxi people – one of China's ethnic minorities, and Lijiang, their principal town, is a UNESCO World Heritage Site. It looks glorious in the guidebook and I can't wait.

But I'm off to lunch now. Will it be a taxi ride followed by steak and kidney pie at the pricey but unashamedly western 'Crystal Palace' or goose webs with black moss at the café round the corner? There is a Chinese saying that if you don't eat it, someone else. One this occasion I think I'll leave it to that 'someone else' and hail a taxi.

马年

THE YEAR OF
THE HORSE

ma nian

CHAPTER 12

Trains, Planes and Automobiles ... and Bikes, Boats and Motorcycles too

March 2002　　2002年 三月

A few weeks ago I returned from spending the most wonderful Chinese New Year in Chengde, north east of Beijing. I first met Jerry, our Chinese host, last summer, in Shanghai, when he and a friend approached me with that mind-numbing enquiry 'Hello! You speak English?' Undeterred by the weary response, (I'd already been asked the question at least a dozen times that morning,) he followed it up with a barrage of further questions including, inevitably, where I was from. Although I generally reply 'London' and then make to move on, on this occasion, and probably attempting a bit of one-upmanship too, I added that no, I wasn't here on holiday, but that I lived and worked in Tianjin.

'That is good. I am a student in Tianjin.'

'Like heck you are!' I thought.

'Maybe we can meet next term?'

'Maybe,' I replied, in as non-committal a tone as I could muster. And so the conversation went on ... and on.

To cut a long story short, though, it turned out that Jerry was indeed a student in Tianjin – as well as being a really genuine sort – and consequently we met several times in the run up to Christmas. An invitation to spend Chinese New Year with his family followed a few weeks later, and I accepted like a shot. However, plans were thrown into immediate doubt when Denise and David, family friends back in England, asked if they could come over to visit me at much the same time. Dare I ask if we could all come and stay, I wondered? Well, I dared, and the instant reply was one of sheer delight – yes, of course we could. What an opportunity this was to be.

Chinese New Year's Eve, and the K711 fast train to Chengde made just one stop, at a town about two hours from Beijing called Xing Long Xi An. Although, as a rule, I have long since stopped trying to decipher these place names, this time, as I had company and actually knew all the words – or at least thought I did – I decided to show off a little. 'Xing' means star, I said, 'long' is dragon, 'xi' is west and 'an' peace. A very nice name we agreed. Actually, rather *too* nice for that little bit of it we could see from the railway carriage. I was beginning to have my suspicions, and, of course, you don't have to have lived in China for more than a few months to discover that absolutely everything to do with the language depends on the tones. Thus, sadly, my translation, whilst undeniably poetic, was totally inaccurate; out, as ever, by a million miles. Come to think of it, though, I think I might have been more surprised if I had been correct. Xing Long was an extraordinarily grimy looking place, with a thick pall of smoke hanging over it in the still morning air. And although it was set amidst spectacular mountains, it was, we agreed, totally unworthy of the fanciful name I had bestowed upon it.

I think we were the only westerners on the train, which was fairly full even in soft class, and bursting at the seams in the hard class carriages. Chinese New Year is that time of year when just about everyone in south east Asia goes back home to see the folks. As a result, getting rail tickets is almost impossible without the services of a travel agent – in my case the ever-faithful Louie from China Travel Service. But although it was a comfortable express, few if any of the passengers seemed to be taking much pleasure in their four-hour journey. Even the sight of the Great Wall an hour and forty-five minutes or so outside Beijing provoked not a ripple of interest. Of far greater consequence were the countless purveyors of this and that who came through the carriage in never ending procession, gratifying the seemingly insatiable appetite of the Chinese for pot noodle and sunflower seeds. But we got our coffees, even if, as I suspect there was a bit of a mark up on the price – a sign, maybe, of China's newly won membership of the WTO. 'Maybe … maybe!' *Hmm.* Now that's a bit of Chinese culture I've picked up.

Jerry met us at Chengde Station, which, like just about everything else in China, (until the past few days anyway,) was decorated in red and gold. Cheerful, patriotic, supposedly lucky and certainly very traditional, (if a trifle gaudy to western eyes), the decorations, rather sadly, also served to heighten the general drabness of the town itself. Northern China is, of course, very dry in the winter months, and so dust on buildings, pavements, trees, shrubs, everywhere in fact, never really gets washed away. In Chengde though, things are made even grubbier by the presence of steam trains (I think we counted thirty-nine during our first night's interrupted sleep) and the Chinese obsession for brooms and sweeping. This latter pastime never ceases to perplex me, and in Chengde the sweepers seemed to tackle their work with a particular vengeance. But here, as indeed everywhere else for that matter, the job really only serves to disturb the dust and, so far as I can see at least, is of absolutely no benefit whatsoever.

New Year's Eve itself was spent in the magnificent Puning Temple – the Temple of Universal Tranquility, complete with its dozen or more resident monks. We arrived at 9.00 p.m. to find it spectacularly illuminated and spectacularly cold – something that even two sets of thermal underwear could not keep at bay. Several people in the crowd were sporting clever little chin and nose muffs – how I envied them, and how I wished for a cup of something warming. But, alas, the only warmth came from the burning of paper spills and incense sticks in the huge braziers that were to be found in front of most of the Buddhist shrines. Fireworks from the town itself periodically lit up the night sky and the noise of firecrackers increased as time went on. (At the time, I had completely forgotten that daily life would go on to a constant accompaniment of firecrackers for the duration of the Chinese New Year celebrations – i.e. the next fifteen days.) Monks and fireworks might well be an unusual combination, but the effect was quite agreeable nonetheless. And, although we were hardly the focus of attention, it was clear that the monks had had word of the three western faces in the crowd, and, it has to be said, many were momentarily distracted from their devotions.

Although I had visited Puning Temple before, this, in fact, was my third visit to Chengde, on this occasion the night air added a certain atmosphere to the place. Details that had, hitherto, passed quite unnoticed were disclosed, and the presence of our Chinese friends meant that many of the temple's mysteries would be explained. At the rear of the furthermost pavilion, for example, is a set of steps leading into a garden where the railings have been covered by hundreds and hundreds of padlocks. 'One lock – one hope!' explained Jerry solemnly. I certainly have my own hopes (but I'm ashamed to say, few resolutions) for this, the Year of the Horse – though it's a pity my horoscope is somewhat downbeat about those of us born in the Year of the Tiger. I am destined, like the Flying Dutchman, to wander alone over the face of the earth – for the next twelve months at least. How I wish I had been born a rabbit or an ox – they're due to have a lot of fun.

Staying with Jerry's family, we were most definitely 'honoured guests' (they had actually redecorated their apartment in honour of our arrival.) and we almost lost count of the number of meals we took in the lively company of hosts of relatives and friends (most family friends seem to be described as aunts/uncles/sisters/brothers or whatever), processions of visitors and dozens of phone calls and photo shoots. The *bai jiu* flowed freely although we stuck to the local beer, (cheaper than bottled water incidentally) as we ate our way through upwards of fifteen different dishes at a time. Traditional new-year fare consists primarily of *jaozi* – a sort of boiled dumpling which you dunk in vinegar. Unfortunately, when hot they have a tendency to slip through your chopsticks with disastrous effect. A little vinegar goes a long, long way believe you me. Most of what we were offered was delicious – the fish and the one thousand and one varieties of mushroom in particular – although I was less sure of something which was possibly (probably actually) leg of toad, the seaweed, tofu and fat noodle hotpot, and the whole chicken (and yes, I mean *whole* chicken) in caramelised batter.

Jerry's family had so little, yet what they had they shared with such pleasure. Furniture excepted, we almost had more in our suitcases than his immediate family had in their apartment or his aunt and uncle had in their tiny lean-to shop with its two little back rooms close by. Our hosts had registered our presence with the Public Security Bureau of course, and it turned out that we were probably the first westerners to have stayed in Chengde not to be based at one of the hotels. A privilege indeed. We were also the only first-language English speakers many of our new-found friends had had contact with. Thus, with the help of those who could translate, we chatted

Aunty's shop, complete with its New Year lanterns, in Chengde, Hebei Province. The Chinese characters above the door read 'bian min shang dian' – convenience store.

non-stop about every topic under the sun, as we were taken round the Imperial Summer Resort for sight-seeing and the obligatory sleigh ride on the ice. (We opted for the donkey rather than the goat-pulled variety by the way.) I also had a quick go on one of the little sit-down sledges such as I had seen in Tianjin. Unfortunately, though, it went mighty fast and I never really got the knack of steering the thing.

Our visit the following day was to the Putuozongsheng Temple – a World Cultural Heritage site and built to celebrate the sixtieth birthday of the Emperor Qinglong. It is actually a scaled down version of the Potala Palace in Tibet, and we had the place more or less to ourselves for the entire morning. Although magnificent, it is sadly in need of some fairly serious preservation – and pretty sharpish, too. But who will undertake such a task? Without wishing to sound too patronising, it is probably the case that the Chinese themselves would be more than happy to turn it into some sort of tacky theme park, and one shudders what would happen if the likes of Richard Branson or some other western entrepreneur were to hear of it. The place needs a benefactor with no ulterior motive – if such a person exists; someone who would plough any profits back into the temple

111

itself rather than lining his or her own pocket. Left in the hands of local officials (as it most surely will be) it will be a miracle if it is not wrecked by the end of the decade. For it is a sad fact that China has a poor track record in this respect. Of the eight thousand ancient monuments that apparently existed in Beijing around a hundred years ago, for example, seventy-eight, I am told, now survive. And whilst the Brits and the western allies are partly to blame for this, the Chinese were and still are pretty good at cultural suicide too. As I write, something I read a year or so ago now has just come back to me. It is that we expect people to die, just as we expect our own lives to end, but that the destruction of a monument is something else. Such things are built to outlive the creator. Through negligence if nothing else, Putuozongshen is most definitely at great risk.

In return for Jerry's family's hospitality, it was our pleasure to ask him to accompany us on a trip to Yangshuo, an hour or so by road from Guilin. Although we had quite expected him not to have travelled by plane before, what we did not anticipate was that he had never stayed in a hotel or been in a proper bath since infancy. It is the little discoveries, things like this, that you rarely glean from a book or get from an organised tour of a place, that make living abroad and getting to know the ordinary Chinese man or woman so fascinating. Although the hotel (and bathroom, too, I hasten to add) were fine, it was a pity that our China Southern Airlines flight was not quite the world's ultimate travelling experience. Squashed into our seats, the pilot chose to entertain us with a curious medley of what I can only assume was somebody's all time favourites including 'Home on the Range', 'Poor Old Joe' and 'The Old Folks at Home'. Without doubt the perfect accompaniment to a tepid Sprite or Coke. G and T – *meiyou*, whisky and ginger – *meiyou*, beer – *meiyou*, wine – *meiyou*, orange juice – *meiyou*. Perhaps British Airways really isn't so bad after all.

Yangshuo is the consummate place to unwind, with its pavement cafes and market stalls set amidst truly magnificent scenery. The Karst Café was a particular favourite – just round the corner from the little internet bar where one was promised assistance from a staff who would serve you 'soul and body' – and where I, unashamedly, ordered huge western style breakfasts every morning. From the comfort of an upstairs room, and through open French windows, I drank in the general ambience of the place, reflecting on the day just passed or musing casually on the day ahead. The scenery of the Li River is justly famous the world over, and whereas there might well be a degree of artistic licence in the pictures that are to be found in Ancient Culture Street here in Tianjin or in Chinese restaurants the world over, they are no exaggeration or flights of fancy. Yes, this was definitely the sort of five-star experience I felt I deserved and strangely a place where we probably felt more at home than our Chinese companion.

I have to confess that I have not really ridden a bicycle since first coming to China eighteen months or so ago. Tianjin's chaotic traffic has meant that I have not even been so much as tempted. But bike rides are most certainly the order of the day in Yangshuo, and hire shops abound. One trip took us, by way of a leisurely boat trip and a quick look at an ancient banyan tree, to Moon Hill – an arch of lime-stone rock shaped like a crescent moon. The ride was surprisingly easy given the fact that the area is mountainous – in fact I don't even remember changing gear. The actual hill was fairly busy, but as most visitors kept to the main path, it was easy to lose the crowds. Less easy was to lose the trinket sellers – at Moon Hill, even the time worn phrase *bu yao* was to no avail. Persistent just wasn't the word. Looking back on it I still feel just a little bit guilty that four or five Chinese ladies traipsed up and down that mountain without so much as selling me a bottle of water.

The Chinese concept of economics present in this sort of behaviour still astounds me, and friends and I frequently share stories of similar bizarre experiences. But, of course, at the root of it all, is the simple fact that China is a country where there is far more time and far more labour than there is money. The Chinese people have not yet reached the stage of economic 'development', if indeed that is the right word, where they realise that time *is* money. With bikes for example, they don't see what we might call the economic nonsense of charging a customer one *yuan* (less than ten pence) for spending fifteen or twenty minutes putting a patch on an inner tube, rather than spending five minutes installing a completely new tube and charging fifteen *yuan* for time and materials. Barbara, my American friend, told me the other day of the time she took her bike to a repair man in Tianjin. As her rear tyre was constantly flat and about one-third of the spokes in the wheel were broken, she asked her local bike man to make everything new. Later in the day she proudly rode off with

113

shiny new wheels and spokes and a wonderful new deep-tread tyre only to discover that the thing was flat again the next morning. It turned out that although all the exterior parts were new, they had put the same old, frequently patched inner tube back inside. And when she took it back once more for repair, they once again patched the tube up – they would not even consider replacing it!

But I digress. One other short excursion Denise, David and I made was to Fuli – this time by motorbike and sidecar. I've no real evidence, but my feeling is that Yangshuo itself was probably like this ten or fifteen years ago – before it became the backpackers' Mecca it is today. True, there was no place to sit and enjoy your *pijiu* and the 'Three Sisters Café' on the banks of the river was well and truly closed, but we had the little town to ourselves and enjoyed it enormously, as did we the cormorant fishing that same evening. I had seen cormorant fishing before, last summer in fact, but on that occasion it was from a huge boat that could have taken a hundred or so passengers. (The fact there were only four of us and that we had the craft to ourselves was by the by.) From Yangshuo, however, our experience was the real McCoy – a fisherman, half a dozen birds and us on a tiny, noiseless vessel in the middle of the night.

Although there is no shortage of budget style accommodation in Yangshuo, we stayed at the fairly opulent 'Paradise Resort' – conveniently located at the end of West Street and just a short stroll away from the river, market stalls, cafes and what have you. It is well run too, and good value for money, with large, well-appointed rooms and, I am sure, a fine if somewhat eclectic restaurant. There must have been some sort of weird 'hotpot promotions week' going on too, as the chef's 'specials' included field snail hotpot, yellow weasel hotpot, diced dog hotpot, and boar and bull genitals hotpot. Surprise, surprise, we steered well clear and ate out. However, we did decide to use the free welcome drinks vouchers we found in our rooms, and chose to save them for our last night – as a special treat of course. Thus, it was with no little anticipation that we presented them at the lakeside bar on the Saturday night. Strange, but as we did so, the extensive and expensive drinks list we had seen earlier mysteriously disappeared to be swiftly replaced by a truly miserable selection of soft drinks, tea, coffee and beer. Two *yuan*'s worth of *pijiu* between four was just a little stingy we felt for a hotel that charged round about five hundred *yuan* per room per night.

Chinese New Year is now officially over, but the sound of the fire-crackers has not abated, and back here in Tianjin explosions are commonplace. One reason is the fact that I live in an area of the city that is being rapidly developed, with buildings shooting up right, left and centre. (Actually, the same could be said of Tianjin as a whole – most of China too, come to think of it.) Chinese firecrackers are set off whenever a family or some business moves in, both to frighten off evil spirits and to bring good luck. Consequently, my home is far from the oasis of tranquility it should be and it's far more peaceful at school. The actual building work goes on for at least twelve hours a day as well, the sledge hammers started up at about 6.30 this morning, with the construction workers literally living on (or rather 'in') the job. And although the twenty or so westerners that live in my part of Tianjin are all known by sight, we still provoke interest and a little amusement from the builders when we cross the street to go to the market or the shops or to find a place to eat. Talking of which, a pretty good restaurant offering both Asian and European cuisine has just opened just over the road. 'Asrope.' *Hmm*. Not a name I would immediately have chosen. I assume it's a sneaky combination of Asia and Europe, but to me it sounds just a bit dubious. But 'Asrope' it is, and give the management their due, they could have called it 'Euria' which would undoubtedly have been worse. And although you can't buy the locust kebabs, sparrows-on-a-stick, intestines *varieuse*, deep fried chrysalises or black ectoplasm that you can get in Diagon Alley*, they do great seafood. In fact, as ever, all this talk of food is making me just a bit hungry. 'Asrope' here I come!

---

* Talking about Diagon Alley, which, as I have assured people before, actually exists, (it's up the road in Beijing in fact,) friends reliably inform me that there is an even more esoteric street in La Paz, Bolivia. There, there is a Witches' Market, where, for a minimal amount, you can get amulets for most things in life, a llama foetus for burial under that new house, and many strange and wonderful brews to add aroma to the street and 'lead to the pencil' – whatever that might mean!

CHAPTER 13

Crouching Toilet, Hidden Loo Roll

May 2002   2002年 五月

It's not every day that Tianjin hits the international news, but, to my certain knowledge, it has done so at least twice already this year. First, we had an AIDS scare early in 2002 and then, more recently, a truly awful dust storm, when, towards the end of last month, goodness knows how many cubic metres of the Gobi Desert was deposited on the hapless citizens of Beijing and Tianjin. It was most peculiar and, so far as I have been able to ascertain, came without any warning. We simply woke up to an ominous, orangey dusk-like light, which never really brightened. Although it wasn't a storm in the violent wind and pounding rain sense, more like a dense smog in fact, it was something I had not experienced before, and when, after twenty-four hours or so it eventually cleared, Tianjin, never the cleanest of places, was left in an unutterably filthy state. The light drizzle too, which fell for part of the morning, far from clearing the air, just seemed to bring down more of the stuff from the higher reaches of the atmosphere. The gangs of car cleaners must have had a field day the following morning.

Our other claim to fame, if you can call it that, was when Reuters, (but interestingly, neither local nor national press,) reported a minor AIDS scare, with news of attacks by enraged victims armed with syringes of blood apparently driving dozens to get tested. AIDS sufferers, we were told, angry at hefty drug prices and inadequate government care, randomly shot blood from syringes on *Binjiang Dao* – one of the busiest pedestrian shopping streets in Tianjin, and quite near to where I live. The rumours spread rapidly and there was quite a lot of panicky talk from amongst our Chinese staff at school. One of our classroom assistants even said she was going to Beijing and not coming back until it was all over. Unsurprisingly, the Tianjin alarm came as the Chinese government, ending several years of official silence, is beginning to face up to the threat of AIDS. In fact, the western press reported a scandal early last year in the central province of Henan where, in some villages, HIV infection rates surged as high as 65 percent after residents sold their blood to the transfusion services. It was, of course, these hapless Henan peasants who were blamed for the Tianjin incident.

But onto brighter things. I have just spent a couple of hours in one of my favourite parks in Tianjin – *Jinganggongyuan* – in the north east of the city. It's a tiny little place really, much smaller than the length of its name might suggest, and dwarfed by massive construction sites all around as well as the mighty double-decker Jingang Bridge which crosses the *Hai He* River right next door. But it is a better maintained park than most, surprisingly quiet, and at two *jiao*, (rather less than two pence), undoubtedly good value for money. I often spend a happy hour or so there simply people watching. Today, as well as the score or so of old men in Mao suits and hats giving their caged birds an outing – while the birds sing their hearts out, the men drink green tea from small thermos flasks (up-market) or old jam jars – there was an elderly lady engaged in the most fantastic contortions on the climbing frame, and, as a real bonus, a special offer on kidney bean and green pea iced lollies. The park itself is usually one of my ports of call when I go for a wander around the *hutong* in this part of the city. Elsewhere, these mazes of alleys are being demolished with frightening rapidity, but here they remain relatively untouched, for the time being at least, and afford a glimpse into a China which is fast disappearing. Incidentally, public opinion over Tianjin's extraordinarily rapid demolition programme which, unofficially at least, is all being done in readiness for the 2008 Olympics, is, more often than not, soothed by statements about the need to clean up the environment, remove health hazards or whatever, or else won over by insinuations that it is the people who live in these little streets (along with the Henan peasants of course) who are the main causes of crime. The nearby Dabei Buddhist Monastery is generally on my itinerary, too, when I am in this neck of the woods, along with a wonderful sprawling market and a decrepit pontoon bridge across the *Hai He* – another two *jiao* well spent. If less elegant than the Millennium Bridge across the Thames, which I have not seen but, I gather, is now only *formerly* known as 'Wobbly', it is, I am sure, every bit as photogenic – and probably equally as stable.

Since my last letter, one of my sisters and her family have been across to visit me, for what turned out to be a brilliant if exhausting holiday. Of course, I was determined from the outset to pack in as much as possible, and so it was hardly surprising that we caught the train from Beijing to Tianjin on our first afternoon by the skin of our teeth. The martial music that accompanies the departure of most express trains was already over as we hurried down the platform in search of carriage twelve or whatever. But, horror, not only was there no number twelve, but neither was there any time to stop and consider, rationally, why this might be the case. We bundled into the nearest carriage, to be halted in our tracks by a rather glamorous uniformed attendant who was, no doubt, trying to tell us to get off as the train was itching to go. A streak of arrogance rose to the surface and I decided I wasn't having any of it. 'I don't know what you're trying to say, luvvie, but we need to catch this train!' We clambered aboard. As the train left, my niece Jenny tended her bruised knee, she had fallen over in the rush to buy the tickets, sister Janice rummaged through her rucksack for her inhaler, the consequence of an escalator, a mighty long corridor, a flight of stairs, hundreds of passengers and the longest platform north of the Yangtse, while Chris and Martin, my brother-in-law and nephew, collapsed in a sweaty heap. 'Welcome to China!' I quipped merrily as the train gathered speed and I made myself comfortable. I glanced at our tickets – we were on the wrong train.

A further blow to my credibility occurred the following day, when we found ourselves on the wrong bus. This time, though, I was not wholly to blame, as I hope will be understood. A trip to the Great Wall is, naturally enough, a must for anyone visiting northern China, and as there is a section of it about three hours away from Tianjin, I am getting to be a regular on the 7.00 a.m. boneshaker to Huangyaguan. The bus is inevitably packed, and so, influenced both by our experiences of the previous day, and to be sure of getting seats, we agreed that we should get to the bus station a good thirty minutes or so early. No problems – we found the correct bus and staked our claim. In fact all was going well, until my sister decided she ought to go to the toilet as there would be little chance of a 'comfort stop' (I love that expression) once the journey had begun. Now, for those of you unaccustomed to the far east, I should say at this point that Tianjin North East Bus Station is not the place I would choose to get taken short, but as *cesuo* was in my vocabulary, I advised Janice what to do. Sure enough, she had a discreet word with the lady bus driver and the two of them disappeared into the throng. Only then did it occur to me that she'd been in China less than a day, and that I should perhaps have mentioned that there was unlikely to be a *western* toilet at the end of her quest.

As expected, the *cesuo* turned out to be an extremely primitive staff toilet some distance away from the bus, along a winding maze of passages, which, when the door was unlocked and my sister ushered inside, was totally devoid of light – natural or otherwise. Janice had no idea what to do or even where she was until, eventually, her eyes grew accustomed to the blackness and she became aware of the hole in the floor and the general ambience of her surroundings. But things were to get worse. There being no sound, and probably sensing some problem might have arisen, the driver apparently went in a few minutes later as well and proceeded to chat away to my sister in rapid Chinese – a well intentioned effort to reassure her maybe. Janice, incidentally, was by this time squatting somewhat anxiously in the corner, hoping beyond hope that there might be some toilet roll – which of course there wasn't. I won't elaborate further, except to add that no sooner had the two of them got back to the bus, than the driver began to recount what was evidently the 'crouching toilet hidden loo roll' story to the amusement of the other passengers. Lots of glances in our direction, much hilarity, and, as more people got on, further re-tellings of the tale, no doubt with little personal embellishments from those passengers who had heard it all before and felt they had something to add. Both subject and story-teller had clearly achieved something close to celebrity status.

'But what has this got to do with the wrong bus?' I hear you ask. Well, a couple of hours later, I confirmed with the lady driver, in my best Chinese of course, that the return journey, *laihui*, would be at three o'clock, *sandian zhong*, and thus, following an exhilarating horseride and walk on the Wall, we returned to the little bus stop in Huangyaguan with about fifteen minutes to spare. We waited and waited and waited, until, just as I was beginning to wonder whether my Chinese had let me down yet again, an antique bus came round the corner. Although it wasn't bound for Tianjin, it *was* going to Jixian, a town on the way, and as I was fairly sure we would be able to catch a Tianjin bus from there fairly easily, we got on and settled down for the bumpy ride. Quite what it was that made my sister look out of the rear window I never did ask, but ten or fifteen minutes into our journey, she glanced out the back to see her driver friend in the bus behind. The driver waved, Janice waved back, and then frantic gesticulations started as the second bus pulled out, dodged the oncoming traffic and swerved in front of our bus causing it to stop pretty sharpish. The two drivers exchanged a few words, out we got, changed buses, and after many thankyous and much laughter were on our way again. Nowhere but China we thought.

The main journey of our holiday was a very different affair though. Two days of comparative peace and semi-luxury in a soft sleeper on board the T61 from Beijing West to Kunming – a distance of over three thousand kilometres. This was only the second time I had been to Beijing West Station – the biggest and either the most impressive or vulgar station in Asia, depending on your taste. As it is also a place where it doesn't pay to get lost – it handles up to 600,000 passengers per day – and not wanting a re-run of my experience there last autumn – when again I only just caught the train – we decided we ought to get there in ample time. And so it was that we settled down in the sumptuous leather armchairs of the soft seat waiting room for half an hour or so, got ourselves generally sorted and stocked up with provisions for the journey. And a short while later, as the train pulled out of the station – at 8.00 p.m. on the dot – we toasted our forthcoming holiday with a glass or two of what the label unashamedly called 'spanking wine', and chatted away until sleep finally got the better of us.

Just over twelve hours later we reached Wuhan, and, over break-fast, crossed the Yangtse – an eerily, misty spectacle observed from the comfort of the restaurant car – conveniently adjacent to our car-riage. The flatness of the north east had given way to textbook pic-tures of China – water buffalo and paddy fields, ducks and goats, coolie hats and haystacks. The landscape between Wuhan and the following stop, Changsha – Mao's old stamping ground – continued in much the same vein and, indeed, at times, looked almost as though it had been landscaped by the oriental equivalent of

Capability Brown, with its mountains and rich green meadows. There were some seriously impressive viaducts and tunnels too, no doubt the work of some Chinese Brunel, and a gradual if less startling change in the domestic architecture. Yes, things were becoming very picturesque, although Chinese factories, alas, look much the same wherever you go and all churn out the most appalling filth. Something else which caught my eye though were the little funeral mounds that were dotted here and there. There are many mini-graveyards on the train journey between Tianjin and Beijing – family plots squeezed in between the tracks and the fields like extra large egg cartons with flat stones on top; but here, the mounds were topped with flags, to be replaced further south by what looked like tunnels cut into the side of the hillsides, with white, possibly stone, arches in front of them. I had not seen anything like this before – a research project for my retirement perhaps.

The train was running a little ahead of time when it pulled into Liu Pan Shui at about 8.00 a.m. on the second morning, and where I surfaced after a good night's sleep. The married couple with whom I shared my compartment once more offered to share their breakfast of fruit with me, which I accepted this time, although, to tell the truth, I would have preferred to have stretched my legs on the platform and seen what the station vendors had to offer. I was also rather keen to see any members of the long-horned *Miao* who might just happen to be around. According to the 'Rough Guide', women of this particular ethnic group wear the strangest of hairpieces resembling bolsters made from plaited hair bound round wooden buffalo horns. As luck would have it, though, I was trapped in my compartment by a sizeable group of passengers engaged in what, to the uninitiated, looked like some variant of *tai chi* – I'm told it was called *chi kung* – instigated by our carriage attendant and which completely blocked the corridor. Oh well, maybe another day. I did manage to escape briefly at the following station however, *Xuan Wei*, where I was quite taken aback by the glorious revolutionary music (chorus and full orchestra) being belted out from the station loudspeakers.

By now, the landscape was becoming increasingly mountainous, with stunningly executed terracing almost up to the summits, which were often crowned with clumps of trees. From our vantage point we were able to look down onto and into the little villages of stone and wood, noting not only the mixture of crops being grown (how I wish

I knew what things were) but also how labour intensive the agriculture was – not only in this part of the country incidentally, but all over China. Blossoming trees, too, added to the rural idyll and general charm of Guizhou Province. Idyllic for us, perhaps – relaxing in the comfort of our little air-conditioned sitting room on wheels, with its vase of plastic flowers and giant thermos of hot water.

When, forty-four hours or so later, we eventually pulled into Kunming Railway Station, we were warmly greeted by a representative of China Travel Service who was actually waiting for us on the platform with the plane tickets that were take us, the following morning, to our final destination – Lijiang. Although the red carpet was nowhere in sight, we felt like minor celebrities as he ushered us through to the front of the taxi 'queue' (or at least what passes for a queue in China) to be whisked off to the Camellia Hotel – highly recommended if you are ever in these parts. Kunming itself seemed a lush, relaxed and friendly place, although I personally found the number of beggars, some of whom had a truly shocking degree of disability, quite disturbing. But, it certainly looked as though it might be the sort of place worth spending time in, although, for now, it was merely to be a stopover.

As if the rail journey to Kunming hadn't been spectacular enough, the flight to Lijiang was spellbinding – forty minutes in a cloudless blue sky across the most magnificent terrain imaginable and culminating at the foot of the poetically named Jade Dragon Snow Mountain. More than once we were actually lower than the mountain tops on either side of us, and almost on a level with the little villages that were dotted on those remote peaks where the land was fertile enough to be terraced and farmed.

Lijiang Old Town, the home of the *Naxi* people, is quite exquisite, and our hotel, the Ancient Town Inn, was just inside the entrance – a low two-storey house set around a traditional, secluded courtyard. Conveniently placed armchairs there, and the open-air balcony up the stairs at Lamu's House of Tibet on the other side of the street gave us two perfect vantage points from which to observe the bustle of every day life, and the opportunity of scribbling these few notes whilst basking in the early-morning sunshine and enjoying warm Naxi bread and Yunnan coffee. I always meant to try the yak meat, yak butter, yak milk … but somehow never felt quite up to it. Lijiang itself is criss-crossed by deep streams – tributaries of the Jade River which divides at the entrance to the Old Town, and these streams are the focus of much of the activity – from hair-washing to food preparation. One restaurant kept its fish in a nearby drain, presumably to keep it alive and fresh (sic) until the very last minute. As someone used to the chaotic roads in Tianjin, an added bonus was that the streets were traffic free – no vans or cars, no motorised belt driven vehicles with handlebars or even bikes. Just people and a handful or so of woolly bonsai-sized dogs which seemed to have the run of the place. It was the cats, curiously, that seemed to be on leads.

The 'Rough Guide' considers Lijiang to be rather like a cultural theme park, and I must confess it is certainly geared up for visitors. But to what extent the Naxi women in particular were dressed up for the tourist or simply wearing what they would be wearing anyway is difficult to ascertain. Similarly, the musicians of the Naxi orchestra – were they rapt or bored out of their minds from giving their nightly performances in the company of irksome Eileen, her introductions were regularly twice as long as the pieces themselves, in an auditorium full of noisy, trigger-happy photographers? And what about the all-male funeral procession, with its firecrackers, laughter and gaudy hand-held banners? Genuine, or an episode from the 'Truman Show'? One thing that was undoubtedly authentic though was the Dongba language, spoken by almost all the people we met; Mandarin is very much the second language in Lijiang. The written language, too, was quite different from anything I had seen in China before, and took the form of highly stylised pictograms, for all the world like the hieroglyphics of ancient Egypt.

Although some of Lijiang's streets are very commercialised, a few minutes wandering up the little alleys and across the tiny bridges will take you to a different world where, at every turn, there is a photo opportunity, be it a group of men coming home from their day in the fields or a glimpse of family life in a cluttered courtyard. Here, I suspect, you are as close to the real Naxi culture as you are likely to get. And if we *were* intruding, there was no sign that we were in any way unwelcome. Theirs was not a show being put on for our benefit. We were simply surrounded by kindness, curiosity, well-meaning advice and good humour – from the lesson in chopsticks offered to my brother-in-law to the grave warning, involving some typically inscrutable Chinese logic, to avoid a particular street peddler: 'He has a tattoo. He is from Shanghai. He is a bad man.' Q.E.D.

Lijiang, Yunnan Province – the home of the Naxi minority people.

Dr. Ho, China's most famous medicine man, outside his clinic in Baisha, near Lijiang, Yunnan Province.

Jade Dragon Snow Mountain dominates the skyline in Lijiang, and thus a visit there was a must. To give you some idea, Lijiang itself is, at 2,400 metres, pretty high up and already a good thousand metres higher than Ben Nevis – and we wondered why it got cold at night. The summit of Jade Dragon Snow Mountain, however, is higher than the Alps, and even the cable car drops you off at the height of the Matterhorn. Is was hardly surprising, therefore, that we all suffered from a bit of altitude sickness, and were forced to reflect, in a sober and even humble manner, how unwise we were to have scoffed at the menu in the café at the base of the cable car where one could have bought a range of truly useful merchandise – from a cup of hot chocolate to a bag of oxygen. The view from the cable car was, as you might expect, spectacular if a little scary, particularly when the wind caught us and rocked the gondolas – it would have been a long drop into one of the mountain's nineteen glaciers. And hardly less scary, for me at least, was a sort of bob-sleigh ride I went on in a car inner tube – something that I was talked into doing by Martin, my teenage nephew. Yes, there was a sheer drop beyond that dangerously low embankment. It was bitterly cold at the top too, so we were feeling thankful that our thoughtful taxi driver had had the foresight to pack a plastic carrier bag of extra warm clothes for us. However, on opening the bag at the summit anticipating scarves, hats, gloves or better still fleeces and woolly jumpers, all we found were a number of thin cotton Dongba outfits for my niece and sister to pose in for photographs.

Such was the soporific atmosphere of Lijiang that provisional plans to visit Dali and Tiger Leaping Gorge got the thumbs down. Instead we opted for the nearby village of Baisha, which nestles right at the foot of Jade Dragon Snow Mountain. We booked a taxi for the return trip, but no sooner had we got out than we were accosted by a trio of Naxi women who, clutching a gigantic tape-recorder, dragged us along to join their impromptu dance at the edge of the carpark. Ten exhausting minutes later we were released and after a quick dash through an avenue of market stalls that had been hastily manned during our dance, it was clearly a delaying tactic, we arrived at one of Baisha's main claims to fame – the Liliu Temple with its beautiful Dongba frescoes. With the cheerful sound of children from nearby Baisha County Primary School playing football in the background, we were privileged to have this gem of a

125

Diorama in Shaolin, Henan Province, birth place of Kung Fu.

temple more or less to ourselves for thirty minutes or so. Following
the track upwards towards the mountain we eventually met up with
Baisha's main street and bumped into the little town's second main
attraction – the renowned Dr. Ho, a practitioner of traditional
Chinese medicine and quite a big shot in these parts. I had read a
little of the 'Dr. Ho Phenomenon' before setting out, and so it was,
perhaps, with some scepticism that we entered his clinic where we
were entertained, as expected, with much chat, countless press cuttings and copious cups of his special 'healthy tea'. Dr. Ho has a working knowledge of two, or was it three thousand different medicinal
herbs, and has received more visitations and accolades from public
figures than you or I have had hot dinners – facts that he was more
than keen to elaborate upon. Nevertheless, our forty-five minutes
or so with him was completely fascinating and, we all agreed, time
well spent.

Sadly though, our spell in Lijiang was over all too quickly and it
was soon time for us to return to the real world – for my sister Janice
and her family, Beijing airport, and for me, the train back to Tianjin.
Like so many other places I have been privileged to see, a second visit
would be wonderful; but although I have now officially renewed my
teaching contract for a further year, my list of 'must sees' grows ever

longer, and realistically, I must conclude that a return is probably unlikely, perhaps not even sensible.

So, that's it. I've gone on quite long enough. My thrilling if inconsequential adventures with the kung fu monks of Shaolin, along with some more prosaic memoirs of the splendid Longmen Grottos and, hopefully, graphic reflections on the quick canter I had along the sandbanks of the Yellow River must remain until next time. I bet you can't wait!

CHAPTER 14

A Tianjin State of Mind

June 2002   2002年 六月

Having rather less than a fanatical interest in the beautiful game myself, but with most of China seemingly totally immersed in World Cup culture, both colleagues and students at school are in a complete frenzy, the present circumstances have opened one of those so-called windows of opportunity you read about from time to time and have lent themselves very nicely to a bit of letter writing.

I got my preferred variety of cultural fix two or three weeks ago when I attended a performance of 'The Merchant of Venice' in Beijing, given by the Royal Shakespeare Company. It was the company's first Chinese tour and I think I would probably have gone anyway, to wave the flag and all that; but with the set having been built by an old schoolmate and with Jo Keating – a good friend from my Dorset days – as stage manager, there was that extra incentive to be there. A coach load travelled up from Tianjin (getting back by train late at night is always difficult) and all of us, I think, were suitably impressed with the production. Visually it was stunning – but then given my connection with two of the company I suppose I'm obliged to say that. Actually, though, set, lighting and costumes were all wonderful, and the music too, apart from an anachronistic little sing-along in part two, was most effective and largely unobtrusive in helping create the appropriate atmosphere and in heightening the action when needed. In fact, once I had got over the first five or ten minutes and adjusted to Shakespeare's language, (*wo bu dong* as we say over here – I don't understand,) I settled down for a superb evening.

The play was my first dose of western culture since 'Messiah' just before Christmas and possibly the first ever encounter with western

Jo creating a disturbance in Beijing.

culture for a fairly large proportion of the audience. The tickets, for example, as well as reminding patrons to switch off their mobiles etc., also stated, quite categorically that they had to dress neatly, refrain from wearing slippers and to enter the auditorium in an orderly manner. This last must have come really hard. There were no big names in the cast, and as a result, the whole thing came across beautifully as an ensemble piece. Clearly Shylock dominated the stage whenever he was present, but he did so because of the role he was playing and not because he was some big soap star enlisted to boost flagging ticket sales. So three cheers for the RSC and if you get to see this touring production yourself, you won't be disappointed.

For ages now I have been of the opinion that all important events or decisions in China are at least formalised if not actually decided over a banquet in a glitzy restaurant. It therefore came as no surprise that Windy's wedding should follow the established pattern. Windy (and yes, it *is* Windy and not Wendy) is one of our Chinese teachers at School, and a good personal friend, so I was very pleased to accept her kind invitation. As this was the first Chinese wedding I had had the privilege of attending, I was obviously anxious to do things properly. What do I wear? for example, what do I give the bride and groom? (of course), and do I have to stay to the end? (invariably the most important question of the lot). As to what to wear, it seems that weddings are much the same as any other occasion in China and that really anything goes – Chinese slippers excepted of course. The Chinese seem to have little concept of what we might call 'dress sense' – but then, why should they? At school for example our female Chinese staff regularly alternate the wearing of evening dress, jeans, cut-off shorts, traditional *qi pao* and miniskirt. Thus, even at an occasion as significant as a wedding, posh frocks for the ladies or suits and ties for the men were far from universal. Indeed the only common element in people's dress were the lucky red hair slides most of the ladies wore – distributed in the same way as we might give out carnations for our buttonholes back home. Presents were similarly easy, but here there was almost complete uniformity – hard cash – put in special red envelopes and placed in plastic carrier bags clutched by the bride and groom as we entered the dining room. I believe some newlyweds use this money to offset the cost of the reception.

The marriage itself was registered twelve or so months ago, but with the joint reading of the vows, it was now *official*. 'What does that mean?' I asked Vera, a rather straight-laced Chinese teacher on our staff. 'Just that they can have sex!' she replied in quite a matter-of-fact tone of voice. Good for them I thought, and quickly downed a glass of *bai jiu*.

Windy herself always manages to look stunning even on an off day, but on her wedding day she excelled herself, changing her ensemble more than once during the course of the afternoon and looking more and more glamorous with each outfit. With her husband, she came round the various tables for small-talk and endless photocalls featuring miscellaneous combinations of friends, family and sundry worthies. I am sure they couldn't have had so much as a mouthful of food all afternoon. Surveying the guests though, I noticed to my surprise that one of our more youthful Chinese teachers, Freda, was not there. Had there been some bust up I wondered. But on asking the reason, in as diplomatic a way as possible of course, I was told that it was because she was pregnant. Traditionally, to invite someone who is in such a condition is extremely bad luck. Far worse luck having to invite one's inebriated boss I should have thought, (I can't imagine that going down at all

well back in Britain), especially when he insists upon making a
speech through an over-reverberant PA system and proposing a toast
or two, or three …

No-one can accuse me of having allowed the grass to grow
beneath my feet since coming to China, and, given a free weekend,
mini-breaks are very much the thing. Shortly before my birthday for
example, a group of us flew to Zhengzhou, just south of the Yellow
River, for a number of fairly gruelling excursions to nearby (sic)
places of interest. Zhengzhou itself is dreary, memorable only for the
journey from the airport to our hotel, when we were entertained, if
that is the right word, by Winnie, our hugely incompetent singing
tour guide. This young man, alas, had almost less English than I have
Chinese and was sacked the following morning, but not before he
had sung his heart out. 'Thankyou for the clap!' he murmured tear-
fully as he sank inexorably towards his fate.

The next day, Kaifeng and its so-called Iron Pagoda were number
one on our agenda, and although we did manage to convince our
driver that a 6.30 a.m. start was not quite in order, we were still on
the bus mighty early for the two-hour run. Built in the eleventh century, the Iron Pagoda is actually made of normal bricks, but covered
in specially glazed tiles that make it look a little bit like iron. It is
an impressive structure though, and most of us got to the top for
the view of Kaifeng – a town that looked far more interesting
that Zhengzhou, and where the city walls are original and more or
less intact too. But there was a strict no lingering policy and we
were quickly whisked back to Zhengzhou, where the entire city was
apparently without electricity thus making for a protracted lunch
stop, and onto Shaolin, tourist blackspot, and home of the famous
kung fu monks.

Each year, thousands of Chinese and not a few foreigners enrol at
Shaolin's martial arts school, where according to legend, monks,
seeking relief between long periods of meditation, imitated the natural motions of birds and animals, developing these exercises over
the centuries into a form of unarmed combat. Certainly there were
monks to be seen, but those that I saw amongst the hordes of tourists
looked neither venerable nor deadly, but were of a disappointingly
everyday variety. Nevertheless, much of the kung fu that is known in
the west accredits its origins to the monks of this small mountainous
region of China, and in the adjacent town literally hundreds of boys

and young men could be seen practising their skills – and pretty impressive some of it was too. Less impressive were the numerous stalls selling unappealing snacks, ice-creams and shoddy souvenirs, while the temples themselves were a bit on the average side to say the least. But the so-called Thousand Buddha Hall was better than most, with its forty-eight deep depressed footprints that are said to have been left by the monks practising kung fu in far-off times.

Luoyang, where we stayed for our second night, was an infinitely nicer place than Zhengzhou, and with our hotel situated next to one of those Chinese market-cum-restaurant streets that I love so much, I was as happy as could be. Although it is apparently known to hor- ticulturists as the peony capital of the world, we missed the best of the displays by several weeks. However, not having a great deal of time for peonies myself I wasn't overly disappointed. For me, Luoyang's proximity to the fabulous Longmen Caves was far more important. Although not as spectacular as the grottos at Datong which I visited last summer, they are still highly impressive, forming a wonderful treasury and gallery of Chinese Buddhist art, with around a hundred thousand images and statues of Buddha and his disciples carved into the limestone cliffs on the banks of the Yi River. Of course, there has been much damage, and, sadly, not only from the ravages of time – they are all about fifteen hundred years old. Regrettably, but I suppose predictably, European and North American explorers have left their mark, doing little to enhance the place in the process, and what they left behind Mao's Red Guards managed to just about complete. But it was still a most uplifting place to be – despite tourists posing in the lotus position in several of the empty niches.

From the Longmen Caves (for once accurately translated by me – and to much acclaim I might add – as 'Dragon Gate' caves), our next destination was the Yellow River where we were to spend our final afternoon before heading back to Tianjin. Now, the 'Lonely Planet' is my constant travel companion, and I had read about the road between the grottos and the Yellow River and the opportunity it afforded to see some of China's cave dwellings. Up to a hundred mil- lion Chinese people apparently live in cave houses cut into dry embankments or in houses where the hillside makes up one or more walls – a fact the luckless Winnie knew nothing about, (and that his successor, too, dismissed as being of little consequence come to think

In the saddle in the middle of the Yellow River, Henan Province.

of it). However, I was both keen and persistent, and managed, with a little difficulty, to photograph a few of the dwellings that lie adjacent to the road. Some were clearly derelict, but others had the red and gold couplets left over from Chinese New Year which indicated, I was fairly sure, that they were still in use. However, we could not persuade the coach driver to stop or even slow down for that matter, and, for the troglodyte experience, we had to make do with a subterranean restaurant at Huayuankou – definitely not recommended if you ever find yourself in the area. The River itself was great though. To quote from the 'Lonely Planet', it has 'always been regarded as *China's sorrow* because of its propensity to flood. It carries masses of silt from the loess plains and deposits them on the riverbed causing the water to overflow the banks. Consequently the peasants along the riverbank have had to build the dikes higher and higher each century. As a result, parts of the river flow along an elevated channel which is sometimes more than fifteen metres in height.' The effect is indeed extraordinary. We travelled a few miles upstream by hovercraft (a first for me) and disembarked on a large sandbank in the middle of the river where I bravely volunteered to go horseback riding. I have the photos to prove it too.

My birthday bash early in June, was in Beidaihe, when a dozen of us went for a weekend to the Guesthouse for Diplomatic Missions – who could resist a hotel with a name like that? Not unlike an old Pontins or Butlins holiday camp, but mercifully without the amusements, the hotel was made up of assorted buildings in various stages of decay but all with the most wonderful sea-view balconies. Here one could, if one should happen to be so inclined of course, sit in rattan armchairs, make small-talk and drink birthday cocktails until the small hours. It was, no doubt, a Party guesthouse in days gone by, and its private beach was presumably once the preserve of the party cadres. However, this sort of official hierarchy, publicly at least, seems to be slightly on the decline – for which the vast majority of the population can be well and truly grateful. But even though the beach is now open to the general public (or at least to those who can afford to stay in the Guesthouse) there are many areas that still remain off-limits to those without the necessary *guanxi*. These 'connections', for want of a better word, continue to play an important role over here in getting (or not getting) what you want/need/deserve in life, and for all its socialist ideals, it is clear that China is far from being a level playing field in this respect. However, there are a few rays of sunshine in what is still a generally depressing and distasteful picture. It was good to read reports of a recent speech by Chinese Prime Minister Zhu Rongji a few weeks ago, for example, when he spoke of *serious* corruption amongst government and party officials – a mighty strong term to use. Addressing the National People's Congress in Beijing, he attacked official 'deception, extravagance and waste' and criticised local authorities for building ostentatious offices and lining their pockets by fair means or foul, whilst failing to pay wages on time. In a country where the undeserving rich generally seem to rule the roost, it is a pity that Zhu, who is well liked and one of the, possibly, few good guys in positions of authority, will be stepping down in a year's time. Perhaps the road sign Beijing which warns passers-by that 'the slippery are very crafty' is not so much Chinglish as a warning to that naïve that there are a number of unsavoury characters about.

The Chinese themselves took to bathing in the sea about one hundred years ago when Beidaihe developed from small fishing village into one of the major seaside resorts in the north of China. Originally patronised by European diplomats, missionaries and businessmen,

John Affleck who lived in Tianjin in the '30s, remembers going there with his family as a small boy, staying, no doubt, in one of the many villas that were built at the turn of the century, a few of which still lie half-hidden in the woodlands. We travelled there by express train after school on the Friday, each doing our own thing the following day before meeting up at *chez* Grierson in the evening for a few drinks and an impromptu concert before (*and* after) a barbecue on Saturday night. About half the group sing in a small expat choir I run in Tianjin, so, of course, the quality of the singing was arguably a little more sophisticated than might have otherwise been the case. To tell the truth, to imply the concert was totally ad lib is not strictly accurate – I did pack a bit of music in my bag … just in case anyone should ask.

Reds, a Chinese friend, and I went to Nandaihe, about four or five kilometres away on the Saturday afternoon. We hired one of the little motorbike-rickshaws that ply their trade in small towns everywhere and our return trip, including the stopover which was in excess of an hour and a half, was a mere thirty *yuan*. Nandaihe's chief attraction, totally unexpected too, was a sort of ski-lift which took you about half a mile out to sea and dropped you on an artificial island devoted to the sort of amusements that the Chinese love but which I could well do without – synthetic rocks with fountains and waterfalls, a dusty, cavernous restaurant (closed of course), karaoke galore, fake temple with bell, electric fireworks, bungee jumping and such like. They did have a rather large helter-skelter that deposited you unceremoniously in the sea, that in retrospect I wished I'd had a go on, but at the time I fear I chickened out.

At the start of our journey on the ski-lift we heard a bit of a commotion and, looking down, saw a couple of Chinese ladies, cameras at the ready, anxious to take our photographs which would be developed by the time we took the ride back. I just wish I had had the foresight to have my camera at the ready too; far more amusing than the two of us sat in a ski-lift would have been the shot of two ladies running along the jetty, wearing what I have come to call 'Great Wall Shoes'. I refer to a style of utterly hideous footwear peculiar to the Chinese, I think, and possibly even a cultural reaction to bound feet. Great Wall Shoes have toes a good six inches longer than need be and must make ordinary walking, let alone running along jetties, a total nightmare. Hence the proclivity for women of any age to wear these

135

Chair lift to the 'amusement island' at Nandaihe, Hebei Province.

when climbing the more hazardous sections of the Great Wall or sprinting beneath a middle-aged man on a ski-lift.

The other photographic encounter of the weekend was during a thirty-minute trip around the bay when about twenty Chinese holiday-makers and I bundled on to an ancient fishing boat. (As I have suggested before, your average Chinese is as likely to fly as he is to queue in an orderly fashion.) The boat hadn't even untied before the photographs started, and I reckon upwards of two hundred snaps were taken, many, I venture to suggest, cunningly contrived to include me. Perhaps they were as taken with my hat as I was with their shoes. Or perhaps they just knew it was my birthday.

Booking in and out of Chinese hotels, something I have done many times, still remains a strangely elusive art. There always seems to be an extraordinary amount of checking and counter-checking to get through. On leaving the Guesthouse for Diplomatic Missions, the management tried to hang onto the six-hundred *yuan* deposit we had paid for the rooms claiming that there was a towel missing – i.e. implying that one of us had nicked it. Regrettably, the experience became just a little unpleasant and, rightly or wrongly, I became quite angry – not only at the distress it was causing one of my friends in particular, but also at the very idea that a group of teachers were likely to go around amassing private collections of hotel towels. The incident was over in about ten or fifteen minutes, and fortunately we didn't miss our train back to Tianjin, but it left a bad taste in our mouths all the same. Although I would still maintain that the average Chinese person is charming, as friendly as you could possibly wish, honest and totally sincere, there is, at the same time, an almost complete lack of trust (and possibly even respect) between petty official and the ordinary man/woman in the street.

There was confusion of another sort the last time I stayed in a hotel in Beijing too, where renovations added to the general pandemonium of booking in. I've used the Song He Hotel many times, as it is central and actually quite good. However, I have yet to perceive any semblance of a system when it comes to arriving and departing. Our arrival this time was made all the more exciting as we had used an 'illegal' taxi from Beijing airport, a nice guy in a little van with a solitary, intermittent windscreen wiper, who wanted his money up front (no problem there) who, I think, got lost *en route*, and who, on finding the hotel, couldn't find the front door as the whole place was bandaged in red, white and blue plastic sheeting. We eventually found what had hitherto been the tradesman's entrance and scrambled up a couple of flights of stairs to the reception area which had been temporarily relocated to the second floor, where, as ever, chaos reigned, and where a bevy of charming if somewhat flustered receptionists could be glimpsed behind mounds of paperwork, wires and dodgy electrical appliances. The deafening noise of the hammers and pneumatic drills made our communications, never easy at the best of times, more difficult than ever, but, as we were in no rush, it was easy to put it all down to the inimitable Chinese experience. After all, we did manage to book in in under an hour.

The art of Chinese cookery is another one of the skills that I had really intended getting to grips with over here, but restaurants and market stalls are so plentiful and food so cheap and good (and utterly fascinating to watch being prepared) that I had, until recently, virtually given up the idea. But then, as is often the case in China, the unexpected happened. I had already been invited to lunch one particular Sunday, when, the day before, I got a call to ask if I would like to help prepare the meal as well. As it was to be *baozi* (Chinese dumplings) I readily agreed, and the following morning I was to be found in the company of a delightful Taiwanese Chinese lady whom

I had met some months previously whilst showing some friends around Ancient Culture Street here in Tianjin. I think I made a good attempt at kneading the dough, rolling it into thin pancakes and then making little parcels containing combinations of the various fillings that I had made whilst the dough was rising or whatever it does: minced pork, finely chopped mushrooms fried in olive oil, green beans with dried shrimps, chervil with aniseed, and chopped Chinese leaves with spring onion. I became quite proficient at stirring the water in the huge saucepan so the *baozi* didn't stick and adding cold water from time to time so as to allow the contents to re-boil. The fried variety (*guotie*) were quite a success too and my batter of flour, water and a sort of balsamic vinegar was spectacular. The preparation time for a meal for three was roughly three hours though, and I was ravenous by the time we sat down to eat; but even given my cack-handedness, I cannot see how it could realistically be cut to less than two. One wonders, therefore, how the local market vendors can possibly make a profit selling polystyrene take-away boxes of both *baozi* and *guotie*, all freshly prepared and in a range of exotic fillings, for a few measly *yuan*.

Term ends in just over three weeks time, and a group of us have decided to travel home on the Trans-Siberian railway – five days from Beijing to Moscow, two further days to Cologne, and then on to Brussels and Waterloo. There can't be too many people who have made that journey, and, in a sort of masochistic way, I'm looking forward to it very much. I was invited to renew my contract at School for a further year too, which, after a little consideration, I accepted. So although I do not see myself as a 'lifer', I will be back in the far east by the end of August, and, if all goes well, look forward to indulging myself once more and scribbling a few more traveller's tales before the year is out. But for now, it's a cup of coffee in my brand new Golden Jubilee mug, courtesy of Jo and the RSC, while I attempt to get onto the internet and zap this letter to you.

CHAPTER 15

Five Go Mad in Moscow

September 2002   2002年 九月

I made a hasty getaway from the end of term staff karaoke, really not my idea of fun, in order to pack for what was to be one of the most exciting journeys any of us had undertaken – travelling home on the Trans-Siberian Railway. Four friends and I had been mulling over the idea for several months. It certainly looked like an adventure, and at fifty-two, adventures do not come every day, but with two weeks of in-service training scheduled for the beginning of the holidays, ten days on a train would have eroded far too deeply into what time was left to us. But then things changed for the better. As a staff we agreed that we would 'devolve' one of the two weeks we had planned and all take our TEFL (Teaching English as a Foreign Language) course on Monday evenings after school. And then, when it came to planning worthwhile activities for the remaining week, we discovered that we really only had enough to justify two days, thus releasing three further days. Add those to the devolved week and take into account the weekend in between and, hey presto, ten days. We made our reservations with 'Monkey Business' in Beijing without delay.

In-service training days for teachers began about fifteen or so years ago, if my memory serves me right, when they were called Baker Days after the then Secretary of State for Education. I don't think any of us in the teaching profession ever doubted the potential value of such days – for preparation, worthwhile development activities, planning meetings or training generally. But, looking back over fifteen or so years' worth of them, I cannot honestly say they have been an unqualified success. New initiatives, sometimes ill thought through and often short lived, and which, by design perhaps, made you feel evermore inadequate; reams of paperwork to justify some crank's latest brainwave or Ph.D. thesis; dreadful, harebrained things, fortunately a passing phase I think, called cross-curricular issues ('themes' and 'strands' I believe they were called) ... I shudder as I write. Occasionally something good would crop up – a guest speaker maybe, for whom education was a passion and who might be genuinely inspiring – but, I am afraid to say, I found more than a few of them a bit of a waste of time and one or two even insulting to a teacher's intelligence and integrity. How wonderful, therefore, to have had the clout to be able to suggest that our three 'spare' days might be better spent as holidays, secure in the knowledge that all of us would spend a sizeable chunk of our free time on school business anyway. I am reminded of something I read years ago now, when some bright spark abbreviated Baker Days to 'B-Days'. Everyone knows what 'bidets' are there for, but no-one really knows how to use them properly.

Day One began rather earlier than expected with thumping on our bedroom doors at 5.10 a.m. – Jeanne, ever meticulous when it comes to detail, had set her alarm wrongly. However the extra hour did enable us to indulge in longer showers than we had planned, as well as giving us more time to check out of our Beijing hotel, where, as ever, the lack of any perceivable system was apparent from the outset – something, incidentally, that always needs to be taken into account when planning a journey in China. A short walk to the station followed, where, after a little bit of hanging around, the man from Monkey Business showed us into the compartments that were to be our homes for the next six days. I was delighted. A couple of bunks, an armchair, a ferocious fan, a small table (with giant thermos flask beneath of course), a proper western toilet at the end of the corridor, and, to our astonishment, a shower cubicle per pair of cabins. All was spotlessly clean and the shining Formica was a joy to behold. The only omission, to our surprise, was that there were no towels. But there was no time to address this oversight and to the accompaniment of martial music and an entire platoon of station staff standing to attention, the weekly K3 service for Moscow via Ulaan Baator departed at 7.40 a.m. on the dot.

We had been going less than a couple of hours before the dreary flatness associated with Tianjin and Beijing changed for the better. The train reached the Western Hills and, not long after, began following the line of a sizeable chunk of Great Wall. The mountains soon

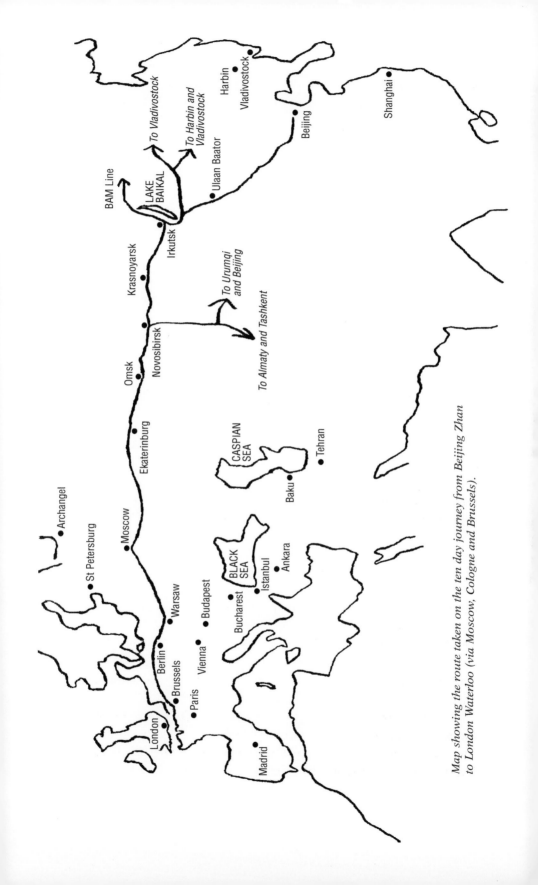

Map showing the route taken on the ten day journey from Beijing Zhan to London Waterloo (via Moscow, Cologne and Brussels).

gave way to vast loess plains though, punctuated by patches of curious tall trees not unlike poplars. Whether naturally, or as a result of cultivation, these trees had few, if any, branches of appreciable size. Instead, their trunks seemed to be covered in small twigs coated with thick green foliage with an extra thick bit of thatch on the top. In the distance, and with the presence of a little mist to give the scene some atmosphere, they looked like herds of strange, graceful animals or even enormous birds – ostriches maybe or cockerels, perhaps even dinosaurs waiting expectantly for something to happen. Almost certainly the trees have been deliberately planted, and, judging by the nature of the fine loess soil, probably planted to slow the desert's relentless approach on Beijing. They have certainly turned out strangely though, but then with so much of China extremely peculiar to behold, why should trees be any different?

We had been given meal vouchers for the Chinese restaurant car and so, shortly before noon, we wandered down to take our places, looking forward to a drink and a leisurely lunch before curling up with a good book or, it being the first day of the school holidays, an afternoon nap. None of it. 'Please, you must hurry!' we were urged in broken English. 'The Americans ... they are coming!' Nothing could have induced me to eat up faster and so, rather earlier than I had expected, I settled down in our compartment for an hour or so's read. What luxury. Being teachers, we had all brought lots of books with us – I had the complete Professor Challenger stories by Sir Arthur Conan Doyle (utterly dreadful, but what a fantastic job some enterprising drama students could make of 'The Poisoned Belt'), a murder mystery actually set on the Trans-Siberian, Vikram Seth's beautifully written Chinese travelogue 'From Heaven Lake' and the programme for this year's Edinburgh Fringe Festival. I made a start on choosing the shows I would go and see.

Gazing out of the window for long stretches of time, the scenery was strangely, almost hypnotically beautiful: mysterious patterns of deep valleys with vertical sides, carved into the land by the combined forces of wind, rain and man; the odd patch of dinosaur trees; field upon field of crops and numerous small villages with single-storey houses and large walled courtyards of the sort that are being pulled down every day in Tianjin. The city of Datong, of course, was a mess, as only Chinese cities can be. By about teatime though, this landscape was gradually replaced by sandy grassland, punctuated with the occasional ragged bush or stunted tree – scenery that was eventually to become the steppes of Mongolia and Siberia. Sadly, horsemen were not to be seen on this first evening, merely the occasional truck making determined if somewhat erratic progress through the alternating patches of coarse sand and grass.

As dusk fell we approached Erlian and the Chinese side of the border with Mongolia. Here we were required to disembark for an hour or so while the bogies were changed. Russian and Mongolian railways operate on a slightly wider gauge than do Chinese trains and, I believe, those of the rest of the world. It was a warm, dark night as we wandered out of the station building and through the bustling night market with its cheap stalls, shops, cafes and rickshaw men. Towels were number one on our list. Expecting the search to last forever, lo and behold, the first shop we went into had a great pile on the counter – at least we thought they were towels. In fact they turned out to be packets of noodles, not that that mattered a single bit. A little skilful mime indicated what we wanted and although the shopkeeper didn't sell them himself, he knew a man who did – of course. We sat down to a late night snack of lamb kebabs and beer while our shopping was done for us.

Boarding the train once more and then crossing into Mongolia itself seemed to take an absolute age though. As well as the lengthy wheel changing, the passport checks were very protracted and we had some confusing customs declarations to sign too, the result being that it was a little after 2.00 a.m. before we pulled out of Dzamyn Ude and were actually on our way once more. However, another ten or twelve hours were to pass by before we reached Ulaan Baator, the only city in Mongolia I had ever heard of.

At first, the terrain was not so unlike that which we had left behind in China, although it was definitely becoming hillier and greener as we headed north. But there was also something strange about it that I couldn't quite place at first. Later it was to dawn on me that, whereas virtually every spare inch of land in China is cultivated, here it is all grassland, stretching as far as the eye can see. It is against Mongol belief to dig or till the land, to 'break the slumber of the earth'. There were a few towns or villages en route though, and occasional collections of yurts to be seen, the Mongols call them *ghers*, along with herds of stocky Mongol horses and small groups of camels, cattle or gazelles. The villages themselves consisted of highly

Our luxurious apartment aboard the Trans-Siberian.

Martin made great friends with the Russian dining car attendant.

photogenic single-storey dwellings in bright pastel colours such as you see in pictures of Russian peasant scenes – lots of blues and greens – alongside, inevitably I suppose, exceedingly dreary low-rise flats. But although there was ample sign of human habitation, there were few actual men, women or children about. Certainly no Mongol hordes – just a benign old boy on horseback driving half a dozen or so ponies. Hardly the warrior-child of Genghis Khan. We pulled in briefly at Choyr mid-morning where the silver-coated statue of the first (only?) Mongolian astronaut could be glimpsed behind the station building, and, battling our way through the platform vendors, stretched our legs and loaded up with provisions – Coke, Sprite and something that looked like kaolin and morphine called *airsag* – fermented mares' milk – included. Apparently Mongols can drink up to ten litres a day. My secret stash of Nescafe provided a useful alternative.

Not long into our second day, and we were already giving many of our fellow passengers names or at least characters. There was the serial killer of course, thinly disguised as an Ozzie pilot working for Dragonair out of Hong Kong, Miss Marple's lover (an African diplomat supposedly with the UN), and the very strange man in the woman's wig and two-piece suit, who although initially our 'prime suspect' was, in all probability, a red herring, travelling simply to confuse the plot. Of course there was no plot as yet, as no crime had been committed, although the attentions of one particular middle-aged man towards a young boy in Erlian and later towards another youngster on the train could have been humorous had they not been so disagreeable.

As we got closer to the capital, there was more woodland to be seen, birch and pine, and more sign of civilisation too, with bigger and more frequent villages, Ulaan Baator itself being a strange mixture of soviet style flats and groups of *ghers* surrounded by wooden fences. It was a twenty-minute or so stop, and a fair number of passengers disembarked – including many of the other westerners on the train. Although we had been travelling on a single track line for some time, from here to Darhan, Mongolia's second city, and from there to the border at Sukhebaatar, we made particularly slow progress, making repeated use of passing places to allow huge trainloads of timber to come through. But we were in no rush, and the extra time was well spent sharpening up our game of Canasta. The boys thrashed the girls I'm pleased to say.

Day three began at Ulaan Ude, around two hundred and fifty kilometres inside the Russian border, and close to the junction of three of the Trans-Siberian rail routes. We guessed that the time was around 4.45 a.m., what with protracted border crossings and changing time zones we could make little sense of our watches or the timetable, but already it was hot. Although there were no station vendors on the platform, there were a couple of promising looking shops that were already open, but alas neither Chinese *yuan* nor our US dollars were of any use, and there was no sign of anyone prepared to do any currency exchange – either legally or on the black market. Disappointed, we headed for the dining car which had miraculously changed from a Chinese one to a Russian one, and at 5.00 a.m. or thereabouts settled down to a hearty breakfast of bread and cheese, fried eggs and strong coffee, served by a charming Russian waitress resplendent in pinafore and sparkling golden teeth. Fortunately she did accept our dollars, and, as we discovered later in our trip, was more than happy to do a few under-the-counter currency transactions too. The waitress remained a delight for the duration of our journey, my only little niggle about her general demeanor being her method of waste disposal. Straight out of the carriage window.

The lush green meadows were by this time giving way to *taiga* – alternating grassland and forest – and increasing signs of cultivation, including diminutive vegetable gardens adjacent to many of the little timber houses. These were notable for their tarred or corrugated tin roofs and ornately decorated windows. It was a beautiful summer's day as the train travelled its picturesque route along the bank of the Selenga River and, eventually, the shores of Lake Baikal. 'The Pearl of Siberia' is the world's deepest lake and widely regarded as one of Russia's most beautiful natural attractions. Crystal clear, swimmers have been known to get vertigo, and, I read, for the most part drinkable, it is set round with mountains and lined with little settlements of wooden cabins. At over one mile in depth it contains about 20% of the world's fresh water, and, if this were not enough, for three months of the year doubles as the world's largest skating rink. It is also, by far, the world's most ancient lake, and between 70 and 80% of the recorded animal and plant species in the area are found nowhere else in the world. The *nerpa* for example – a freshwater seal – separated from its nearest relative by three thousand kilometres, and the *bug-eyed golomyanka* – little more than as blob of pinkish fat – which lives at extreme depths only to dissolve into an oily spot when it is brought to the surface.

Our train whizzed through lots of little stations, each with long, low platforms and, more often than not, a little gingerbread-style station house, perhaps with a spire. I, for one, certainly expected to see the name *Anatevka* or something else out of 'Fiddler on the Roof' painted on the platform name board. The train did pull up for five minutes or so at a small lakeside station shortly before Irkutsk, but this seemed largely for the benefit of the carriage attendants who bought smoked fish, roubles only of course, as a change from their dumplings and as an accompaniment to the potatoes that they cooked on their little coal-fired stoves at the end of the carriages.

Siberia is already one of the most sparsely populated areas on earth, yet all the evidence points to the fact that the young men and women are now leaving in droves. Promises of 'new lives' made by the Russian authorities in the early '80s, when millions were drafted in to augment a resentful indigenous population, have since turned to naught. Certainly, the decline of the military industries, the decay of the frontier garrisons and, despite its rich mineral wealth, the subsequent general neglect of the area have all had their effect. With the population of 145 million expected to drop to 90 million within two generations, big problems loom. An experiment in social engineering gone wrong methinks. I wonder what lessons the Chinese authorities have learnt from the Russians. Few I suspect. In China's north west Xinjiang province for example, millions of Han Chinese are currently being promised new lives and being drafted in to exploit/work/develop the rich oil, gas and other reserves. Although it is just possible that the area's riches are more accessible than Siberia's, the reconstruction of Xinjiang is by, with and most definitely for the Han Chinese. If nothing else, this 'go west' drive has embittered the Uighur population who feel diluted and trampled upon. We certainly live in interesting times.

We reached Irkutsk, capital of eastern Siberia, shortly before midday, Lake Baikal having been left behind, sparkling in the midsummer sunshine. The city didn't look to me the sort of place one would be likely to rush back to, although the 'Lonely Planet' spoke quite highly of it. But as the nearest centre of any size to the lake, quite a number of travellers did get off, presumably to continue their adventures there. What with the earlier exodus at Ulaan Baator, 'superior deluxe class' was, by now, getting quite empty – making it all the more difficult to get attention when I was trapped in the shower cubicle. Alas, I missed the afternoon's main attraction – a field of topless Siberian ladies with hoes and pitchforks. Ah well, another day maybe.

Waking up on day four, I had no idea what time it was – my watch had stopped at 6.25 – a time I later discovered we should not even

Lake Baikal, Siberia.

The bridge over the River Yenesei, Krasnoyarsk.

have reached by then. We were running late, this I knew, but beyond that nothing. There was at least one advantage of being late though, as I was able to see the River Yenesei at Krasnoyarsk during daylight hours – something we had been scheduled to cross at 3.00 a.m. The river itself marks the border between east and west Siberia and the one kilometre bridge was pectacular. It was the river I particularly wanted to see though, as I had long been interested in the little country of Tannu Tuva, the capital of which, Kyzyl, lies a few thousand kilometres upstream of Krasnoyarsk itself. It is one of those countries that you hear about once and then, all of a sudden, you come across references to it wherever you are. I have a dream of visiting Tannu Tuva one day – maybe I will take the train once more, alight at Krasnoyarsk and find a boat.

The Siberian scenery continued in much the same vein as before – birch, pine and lush grass with an abundance of wild flowers – cowslips were certainly no rarity here. Homes, both new and old

148

*Welcome to Europe –
the border between
Asia and Europe, near
Ekaterinburg.*

*Journey's end (phase
one anyway) –
Moscow Jaroslavski
Station.*

were attractively constructed too, and the whole area was far from
being the barren and cheerless place that Chekhov would have us
believe. But then, it was midsummer and the sky above promised a
fine day. It was mid-morning when we stopped at Marinsk where we
exchanged our roubles for a gourmet feast of pizza, bread, eggs,
tomatoes, salami, potato pasties and onion doughnuts, washed down
with local beer.

A few hours later we reached Novosibirsk, Siberia's biggest city,
with a great modern station resplendent in its fresh coat bright green
Sandtex. Novosibirsk marked our last chance of a quick return to
China via Almaty and Xinjiang province, but we were not really
tempted. The place looked quite decent, views of the city from the
railway line giving us occasional glimpses of buildings rather more
gracious than your average soviet style block of flats, while the River
Ob was most impressive, as was the beautiful domed roof of what I
think was probably the Alexander Nevsky Cathedral. Our last stop

149

before turning in for the night was Barabinsk which we reached at about 9.00 p.m. Dark, cool and damp, it smelt just like England and was a paradise for mosquitoes.

By now I was well used to the gentle, rocking motion of the train as I settled down in my bunk. The clattering of the points were generally soothing, although the sudden lurches, some of which almost catapaulted you out of your bed, were less restful. But all in all, I slept well, and it was not until we pulled into Tyumen, the oldest city in Siberia, at around 8.00 a.m. on the fifth day that I woke up from a particularly sound night's sleep. Staggering out onto the platform, half asleep, to buy something for breakfast, I bumped into a young Russian girl who spoke excellent English and asked her if she could find out if the eggs that were on sale had been boiled. Expecting her to engage in conversation with the stallholder I was surprised to see that she merely took an egg in her hand and spun it around a few times before declaring that they were.

Tyumen was a colourless place of dull concrete flats as was Ekaterinburg (aka Sverdlovsk) which we reached at around 1.00 p.m. the same day. I am not quite sure what I was expecting here, but it seemed so grey for a city with such a colourful if rather ignominious reputation. As we pulled out of the station though and continued our journey westwards, I just managed to photograph something interesting – the small obelisk on the left-hand side of the tracks which marks the boundary between Asia and Europe. Perm was to be our next stop, some four hundred kilometres away, and I was looking forward to a break in the general flatness of the scenery. Beautiful though it was, it had been more or less the same for three days now and a bit of variety was called for. The map clearly showed the railway line pushing its way through the Urals, and I became quite excited at the thought of a few long tunnels and maybe a lofty viaduct or two. But although there were a few very nice hills here and there, there was no sign of any mountains at all. A bit of a disappointment really, as was Perm come to think of it. Once called Molotov, home of the cocktail (and the hair-do too maybe) it looked to be a city of few charms.

Having slept through Kirov, which we must have reached at around 2.00 a.m., I woke at around 7.00, shortly before pulling into the formerly 'closed' city of Gorki – the place where soviet dissident and Nobel peace prize-winner Andrej Sakharov was exiled – for what was to be our last morning on the K3. Perhaps it is still closed, I wondered, as we crossed the dramatic rail/road bridge over the Volga, for I could find no mention of it in either the guidebooks or the maps we had with us. But, on further investigation, I discovered the place is now called Nizhny Novgorod, presumably in an effort to rid itself of its disreputable past. I assume Russian and Chinese dissidents are of the same breed, and that their offence is simply to refuse to recognise the infallibility of the regime they happen to live under.

Following our final meal in the dining car, and after bidding our Chinese carriage attendant *zai jian*, we disembarked at Moscow's Jaroslavski Railway Station at around 2.30 p.m. having travelled well over seven thousand five hundred kilometres in, it has to be said, considerable comfort. Arrangements proceeded like clockwork, and sure enough the local 'Monkey Business' man was on hand to meet us and take us to our hotels. But impressions, alas, were not particularly favourable, as Moscow was in the middle of a heatwave and our little room was devoid of any of those little luxuries that make living in such an environment pleasant or even bearable. No tea or coffee making facilities, no air-con, no nothing.

We spent our first Moscow night in the lively company of Alexandra, the friend of a friend of one of our colleague's sisters. A tenuous link really, but she was extremely knowledgeable, had excellent English and, being rather larger than life, determined to squeeze as much of the city as she could into our fairly tight schedule. Our first port of call was the Arbat, the so-called 'soul' of Moscow, originally populated by the aristocracy and now a fascinating area of old buildings, courtyards, and, inevitably, market stalls. From there we visited one or two of the famous Moscow metro stations – all marble affairs with socialist-realist mosaics and statues – before settling down to a typical Russian meal, I had borsch of course, rounding it all off with what Alexandra called a 'stroll' to see the Kremlin and St Basil's cathedral at night. More like a route march really, but, truth to tell, well worth it. From the opposite bank of the Moskva River it looked quite unreal, as though it were confectionery or a beautifully crafted child's toy.

It had thundered during the night, and as a result the following day began refreshingly cooler than before. I had arranged with Alexandra to see some of the other sights of Moscow – the boulevards, some outdoor sculptures, the Bolshoi, one or two churches – including the

Anglican Church of St Andrew (built by a man from Bolton) – before meeting up with the others on the steps of St Basil's for a tour of the Kremlin, Red Square, the KGB headquarters, the GUM toyshop and a drink and a meal in the John Bull Pub, one, no doubt, of many English pubs in the city. I was surprised how colourful and relaxed Moscow was – I think I was expecting something rather more austere. After two years in China, the cost of things came as a bit of a surprise though – a taste of things to come no doubt. There were a lot of little idiosyncrasies, too, that helped make Moscow memorable. Alexandra herself must take pride of place here, followed by an introduction to the work of the 'Ministry for Extraordinary Situations', (and yes, it actually exists), and finally the concept of 'face control' at the numerous nightclubs in the city, where, if you face doesn't fit, for whatever reason, you simply don't get in. But I liked it; I loved the churches in particular, and felt that it was definitely a place to return to if ever I were to get the opportunity.

We caught our new train, the East-West Express, (a bit of a misnomer that one) from Moscow's Beloruski Station at 11.40 p.m., and were eventually installed into our tiny, but nevertheless pretty comfortable sleeping compartment about an hour later – the bed mechanism having eventually been un-jammed. The train seemed so small compared with our spacious 'salon' on the TransSiberian. It was as though it had been built two-thirds size, like a woodland railway in an amusement park. But we slept well and surfaced at about 9.30 a.m. having already crossed into Belaurus – customs were to come much later. Belaurus gets a bad press in the travel books, and if the total lack of catering facilities on our train was anything to go by, this is certainly justified. Our meagre supplies were going to have to be rationed. Travelling via Minsk, we arrived at Brest (or 'BPECT' as it is spelt in the Cyrillic alphabet) at 1.40 p.m. Although we had been given customs forms to fill in long ago, nothing resembling a border check had yet occurred, but here, while our passports were eventually taken away for stamping, our train was jacked up and new bogies attached. Huge car jacks raised each carriage, the old bogies were wheeled away and new ones bolted on. It was an awesome sight, and looked extraordinarily dangerous too – especially as several people jumped down to observe close hand, jostling with the workers and half a dozen ancient and wizened women who were wandering here and there selling beer and vodka.

It was 4.15 before we eventually left, but minutes later we were crossing the River Bug and pulling into Terespol, Poland. After eight days, how reassuring it was to be able to read station signs once more. However, it was 5.20 before we were clear of Polish passport/customs control and on our way once more – the previous ten or twelve kilometres having taken over three and a half hours. My first observations of Poland were not at all happy, I am sorry to say. Graffiti everywhere – particularly on the sides of the trains. I am fully aware that there are many who consider it an art form, but I am not to be counted in that number. China may be messy but it is almost 100% graffiti free, and although there was a little evidence of it in Moscow, it was nowhere near as obtrusive as it was the moment we crossed the border. The second thing that struck me was far more positive however – the number of new churches – both in the towns and in the countryside. In retrospect, I think I had expected to see a lot more whilst crossing Russia — in Siberia in particular I don't think we saw any at all in the countryside – but here in Poland things were very different, and as we headed towards the setting sun, I sank in a romantic reverie. We could have been travelling into a Samuel Palmer painting.

The romantic reverie to which I referred was, of course, induced by hunger. Fortunately we had bought a little something in Moscow, but that was eighteen hours ago, and by now, we were getting desperate. But arriving at Warsaw at around 6.00 p.m. our fortunes changed for the better, and I was able to convert some dollars into Polish *zloty* and buy some food – pasties, bananas, water and beer. As we were to form part of the night train to Cologne – our carriage was shunted around Warsaw station for almost ninety minutes as we were coupled up with carriages from all over central Europe – I had a bit of time to leave the station, find a *bureau de change* and raid a bakers and a small convenience store. Still no restaurant car though. Very odd.

There seemed to be an undue number of rather officious passport/customs officers in and out of our compartment during the night although we did manage to get a little sleep, before eventually surfacing to find that the train had changed direction – something I always find a bit unnerving – and that we were in the outskirts of Berlin – a place I didn't think we were due to travel through. But all was well, and with ruthless German efficiency, we arrived at Cologne bang on time. The scenery throughout had been easy on the eye – nothing spectacular, but enough to make you realise that England doesn't hold the monopoly on being a green and pleasant land. Three cheers for our carriage attendant too, the fat controller, who had noticed our predicament with regards food and kept us going with coffee and chocolate for a dollar and twenty roubles a shot.

We had made no reservations – neither travel nor hotel – from Cologne onwards, but finding a place to stay was simplicity itself – a great little B and B almost opposite the station – and as for getting my onward tickets to Brussels and Waterloo, nothing could have been easier. Three cheers for plastic! So, after a leisurely afternoon and evening wandering around Cologne and visiting the odd bier keller or two, I settled down for an early night, waking up refreshed and firing on all cylinders to catch the late morning train to Brussels and, thence, Eurostar to Waterloo – first class too, with complimentary champagne thrown in.

So, ten days after leaving Beijing, here I was in London at the start of the Friday rush-hour, looking for the Bakerloo line. It had been plain sailing, and certainly something I would do again, given half a chance – maybe not exactly the same route though as there are five Trans-Siberian lines to choose from. But next time, just maybe, I will arrange to be met at my final destination – waiting for almost an hour for a London Transport 114 bus at the end of it all was not my idea of a grand finale.

✳ ✳ ✳ ✳ ✳

With stories in the western press about a dreadful arson attack on an internet café in Beijing killing two dozen students (all internet cafes in the capital have since been closed), catastrophic flooding in Dongting Lake on the Yangtse threatening the livelihood of tens of thousands, yet another terrible mining disaster in Heilongjiang province, renewed friction with Taiwan, hailstones the size of cricket balls in Zhengzhou killing a score or more people and rumours that boss man Jiang Jemin will not now be standing down at the Party conference next month despite the fact that his term of office is over, I returned to China at the end of the summer, full of enthusiasm, for what will almost certainly be my last lap, and with one final holiday excursion ahead of me. Reds Wang, one of my Chinese friends, had arranged that we should head off into Shanxi province for a few days before the long autumn term.

Shanxi, the name means 'west of the mountains', is *local* by Chinese standards, but even so, the night train from Beijing to Datong took over eight hours. Although I had made this same journey twice before – once when I was visiting Datong itself and more recently as part of the TransSiberian adventure – on both occasions I had travelled in the comparative luxury of soft class. This time though we were to rough it in a hard sleeper. Actually, it was comfortable experience, despite the complete lack of privacy, with well over fifty bunks opening straight onto the corridor, and not so much as a curtain in sight. No air conditioning either, but with open windows and the train's motion, things stayed surprisingly cool. Although I missed the little vases of flowers you generally find in soft class, at least the giant thermos flasks of hot water were there. When I eventually give up my current lifestyle, I wonder if I will ever learn to live without them?

The itinerary for this little jaunt was so determinedly kept secret from me, that I hadn't the heart to tell Wang that I had been to both Datong's chief places of interest, the Yungang Grottos and the Hanging Temple, before. There was no feigned awe on my part though – both are truly spectacular, and were well worth a second look. There was an impressive display of traditional dance at the grottos which served to draw the crowds away from the Buddhist shrines themselves, thus enabling me to spend longer taking it all in than had been possible the first time. And at the Hanging Temple, I also lingered awhile, sorely tempted to investigate a smallish stall piled high with concoctions and various treatments for this and that, including one that claimed to be something for 'getting rid of the tedious'. I'm sure we could all do with a little of that from time to time.

One Datong attraction I had not visited before though was the nearby wooden pagoda in Yingxian – almost a thousand years old and, as such, the oldest wooden building in China. So well built is it that I don't doubt it will still be there a thousand years from now, which is more than can be said for our apartment block in Tianjin, which, at less than eighteen months old, is already looking as though it could be ready for total refurbishment. With a sort of unofficial deadline of 2008 (Beijing Olympics) being talked about as

Above and left: The Hanging Temple near Datong, Shanxi Province.

the completion date for 'new Beijing' and 'new Tianjin' for that matter, one wonders whether apartment blocks of my generation will actually last the next six years. One dare not even guess what they might look like six years after the big event.

Although the grottos, temple and pagoda are all in the Datong area, these three sites are still a fair distance from each other, so we hired a taxi for the circular trip – at a cost of a little over two hundred *yuan* (around fifteen pounds) for around ten hours. The journey was good value in more than one way too, as, half way through, Wong, our driver, discovered, to his obvious distress, that the road to the Hanging Temple was closed for re-surfacing. Ever enterprising though, he proceeded to drive along a partially dried up river bed before coming to an ominously deep ford. Gingerly he changed down and began to drive through the water until the inevitable happened and the car broke down midstream. Still inside, we were almost up to our knees in water before he gave up trying to re-start the engine and our suggestion that we might all roll up our trousers, get out and push was finally accepted. We were joined by two young Chinese men from the car behind and between us we managed to get the taxi back on dry land, but not before the events had been recorded by a coach load of, presumably, Japanese tourists and hugely enjoyed by a half dozen or so local children as well. Amazingly, Wong managed to start the car again and two further, but needless to say shallower, fords later, we pulled up at the Hanging Temple itself – none the worse for our experiences.

The final journey back to Datong too, if rather less adventurous, was no less memorable. We were bumping along the road and I was dozing on the back seat, when I was suddenly woken by Wong's mobile phone playing an irritating snatch from the 'William Tell' Overture. 'Wei!' he answered. There followed a quick conversation and he rang off. 'Wrong number!' my friend explained, at which I began laughing. The scenario had been almost too perfect for that dreadful old joke about why there are no telephone directories in China. I struggled to explain that it was because there were too many Wings and too many Wongs that you were bound to wing the wong number. I am sure that neither driver Wong nor friend Wang got more than the very faintest idea what I was burbling on about.

The following day were boarded the express coach for Taiyuan, capital of Shanxi province, famous for its coal and, I was told after I got back, its prostitutes. Impressions weren't particularly favourable, but it was only a stopping off point for two places that I had long wanted to see; places that were to afford rare glimpses of pre-revolutionary China – the *Qiao Jian Da Yuan*, a large old courtyard house, probably best known as the location for the film 'Raise the Red Lantern' and the ancient walled town of Pingyao. To see both and to get back to Taiyuan at the end of it all, necessitated the booking of a taxi for two whole days at a total cost of rather less than thirty pounds sterling, which, staggeringly, included the driver's overnight accommodation.

Dancers at the Yungang Grottos near Datong, Shanxi Province.

Yungang Grottos near Datong, Shanxi Province.

Qiao Jian Da Yuan, near Taiyuan, Shanxi Province. The mansion was made famous in the film 'Raise the Red Lantern'.

To mark the end of my holidays, and worried in case my photographs did not do justice to the house in particular, I bought a beautiful hardback book as a souvenir, which, I later discovered, contains some extraordinary Chinglish. I quote: 'In cultural viewpoint, residential courtyards are a kind of background culture so close to people. It marks the life with symbols of nationality and time. In artistic viewpoint, residential courtyards are of the multi-dimension art having changed into rocks in the river of time. It makes life so poetic. In historical viewpoint, residential courtyards are of micro-fiches of ethics culture staying everywhere, and of folklore and engineering. It provides life with more concrete internal meanings.' I skipped the rest of this pretentious word soup and concentrated on the lovely pictures. The house itself was built in 1756 and has been left largely untouched since 1949 when the last Mr. Qiao fled to

Taiwan, never to return, a fact curiously omitted from the book. I found its overall shape particularly interesting, in that, given a bird's-eye view, it can be seen to have been cleverly designed in the form of the Chinese character 'xi' meaning 'double happiness' – the character most commonly associated with Chinese weddings.

Pingyao was once an important, highly prosperous commercial centre, home of the first bank in China, and one of the first places in the world where cheques were issued. Inside the town walls, completely intact I think, and dodging donkey carts and pedal rickshaws rather than lorries, pushbikes and cars for a change, we wandered down a maze of narrow alleys, lined with elegant buildings – for the most part only one or perhaps two storeys high. The roofs, as ever, the woodwork generally and the lattice windows in particular, holding paper rather than glass, were stunning. Although many buildings were crumbling, in a sort of genteel way of course, and there was grime everywhere, there was no sign that things were being wantonly bulldozed and replaced with the modern monstrosities that seem to characterise so much of urban China. Renovations here were sympathetic and where actual new buildings were going up, Prince Charles for one would have been absolutely delighted. Indeed, the place was remarkable for the real sense of the past it managed to retain, with no evidence of the Disney-ishness that you find all too often elsewhere. Perhaps nowhere was this more evident than in the beautifully restored Magistrate's Residence in the south west of the city, with its gateways, halls, towers and shrines. Although not all the buildings were original structures, some had, in fact, been restored in recent years, the whole was one of the most tastefully preserved places I have been to in China. I have a particularly soft spot for the small temple there where I drew a wooden batten from a stone jar in front of the Deity of Earth and exchanged it for my personal prediction. Pretty encouraging it was, too.

Before returning to the hotel and our traditional *kang* beds, made of stone and brick, with the facility for lighting a fire underneath in cold weather, we decided we could not possibly leave the place without doing the three things for which Shanxi is most renowned: Pingyao itself is number one of course (I would agree with that wholeheartedly), followed jointly by Shanxi beef and Shanxi vinegar. We spent our last night enjoying a meal of beef *jaozi* dunked in the specialty of the house. Delicious.

Above: The walled town of Pingyao, Shanxi Province.

Left: Pingyao Courtyard.

Left: Brick 'kang' beds, Pingyao.

Below: The Magistrate's House, Pingyao.

To close, and while on the subject of food, I feel I should draw attention to what I suspect has been a hitherto unreported phenomenon. Here in Tianjin we are suffering from a plague, not of locusts, but of hundreds-and-thousands. I have been used to getting a good handful sprinkled onto my ice-cream for a few weeks now, but today, I could truthfully not see the froth on the top of my cappuccino for a layer of the things (as well as a slice of lemon for good measure), and last night there were more than a few lurking in my chicken-and-pineapple. Actually, 'Asrope', the errant restaurant, will have to look to its laurels with the imminent opening of a new place right next door. Here, if dry runs are anything to go by, they are going to have a light show worthy of an Andrew Lloyd Webber extravaganza. They have also been interviewing and presumably recruiting staff for several days, and military-type parades of would-be waiters, waitresses, and cooks have been adding to the general and continuing fascination of Tianjin street life, with dozens of young men and women lined up three abreast, admittedly looking smart but in fact doing very little. Presumably in an attempt to retain existing customers and maybe to woo a few others as well, the management of 'Asrope' have done a little bit of decoration inside, a bit half-hearted though if the truth be known, and have drawing-pinned a few pictures up on the walls, including a largish print of Leonardo's 'The Last Supper'. Possibly not something I'd have chosen myself.

CHAPTER 16

One, Two, Three, Aubergine

November 2002   2002年 十一月

A couple of months or so ago now, a colleague put a copy of a short article she had found in my pigeon hole in the staff room at school. 'I read this and thought of you,' she said kindly. It was a piece entitled 'Precious Memory' about how to counter some of the adverse effects associated with getting older. After a short bout of mock indignation, I put the copy of 'Clean' magazine I was browsing through into the bin, and settled down to read. And it was actually quite interesting – far from being the patronising drivel I was expecting. 'According to the experts, age doesn't inevitably make us forgetful,' I read. 'If our memories do deteriorate it's because we're mistreating them, giving them a diet of junk TV and no exercise.' I've always had what I consider to be a healthy mistrust of the popular theories of so-called experts, but I thought I'd read on, and in the section ominously sub-titled 'Use it or lose it', bridge, crosswords, listening or playing classical music and learning a language were the four key activities the writer, obviously an expert herself, advocated. Well, I've long decided that bridge is beyond me, but I do play canasta every week, with mixed success maybe, but nevertheless with no mean degree of accomplishment, I've taken to doing the (albeit quick) crosswords in the 'Guardian Weekly' over the past eighteen months or so, music is, of course, part and parcel of my job, and thus learning a language seemed to be a fairly sensible thing to do.

Although I have been in China for over two years now, I had not, until fairly recently, thought about taking proper lessons. I learned a little before I came out from my friend Shuzhen Richards in Dorset, but since then I have been shamefully content to memorise a few useful phrases including, of course, the important bits on a menu.

But as the reading of the article coincided with the opening of a new language school a couple of hundred yards up the road, I cast caution to the wind and paid my fee.

There are five of us in my class, all teachers from my school, and we meet twice a week for two hours at a stretch. Believe you me, it's mighty hard work, but, I suppose, it will be worth it – especially if it's going to keep my remaining grey cells active a while longer. So far, at least, Chinese characters have not formed part of our programme, (I think it was the thought of having to learn these that actually put me off taking serious lessons in the first place), and our text book seems almost user friendly, although, of course, there are long lists of vocabulary to learn. But there is also so much chuckling and giggling going on that I think I'd really miss it if I were to give up now and so I'm fairly sure I'll stick the course – which has been the nearest thing to pleasurable learning I have come across for many a year. I do hope though, that our teacher, Wang Laoshi's attention to grammatical correctness is not going to be at the expense of communication. It's the latter that is important both to me and I think to most of my western friends, and as I like nothing better than socialising with the local population, I want just sufficient linguistic skill to be able to enjoy the strange cultural world I find myself in rather than the ability to impress people with elegantly constructed prose.

Although both China TV's 'World Wide Watch' and the satellite channel 'BBC World' -which, incidentally, must be a front runner for the world's dullest TV channel – appear to be uncensored, we have heard only a little about the America/Iraq situation over here, except that (and forgive me if I'm wrong) China seems to have backed the UN over the whole business from the word go. 'Without irrefutable evidence there should be no use of military force, and any action in this regard should be based on UN authorisation,' said Zhu Rongji, China's highly regarded prime minister, a month or so ago now. Fine, but then, of course, China is anxious to remain friends with the USA too, and itself has a vested interested in al-Qaida in that a small number of terrorist incidents in far Xinjiang Province, where the Moslem Uighur ethnic group have their home and where they also outnumber the Han Chinese, apparently have some sort of al-Qaida connection – although quite what this is unclear. If the present UN ultimatum were to break down though, and the USA ended up attacking Iraq without the backing of the UN, it could just follow that a Chinese government crack down on the Uighurs would face little criticism from the outside world. I hope my pessimism is unfounded, for speaking as one who has spent a short while in Xinjiang, I can say, in all honesty, that rarely have I met more delightful, hospitable and generous people. My friends and I spoke not one word of Uighur, those we met spoke not one word of English, and between us we had but a smattering of Mandarin, yet this was enough to provide us all with a feast of laughter and smiles from dawn to dusk. What richness we found there. We were communicating with one another – something that those in high places seem to be increasingly unable to do. How exciting rather than threatening it should be to be able to move from one culture to another and to celebrate the differences between us without feeling superior or that we have a monopoly on what is right. And how privileged I am to be able to do this at the moment.

Staying with the theme of communication just a little while longer, there has been much international coming and going in my own life over the past few months. It was lovely to be able to meet up with my Chinese friend from Shaftesbury and her daughter Anne-Louise in Beijing at the end of August, and my pleasure to be able to have Amanda Lu, one of our Chinese staff from Tianjin, to stay with me in Dorset for a few days in the summer. And while she was with me, I was able to introduce her to some other West Country friends too, John and Elaine Affleck, who were to be coming to Tianjin in September as guests of the Chinese government. John was born in northern China and spent his early years in Tianjin where he was the son of the former British Consul.

Quite how things really happened will probably remain a mystery, but the extraordinarily fortunate order of events would appear to be along the lines of:

- a short article in the summer of 2000 in the Dorset press about my new job in Tianjin
- John and Elaine read the article and decide to get in touch. They phone my former school and Gill in the office takes their number. I phone them back.
- we meet and establish a friendship. John mentions the places he remembers from his childhood – the consulate, the British Club, the racecourse, Astor Hotel, Victoria Park and Gordon Hall amongst them.

- I use John's list to start getting to know Tianjin, and in particular the former British concessions.
- At the same time, I get to know Louie Liu who runs the local branch of CTS (China Travel Service) and whose office is close to the former concession areas. We talk and it transpires that Louie's mother, Mrs. Hang, is very keen on preserving some of the fine old buildings that remain in Tianjin as well as setting up a museum. I mention John of course.
- Mrs. Hang who clearly knows the right people and who, incidentally, is a force to be reckoned with, gets to work on the local government and eighteen months later John and Elaine are invited back to China along with a group of fifteen or so other foreigners who lived in Tianjin in the first half of the twentieth century.

John and Elaine were in China for over two weeks, spending the first day or so with me, followed by a week doing their 'official' bit and then a further period with me in Beidaihe, where John used to go for his holidays, and Qingdao where he was actually born. The official programme looked mighty heavy, and I was truly grateful not to be part of it. An earnest all-day forum on the role of Tianjin in the twenty-first century, interminable banquets hosted by local dignitaries, of whom China has more than its fair share I might add, visits to free trade zones, government departments and whatnot. Not my idea of fun at all. There was at least one short period of respite however, as Mrs. Hang had miraculously arranged for John to visit the former British Consulate where he lived as a boy. Mrs. Hang's passion for preserving what is left of the past is at odds with what seems to thrill most Tianjiners – which is simply to build bigger and to earn money. 'Nobody cares about the old Tianjin!' a laughing and well-educated Chinese friend once told me. But, fortunately, the redoubtable Mrs. Hang does care and, probably using every ounce of *guanxi* she has, (the old consulate is most definitely off limits, being the Tianjin clubhouse for the very highest echelons of Chinese society) eventually found somebody to give us the OK to go inside.

As somewhat of an aside, it has become increasingly clear to me that no-one in China ever likes to take actual responsibility for authorising anything at all – let alone something as potentially sensitive as this – for fear of upsetting someone higher up the ladder. On this occasion at least though, someone somewhere did say 'yes' and John was able to go home.

Unsurprisingly, perhaps, the self-important, uniformed types in the compound that now surrounds the building viewed us with the utmost suspicion and more than once queried the authority of our permit. But eventually we made it and got inside the front door; and once inside, John was in seventh heaven. We quickly discovered that the custodians of the consulate were of a different breed to the officials outside, and as he had his old family photograph album with him, they were soon dashing everywhere, matching photographs of the sumptuous rooms of the 1930s with the rather more austere but nevertheless very tasteful furnishings of the present day. We were allowed over every inch of the place, John reminiscing over details of his boyhood with great affection; an overwhelming experience for him.

Our trip to Beidaihe was a far more relaxing affair, and for me it was particularly nice to be able to stay in the 'Guesthouse for Diplomatic Missions' once more – the hotel where I had my birthday party a few months earlier. I also took the opportunity of re-visiting Shanhaiguan, where the Great Wall meets the sea, and taking a look at the Mengliangnu Temple, dedicated to a certain Lady Meng, whose husband died whilst building the Wall. As the lovely Meng went in search of her husband's body, presumably to give him a decent burial, her tears washed some of the structure away revealing his remains. Overcome with grief she threw herself into the sea. Whether the story is true I don't know, but the temple itself is, of course, a complete fake, and closely resembles a down-market theme park with its series of concrete tableaux, artificial caverns and tacky gift shops. Although I never did find out what the four zebras were for, the temple was, for all its faults, a very pleasant spot for a day out. After all, there's no point in being a purist when it comes to authenticity in China – wherever you are. Take *Gu Lou* – the Drum Tower in Tianjin for example. This was completely and utterly demolished at the beginning of the twentieth century, I suspect by the British, but over the past six months has been totally rebuilt. It looks very nice too – despite the fact that it contains a bell and not a drum. I can't quite work that one out. But I read in our local English language magazine *Jin* that 'in about 1493, the Drum Tower was built at the centre of the city' and that 'over five hundred years later, it is still one

Above: The former British Consulate and childhood home of John Affleck. Now a club for the Party elite, Tianjin.

Left: Elaine and I en route to Beidaihe, Hebei Province.

of the most important monuments in Tianjin.' Misleading or what? It seems that one or two people have very short memories.

Although John's return to his family home was of great significance, it was Qingdao, formerly Tsingtao, and the remarkable discovery of the seaside villa his parents used to own that really crowned his visit. Thanks to my Chinese friend Summer who was able to interpret, the four of us bundled into a taxi as John pointed inland and up the hill in what he was fairly sure was the right direction. We slowly criss-crossed the area until after about half an hour he thought things looked a little familiar. We stopped, got out and retraced our steps a little way. Was this the house? There was a bell on the garden gate and our taxi driver pressed the button. Moments later the owner came down the path, rapid Chinese conversation followed and we were allowed in. 'There were two stone lions at the top of the steps,' John murmured as we turned the corner. We looked. They were still there. It was the right house. Unbelievable. And if John felt anything like the same degree of emotion my sisters and I felt when we 'traced our roots' up in Northumberland in July of this year, then, for this moment alone the entire trip must have been worthwhile.

Although I have referred to the concept of *guanxi* on many occasions, and usually unfavourably, it is true that, were it not for Mrs. Hang's *guanxi*, then none of the above could have happened. Nevertheless, it is, I think, a sad fact that, in China, people succeed not because they are talented or deserving but because they know the right people. Indeed cultivating the right *guanxi* has become a way of life for more than a few people I know – personal advancement taking precedence over integrity. I have witnessed both licking up and kicking down over the last few months, and have seen more than a few people behaving in what amounts to a totally sycophantic manner towards the powerful, rich men without principles more often than not, whilst showing nothing but contempt for the little people. Curiously though, these 'little people' seem to bear few grudges, and neither do they seem to envy those who have more. If anything they are admiring rather than jealous of fortune. I read somewhere that perhaps one of the reasons why the majority of people in China appear to be happier than we are is that most have less to lose than we do. This fits nicely with my long-held belief that the humbler our expectations of life, the more likely we are to feel fulfilled. Nevertheless these things still disturb me. I haven't yet got sufficient mastery of spoken Chinese to ask what compensation the dispossessed families of 'Dog Alley' actually received when their homes and livelihoods were bulldozed last month for example. I look at the little people devoid of any *guanxi* picking over the rubble that remains and feel more than a little guilty when I return to my centrally-heated apartment and log onto the internet.

If I could have my time all over again, I think I might like to be in the travel business. I have mentioned my Chinese travel agent friend Louie Liu already in this letter, but his trips are as nothing compared to those organised by yours truly. Indeed 'Davey Dave's Economy

Tours' as they are affectionately known, are already a firm feature of the expat social scene in Tianjin. The tradition established, a couple weekends ago, I was persuaded (actually I lie, I *offered*) to run a short trip to Datong and Pingyao – places I had visited before but ones I also wanted to show my colleagues. Thus, towards the end of October, a party of eighteen boarded the 9.00 p.m. sleeper from Tianjin to Datong – hardy souls in hard class, and fellow softies in soft. Arriving at our destination an unearthly 5.30 in the morning, we discovered just how cold a strange place can be in the hour or so before dawn. Cold, undoubtedly, but it must be said, far from unwelcoming. We were met at the station by the smiling ticket agent who had our onward train tickets to Pingyao for the following night, and as soon as these had been distributed we spilt up to go our various ways – something, incidentally, the Chinese hate. They'll stick together whatever the odds. Four or five of us found a little café just beyond the station forecourt though where we ordered a bit of food and, eventually, cups of tea. Scrambled egg and tomato is my usual if I'm having a Chinese breakfast and I am a master when it comes to getting my tongue round *xihongshi chaojidan* as it's called. But try as we might we couldn't seem to get any tea – *cha* in Chinese. Not difficult you might think – especially if you've lived in the place for more than two years. In all honesty, though, it took about twenty different pronunciations of this one syllable to get what we wanted. So much for seven weeks of intensive lessons.

When eventually the sun came up it was to reveal a sparkling blue sky that was to remain with us for the rest of the day. Most of the group was heading off to the Yungang Grottos and the Hanging Temple, but as I had been to both already – twice in fact – for two friends and me it was to be a little known section of the Great Wall forty kilometres north of Datong known as *De Shengkou* (Victory Gate). It was here, around five hundred years ago, that troops fighting a Mongol invasion returned in triumph – at the same time as the first version of the Drum Tower was being built in Tianjin maybe. A scene of much activity then no doubt, today it was a rural idyll, totally unspoiled – just us and a few cows. It was just as lonely and impressive as I had imagined it to be, and not a kiosk in sight. How lovely it is not to be disappointed.

We all met up again shortly before our departure for Pingyao, and another night on board a train. Unfortunately, a second early arrival proved too much for four of my friends, who, far from rising and shining, didn't get off the train in time, and to the consternation of some of the group, continued on down the line. Chinese trains are nothing if not punctual. Fortunately, though, all was not lost as it was a slow train, and as we were advised that the next stop was only some thirty or forty kilometres away there seemed little point in worrying ourselves over breakfast. After all, there would be dozens of taxi drivers at the station only too willing to drive them back to Pingyao.

Less than two months ago when I first visited Pingyao, I felt as though I had almost discovered the place. There was scant mention of it in my copies of 'Lonely Planet' and 'Rough Guide', and even a friend's more up to date versions gave it only a short paragraph. But a lot can happen in two months, including the publication of a brand new edition of 'Lonely Planet' which describes Pingyao as one of the 'must sees' of China. It can hardly be a coincidence therefore that the admission charge to the city wall had gone up from eighteen *yuan* (one pound fifty or so) to a whopping eighty-five *yuan*. The Chinese never miss a trick when it comes to money. Our couple of days in the town though, had some very special moments. It was here that I bought a pair of Chinese slippers from a couple of guys who looked like characters from the 'Elves and the Shoemaker', and where one of my friends negotiated a fantastic bargain for a very large and, I was told, extremely rare wall hanging for me, getting the price down from way over twenty five pounds to less than eight. A pity there was an identical one in its place the following morning. The most bizarre sight of the trip was almost certainly that of the dead body wrapped in a shroud being carried on a stretcher by three cyclists, whilst for the cultural highlight, the theatrical re-enactment of a traditional court case at the Magistrates House was quite lovely. The performance that is. I'm used to rowdy Chinese audiences now of course, but this was the first time I have actually witnessed a tour guide, together with ubiquitous megaphone, addressing her party as the performance was taking place.

After the performance, I wandered off into the next courtyard attracted by what I at first thought was the gentle tinkle of traditional Chinese music. Far from it – the sickly sweet strains of Richard Clayderman had triumphed yet again. He's recently taken over from Karen Carpenter as just about the biggest thing in China since the Cultural Revolution by the way. And if this wasn't enough, the atmosphere was further shattered by three or four competing loud-hailers, echoing from several directions at once, each with their reverb turned up to maximum and getting ominously louder by the second. My little siesta in the pavilion where I was luxuriating in the warm autumn sunshine was rapidly turning into something more akin to the concourse at Waterloo station. But then that's China through and through.

A typical Chinese can change from a state of deep sleep, the national pastime. or vacant self-absorption to being a vital member of a vast crowd in the twinkling of an eye. And the bigger, busier and more boisterous the crowd the better. What a gregarious, fun loving lot they can be, I thought, as I viewed the various tour groups, each with identifying baseball caps, and on this occasion, colour co-ordinated anoraks, posing for this photo or that. Interestingly, no photograph in China is complete without at least a couple of people in it. I've been dragged into dozens of snaps in my time, perhaps to make up the numbers or maybe because anything I do needs not only to be viewed with unquenchable curiosity but also recorded for posterity. 'Yi, er, san, qiezi' as they say – which translated comes out as 'one, two, three, aubergine'. I've taken reel upon reel of photographs myself too since I've been here, (they call the images captured on film 'electric shadows' I discovered only the other day) but, almost without exception, the only ones my Chinese friends take any interest in are those containing people. I don't suppose I'd mind too much if they knew who the photographs were of, but they don't. I have got some wonderful shots of mountains, lakes, seashores, forests, ancient pagodas and the like, but no interest whatsoever is ever expressed in any of these little gems.

A rough parallel can perhaps be drawn between the Chinese enjoyment of the noisy and with their liking for bright lights. 'Asrope', one of my favourite local restaurants, did not, alas, last the year. It was crushed into oblivion by competition in the form of a vast palace next door with more coloured lights than an entire carnival procession. I'm sure quality of food had nothing to do with it – it was the shiny new look of the place. Most of the modern buildings in Tianjin are already illuminated in a spectacular fashion – neon tubes, floodlights, electronic bunting, lasers even I shouldn't be surprised, and to compete you really do have to pull out all the stops. Ms. Asrope was clearly way out of her depth. What is strange and, to me, rather sad though, is the dull light that shines out from inside. Low wattage, metallic grey fluorescent tubes provide about as much cheer as a bowl of tepid fat noodles. Is this, perhaps, another indication of the glossy veneer that coats almost every aspect of life in China?

And the subject of glossy veneer brings me nicely to my last paragraph. Although I have enjoyed excellent health whilst I have been in China, a broken tooth necessitated a visit to the 'Tianjin Loving Teeth Oral Health Center'. The truly excellent Dr. Liu, who has never left China, but who has an insatiable interest in life in the west, also delights in practising his English on me when my mouth is filled with sundry appliances. He is justifiably proud of his surgery too – the AICHI clinic (surely it can't be pronounced 'achy') – and the apparatus he has. He introduced his latest acquisition to me as I was being prepared for what I thought was an x-ray. 'This is my electronic brain baking equipment!' he announced proudly.

CHAPTER 17

Sheng Dan Jie Kuai Le

December 2002   2002年 十二月

The autumn term is drawing to a close with the usual frenzy of activity days, concerts, productions, Christmas dinners and parties. Our school bazaar, which seems ages ago now, was a great success – Father Christmas himself was there too, adding a certain *je ne sais quoi* to the occasion – while the weekend before last, my school choir, instrumental group and adult expat choir gave a couple of concerts in two of the local hotels to mark the turning on of their Christmas tree lights. Although the Crystal Palace, a shiny four-star outfit, managed the whole affair quite tastefully (after I insisted we were not going to make a grand entrance gliding down the twin escalators), the Sheraton, a glitzy five-star, went completely over the top – you could hardly move for tinsel and baubles, fairy lights and stick-on snow. The choir was actually singing very beautifully when there was an audible gasp from the audience. I thought, rather naively as it happened, that perhaps they had been moved by the subtle phrasing in the third verse of 'Lo! He Comes With Clouds Descending', but I was wrong. They'd caught a glimpse of a grotesque, waving Santa coming down in the glass-fronted lift that was behind us. Hardly surprising then that, given the nature of the occasion, and the clientele come to think of it, the throwing of the switch to turn on the lights got more applause than all our items put together.

As part of the run up to Christmas, we had a troupe of Chinese acrobats in school last week – not the most polished of performances I have to admit, although quite a few of the children loved it. Perhaps I was missing something, but to me there seemed to be no thought behind the planning of the show. The sight of a couple of guys wandering around on stilts for a bit, doing the odd somersault or two and

175

then sitting on the side of the stage to work out what to attempt next didn't exactly thrill me. On occasion, they even appeared to change their minds mid streams – one who was perhaps about to attempt a half-hearted handstand deciding instead to hop around in desultory fashion. It has to be said that most of the stunts went wrong too, but really that was pretty incidental.

In a way though, this shambles of a show encapsulated much of what I see over here on a fairly regular basis. My latest theory is that many Chinese are, to a greater or lesser extent, little more than willing puppets. Things get done with startling rapidity when the puppeteer is present, but as soon as he so much as turns his back, they simply return to square one – to the humdrum reality of lives largely devoid of incident. For the majority, daily routines are probably so firmly fixed by now that to do anything requiring initiative is most likely *non*-thinkable let alone unthinkable. Indeed, some may well have lost the ability to think at all, let alone to plan or to consider the consequence of their actions. I walk down 'Dog Alley' and see a couple of elderly women in the winter sunshine, wrapped up against the cold, just sitting for hours on end on low stools by the side of the road; a few more vigorous ones engaging in *tai chi* perhaps in a partially built shop; a little girl pulling a lump of polystyrene on a string for a toy; a street-cart food seller asleep with his dark head tucked down on the surface of the cart in front of him, and wonder about the waste of good lives. When I am having a 'bad chopsticks day' I see in this the very worst aspects of capitalism and communism combined. Tianjin in the twenty-first century is a world where brand new toy-town mansions stand ostentatiously alongside decaying *hutong*, where daily life alternates between sleep and an obstacle course of petty bureaucracy, and where ignorance and slumber are probably safe havens. But, it has to be said, I rarely have such bad days. Society here appears so solid and so stable (all the more remarkable when you consider the size of the population) and the Chinese, for the most part, so fantastically happy, that it rubs off on us all. For most of the time, I too am as happy as the day is long, and although I am relishing the thought of bringing my experiences back home to England for Christmas, at the same time I will be looking forward to my return for what will, in all probability, be my last stint over here.

Being fairly efficient about these things, I've now finished most of my Christmas shopping, discovering in the process, not only that the new Harry Potter DVDs have been on the streets for a good few weeks, but that so too have books five, six and seven. All fakes of course and destined to disappear sooner or later. A pity really as 'Harry Potter and the Leopard-Walk-Up-To-Dragon' seems particularly good, featuring as it does a torrid love affair between HP and Hermione along with a surprise visit from Gandalf. Ms. Rowling's lawyers are no doubt onto it, but I heard on the grapevine that the books confiscated by the PSB (Public Security Bureau) actually turned out to be illicit copies of the 'authorised' fakes.

As I have said on many occasions before, the activities of the PSB permeate just about every aspect of a Chinese citizen's life – the Bureau itself no doubt staffed by people who delight in making life difficult and, as I read somewhere, probably staffed by the sort of person who sniffs rubber stamps when the paperwork gets slow. However, Christmas spirit and all that, I am happy to report that I was on the receiving end of some irrepressible assistance in my little DVD shop last weekend – quite the opposite to the indifference one sometimes gets in the big supermarkets or the obstructiveness one encounters when dealing with the Chinese authorities with their forms, red stamps and doubtful 'administration charges'. My problem was not that I was buying illicit goods or that hundreds and hundreds of the things were randomly stacked in cardboard boxes around a room no bigger than the average garden shed, or indeed that the place was bursting at the seams with customers acting as though there was no tomorrow. Rather it was, and is, that the Chinese titles of most films are, shall we say, *poetic* rather than literal translations. I had no trouble with Harry Potter II, but as to the Chinese title for 'Blade Runner – The Director's Cut' I was stumped. Stumped that is until a charming young lady got onto her mobile and phoned first her boyfriend and then, I think, a friend of his who clearly knew someone who was a bit of a film buff. I naturally assumed she was an employee, but it turned out that she was just another customer anxious to help – as were all the other customers in the shop come to think of it. '*Sheng dan jie kuai le!*' they called out as I left. 'Merry Christmas!' (By the way, the title translates as 'Silver Wings Killer'.)

New Culture Market where this particular DVD shop is located, also does a good line in greetings cards, so I thought I'd buy a few to stock up – all in cheery Chinglish of course. A particular favourite declares, a little enigmatically perhaps, 'Peeling knife, dood for you', which, if it is to make any sense at all, clearly necessitates the sending of the companion card which reads 'Thank for you – don't ask why or what the whok thing means the same apolles to you and I'. How very sad, therefore, to read an article in a recent issue of China Daily suggesting that 'People who come across English that is incorrect or confusing can report the offence to the Bureau'. Such a killjoy offer is totally misguided. I am still laughing at the birthday card I have just sent to my sister admitting that 'Her image was deeply impressed on my minp' and at the equally glorious one that proclaims (and I'm sorry if I offend) 'I feel it in my fingers I feel it in my toss'.

So, on that very dubious note, I think I'll settle down to a quick snack and my Chinese homework. Having had several enormous meals recently, I don't see myself managing anything more than cheese on toast this evening. Certainly not for me a repeat performance of the vast bowl of mouth-watering chilli beef with mint I had a while back – the latter served very much as a vegetable by the way (mounds of it too). Nor do I really feel up to a 'caesarian' salad either, although a friend of mine ordered one at our choir Christmas dinner the other day and maintained it was quite delicious. There's no accounting for taste I suppose.

Sheng dan jie kuai le

羊年

THE YEAR OF
THE SHEEP

yang nian

CHAPTER 18

Xin Nian Hao – Happy Chinese New Year to You

February 2003 　 2003年 二月

On my return to school after the Christmas break, I was greatly cheered by thought that, in less than four weeks time, I would be on holiday yet again and celebrating Chinese New Year. *Zai jian* to the Year of the Horse, *ni hao* to the Year of the Sheep. And how time has flown, or should I say galloped. As I write, firecrackers are still heard most nights, and though the season of feasting and fireworks is drawing to a close, a fair number of people, including the students of course, are still on holiday. Alas, not me – I managed just one week's break before having to go back to school for a series of meetings, planning sessions, stints of report writing and, in my case, the chance to complete the final assignment for an English as a Foreign Language course that I have been doing. Although the week was not particularly demanding, it was wonderful to have the opportunity to do things in what UK teachers call 'directed time'. How nice to feel valued and given proper time to do admin and paperwork. And how nice to get that sense of job satisfaction which comes from knowing you've done something rather well simply because you've had the time to do it.

For the Chinese New Year holiday itself, Lynda, one of my colleagues, and I ventured way down south to Fujian Province, flying initially to Xiamen – or Amoy as it once was called. This coastal city, roughly half way between Shanghai and Hong Kong, seemed the perfect place to spend a few days, and as my timetable showed daily flights from Tianjin 'airdrome' as it is called, what could be simpler? The answer to that particular question is 'quite a lot of things' actually. In true Chinese fashion, the publication of a timetable does not in any way imply that there might be a service. *Meiyou* came the reply when I asked the travel agent to book us some tickets. I produced the up to date timetable from my back pocket and showed her the flight numbers. *Meiyou* she repeated, and looked slightly puzzled when I suggested that it seemed reasonable to think otherwise. In the end, of course, she was right, and we had to fly from Beijing. It wasn't that the flights had been cancelled, but rather that there never were any anyway. I may be naïve, but cannot for the life of me see the point of publishing quarterly timetables when an airline has no intention of running a service.

Arriving in Xiamen, we were joined by an expat couple from Shanghai, mercifully not teachers, and the delightful Mr. Chen, a lecturer from Xiamen University who was to be our tour guide and who relished the opportunity of being able to practise his English. Mr. Chen showed us around the beautiful university campus, and we had ample time to explore Xinjie Church and a couple of Buddhist and Taoist temples built quite high up in the mountains, and which, of course, afforded some spectacular views. Although such places generally fill up with Chinese tourists by mid-morning, they tend to be relatively quiet early in the day, and one of the most captivating sights was seeing a lone Chinese man practising his *tai chi* as the sun burnt off the early morning mist. He was as close to his Nirvana as he was ever likely to get in this life I suspect.

One of the most fascinating areas of Xiamen is the old western concession island of Gulangyu, where there are no cars or bikes, and where many of the twisty streets are lined with houses dating back to the early years of the twentieth century. I was particularly keen to visit the place as the guide books invariably refer to Gulangyu as 'Piano Island' – a place where, in times gone by at least, you could wander the streets and hear the sounds of prosperous Europeans playing their pianos in their drawing rooms. Even my 'Lonely Planet', not known for its use of superlatives, waxes lyrical about 'the sound of classical piano wafting from shuttered windows'. I must have an old edition ... or maybe it was just because it was Chinese New Year ... I really don't know ... but the streets of 'Piano Island' were teeming with screaming families and raucous tour groups. And although the occasional strains of Chopin and Debussy could be heard, the music itself was being relayed from tiny loudspeakers placed in and

Looking across to Gulangyu Island, Xiamen, Fujian Province.

Traditional Hakka houses, Yundong County, Fujian Province.

around sundry nooks, crannies and rocky outcrops. But Mr. Chen's gusto was infectious and we loved it nonetheless. He had been born on the island and was buzzing with enthusiasm as he showed us his old haunts. The traditional seafood dinner we had on our first evening was pretty wonderful too – as indeed was our final meal – in the one-hundredth Pizza Hut to be opened in China, situated way up on the twenty-fourth floor with stunning views of the harbour.

On the second day, the four of us, together with Mr. Chen and our driver, set out for Yongding County and the village of Hukeng to see some Hakka earth dwellings (or *tu lou* as they are called in Chinese). The Hakka people are one of China's many minorities; the word itself means 'guest' as they often arrived in areas already inhabited by others. War and economic conditions apparently forced them to leave their original home in Henan Province and as a result the Hakka are now spread throughout southern China and south east Asia. Hence the earthen towers of course, for as guests, it has to be said, they were not always welcome. Round, built of raw earth, four storeys high and holding up to a thousand people, many of these structures look impregnable even today and some still house bustling communities.

Although our tour schedule warned us that the earthen buildings were in a relatively undeveloped part of the country, we were undaunted. After all, we had all lived in China for two years or more, had never thought of ourselves as tourists and probably no longer even considered ourselves travellers. Dare we call ourselves explorers now I wonder? Perhaps not yet. The schedule was quite accurate though, and the area was pretty wild to say the least. Once we had left the outskirts of Xiamen with its acres of palm trees and banana plantations, to suggest that some of the roads were a bit on the bumpy side would be a significant understatement. Many of them were no better than rough tracks, and one particularly long road we took, and between two sizeable towns too, had clearly overspent its budget, despite the toll we had to pay, as sizeable chunks of it had been washed away or buried under minor landslides. Cars were a rarity too, but that was hardly surprising considering the state of the roads, and most people seemed to zoom around on motorbikes. Four on a bike was commonplace and we even saw a five-plus-dog, but that was, I'm pleased say, the record.

I have long since come to almost expect warmth and kindness from the ordinary Chinese I meet, but in Hukeng and in the nearby village of DaDi, the hospitality was quite humbling. We were invited into three Hakka homes on the first afternoon alone – for green tea, home brewed rice wine and to join them sampling tables weighed down with traditional New Year food. Dried sharon fruit seemed to be a local specialty, and I quite took to it although there were a few undesirable side effects. It was hard to believe that these villages were only a few hours drive away from Xiamen. If it were not for the signs of cable TV and the odd telephone, there was little to suggest that the way of life here had changed much for hundreds of years. Without exception, the people we met took such delight in our company that we all felt we had made some true friends. Addresses were swapped with some of them, and e-mail addresses too – for although the villages themselves had no computer facilities, some of the younger people we met were at university in Xiamen or Fuzhou where they had access to such stuff, and after protracted goodbyes, we moved on. No doubt, when the holidays are eventually over, some at least will try and keep in touch.

Above: Connie and friends. Hukeng Village, Yundong County, Fujian Province.

Left: Connie's family home, Yundong County, Fujian Province.

185

We made a particular friend of one young girl from Hukeng called Connie. She latched onto us when we were exploring Zhencheng Tower – the four-storey earthen building where we were to spend the night – the four of us westerners on the top floor; cooking, assorted livestock and toilets far below on the ground. Although most tour guides have a habit of shooing such interlopers away, Mr. Chen generously invited her into our conversation and allowed her to take the lead – she too wanted to practise her English and clearly knew more about the place than he did. She did live there, after all. Later, she introduced us to some of her friends and to her family as well as yet more food and drink was brought in. Connie herself was a student at Xiamen University, although not in the same department as Mr. Chen, and whilst she had passed her exams well enough, she had failed to win a scholarship to allow a reduction in fees. It seemed just a little unfair, because she had good English, a burning enthusiasm to learn and her parents were as poor as the proverbial church mice. But all is not fair in this world, for whilst Xiamen University takes in students from all over Fujian Province, and elsewhere in China for that matter, the first round of scholarships always go to those who live in the city itself (and who probably have the right *guanxi* too) leaving those from the rural areas with barely a look in.

Such is the speed with which things happen in China that, on my return, I was not altogether surprised (if a little saddened) to discover that one of my favourite alleys (or *hutong*) was being bulldozed. I liked this particular back street not only because it was very cheap and very close, but also because here, I always felt, was the real China – the China that is being swept away, or at least under the carpet, with frightening rapidity. The street is grubby, yes, but it is also friendly, rooted in tradition and endlessly fascinating. I love the good food you can buy from the street carts or little pavement cafes, which are now housed in quilted tents as protection from the cold, – no karaoke here – the stalls selling this and that, the clothes and hardware displayed on blankets on the pavement, the trailer loads of fresh fruit and vegetables, and, especially for me, the old man who cuts keys and mends bicycle tyres and who grins and calls out '*Ni hao*' whenever a friend walks past. All this will soon be lost in some entrepreneur or other's thirst for wealth. Now, in Tianjin, almost wherever you go, you can turn the corner and yet another shrine to shopping will confront you – every inch of it positively glowing in the

Demolition in Tianjin.

bright winter sunshine. One just a couple of miles from where I live is even called *Shining Square*. There is a large hoarding on the corner of the rapidly disappearing *hutong* near me that *may* possibly be telling the locals what is happening to them, but I cannot read the characters. The Guardian's far east correspondent recently reported similar developments (?) in Shanghai though, and he, presumably, can read these things. 'We pay respect to the work units and citizens who have agreed to move in order to assist the nation's reconstruction' one of the hoardings there apparently states, while, in case anyone had not agreed, the second made it clear that it was 'every citizen's glorious duty' to do so.

Although I lament the destruction of the old way of life, I do so, of course, from the comfort of a western-style apartment and a rather better salary than that of my neighbours. It is doubtful whether some of the quaint little buildings being demolished have running water let alone sanitation – hence the evil-smelling public toilets on every other street corner in the old parts of the city – and heating/cooking facilities are unlikely to be more sophisticated than a single, substandard charcoal stove. But whereas I, from my cosy perspective, would choose to restore the old almost every time, in China, the trend is very much towards building from scratch. It seems that the average Chinese has little nostalgia for the past in this respect. But whilst the façades of many of these new buildings are undeniably imposing, they are most definitely façades for all that, and there remains a fair degree of superficiality about them. Even the chiming clock that I can hear from my apartment is computerized, the actual chime, no doubt, a digitally enhanced recording of some great church in Florence. Beneath the veneer, or deceit maybe, things are rarely what they seem and generally fail to live up to their promise. Gadgets and systems often don't work properly and there is almost a total lack of customer service when it comes to getting things put right. The result is that you are left with the feeling that virtually everything new thing you see around you is designed for effect and little else. Ultimately, some unprincipled soul has likely made a fat profit too and probably taken the majority of the populace for a bit of a ride into the bargain. Although in post-communist China, a few Chinese are getting very rich indeed – which is, I suppose, an improvement on what things were like in pre-communist days when prosperity was largely in the hands of the Europeans, this new affluence is, sadly, still only for the very few. The vast majority is, without doubt, exploited, while the gap between the haves and have-nots is, I suspect, getting ever wider. And as the haves become visibly more detached and, I have to add, arrogant, they are leaving a large, socially excluded underclass in their wake – people who struggle to make ends meet, with few rights and, individually at least, little influence. So much of what was probably good under the old communist system – job security, social stability, solidarity – things that were probably taken for granted ten or twenty years ago – have now been lost, possibly forever.

But all is far from doom and gloom. No matter who you talk to, the sense of national pride is never too far from the surface, and with considerable justification. Even if you remain unconvinced about the real purpose of the enterprises, there are some extraordinary feats of engineering going on over here at the moment. The massive 'Three Gorges Dam' on the Yangtse is just about finished, while the waters of China's other great river, the Yellow River, have now been partially diverted northwards to become a major source of water in Tianjin's taps. We are told to boil it thoroughly of course, although, personally, I rely on bottled water for drinking and cooking. Which leads me nicely onto one of my other little grumbles. Despite modest success in my Chinese lessons, I sometimes find it harder to communicate than I did before. This, of course, I blame fairly and squarely on Chinese bureaucracy – what else? For gone are the days when I could simply telephone the 'Jinwanruntian Water Company' and, giving them my code (420 – 'si er ling'), would get bottled water delivered in less than an hour. Oh no! For the past few months I have become totally reliant on Chinese friends to perform what was once a simple operation for me. A bit disheartening really, but you see, just when things were getting a bit too easy, they changed the system. In order to get water delivered now, one seems to have to answer a tirade of questions that I simply don't understand. I am also told that phone bills are more difficult to pay these days. Colleagues have informed me that when they went to pay their bills at the bank last week, they were turned away. Apparently the system was changed here too, and one now has to buy a piece of plastic which you then feed into a machine rather like an ATM. 'Why?' one wonders, when, before Christmas, one could pay over the counter and exchange a few simple pleasantries with the clerk. It appears that there is nothing the Chinese official likes better than putting a little bit of a hurdle in your way – presumably in the name of progress but no doubt as a preventative against complacency too. But then, perhaps, the same can be said of officials the world over.

Returning to the subject of national pride though, in the far south west, the much vaunted railway line linking Lhasa in Tibet to the rest of China is proceeding apace while, in an attempt to alleviate enormous urban transport problems in the east, there is now talk of a magnetic levitation train or *maglev* being built between Beijing and both Tianjin and Shanghai. The first commercial *maglev* in the world, in fact, is set for launch in Shanghai later this year, and has just completed its first test run with its VIP passengers 'flying on the ground' at a speed of between two hundred and fifty and three hundred miles per hour. The principal is easily grasped – two opposite charged magnets repelling each other – but the technology is, I suspect, formidable. All very exciting for the future – a pity therefore one has to report that the Tianjin Metro remains closed – as it has been for the last year and a bit.

Quite a number of friends from England are set to visit me over the next few months and Mark from Dorset is with me as I write; and of course, the Great Wall has featured/will feature on most of their itineraries – the pass at Huangyaguan being only two or three hours away by bus or, for less hardy souls, cheap taxi. Although this particular stretch is 'well preserved', which is a euphemism for 'just-about-totally-reconstructed', the Chinese press recently published a depressing account on the condition of the Great Wall as a whole – less than 20% of it is apparently intact. The title 'Great Wall' is, in fact, a bit of a misnomer. It is actually a series of walls built and rebuilt one brick at a time, by different dynasties over the past two thousand or more years. Although academic work is very much in its infancy, it is known that construction began in the reign of China's first emperor, Qin Shi Huang (221–206 BC), he of the terracotta warriors, and lasted into the Ming dynasty (1368–1644AD). However, Great Wall bricks have long been crated off by rural people to be sold (fifteen *yuan* per tractor load is the going rate), while some parts are still being officially demolished to allow roads through or to build residential blocks. Although some of the destruction is the result of individual vandalism, and thus the drafting of laws to protect those parts of the Wall that remain must be welcomed, regional governments must certainly be held accountable for some if not most of the destruction – such as that sanctioned by the provincial government in Inner Mongolia a few years ago. They, of course, got off scot-free – the government over here is almost always above the law – those in authority, are, by Chinese definition at least, invariably in the right. Amazingly, though, if the People's Congress approves a law, it will be the first ever legislation in China to deal with the protection of an historic site.

Even older than the Great Wall, and a good deal further south, details have also been published about the opening of the elaborate coffin of a Chinese general from the so-called 'Warring States' period (475–221BC). Although the general's actual name remains a mystery, it would seem almost certain that the coffin is that of a legendary general who had nine tombs constructed so that no-one would know which one he was buried in. According to the legend, the general died on the battlefield and fearing that enemies would dig up the body, his followers built a line of nine tombs to confound them. Eight mounds, the empty ones, had long been known at the site at Zaoyang in Hubei Province, but the ninth was discovered only last year when contractors began work on a new motorway. Although not on the scale of the Terracotta Warriors in nearby Shaanxi Province, the dig has already unearthed nearly seven hundred items including thirty-three sets of carriages and horses as well as more than eighty musical instruments including a set of bronze chimes, drums, bells, reed pipes, with the original reeds intact, and a twenty-five string zither – the first of its kind to be discovered complete.

And whilst on the subject of zithers, as my contract will finish at the end of the summer term – I have told my employers that I am not seeking to renew it – but while I am still anxious not to miss out on opportunities that may never come my way again, I have decided to take lessons on a couple of traditional Chinese instruments before I go. Expect as progress report next time I write. And despite the problems I encounter from time to time, I will continue with my spoken Chinese too, which I enjoy immensely and which I suppose is good for the little grey cells. In fact, buying some lip salve (*chungao*) yesterday, and notwithstanding the nerves induced by the moderate crowd of on-lookers that gathered around me, my actual request '*Ni you chungao ma?*' presented no problems whatsoever. A pity then about the four shop assistants and the handwritten form in triplicate the transaction required. I couldn't fathom that bit of it out at all and in the end someone had to do it for me. The humiliation of it. I still intend leaving Chinese characters well alone though. A bit of a cop-out maybe, but for my purposes, pinyin is quite enough, although I do have to cheat and write things in my coursebook in anglicised phonetics from time to time. Talking of which, some enterprising soul – I know not whom – has recently published a book for the English speaking Tianjin expat community. Called '*Speak Chinese E – Z*', it does away with the need for pinyin altogether. For example, that useful question '*Duo shao qian?*' or 'How much is it?' comes out as 'Dwaw shaow chee-in?' while '*Wo xihuan Tianjin*' ('I like Tianjin') reads as 'Waw she-hwehn Tee-en jeen'. Some people might find this sort of thing helpful I suppose, but I can't help but feel it might be just another excuse to avoid learning the real thing. I still laugh at my naivety when, just before Chinese New Year, I first saw the book. My immediate reaction was 'What's happened to A, B, C and D?' Never in a month of Sundays would I have considered pronouncing '*ee-zed*' as '*ee-zee*'. I am reminded of the time I played the piano for a Sunday school jamboree a while back and we sang '*I am H-A-P-P-Y*'. I had obviously been singing this same chorus for years without realising what I was on about. It was only when I saw it down in print that the penny dropped. It takes all sorts I suppose.

CHAPTER 19

A Grand Day Out – and Other Tales

March 2003　2003年 三月

I thought I should put pen to paper relatively soon after my last letter to reassure people that life in north eastern China goes on much as before despite the sorry conflict in Iraq, the recent earthquake in Xinjiang Province (three and a half thousand kilometres or so to the west of me) and the SARS outbreak some two thousand kilometres to the south east. My satellite TV channel, BBC World, is utterly obsessed with the first of these three miseries and is, of course, milking it for all its worth. In fact I've just muttered a few oaths under my breath and switched the TV off – the interview with one Randy Gangle being more than I could stomach. Although both family and quite a number of friends have been in touch in recent weeks, concerned about my well-being on the SARS front, the poor people of Xinjiang seem to have been forgotten completely by the outside world. Yet, so far at least, it is this that has affected me the most. I was in Xinjiang, the homeland of the Uighur ethnic minority, not so long ago myself, loved the place (although it has to be said I was not in the earthquake area which was centred on the old silk route town of Kashgar – the actual Province is the size of western Europe) and consider my trip there to be one of the most wonderful experiences of my time over here. Turpan in particular, with its mud walled houses, narrow dusty lanes, donkey carts and chaotic markets was everything I had wanted it to be.

Naturally I am appreciative of the consideration shown by so many friends, but my only contact with the SARS virus so far has been in the form of an e-mail from the Embassy in Beijing advising

British citizens to avoid Hong Kong, Guangdong Province, Taiwan, Vietnam and Singapore. At least that is what I was told it said. I couldn't actually open the e-mail attachment as it was infected with a virus itself! I hear from friends back home though that the Chinese government has come in for some fierce criticism, and for many westerners, its decision, until very recently at least, not to tell its own people about the disease must seem shockingly irresponsible. However, Chinese bureaucrats would argue the exact opposite. The Chinese regime sees disease as a state security issue – tell the public that they're in danger and they might panic, goes the argument. And knowing what I do about the Chinese man in the street, I too can see it from the *official* angle. Without wishing to sound patronising, there is, to my eyes, an immaturity in the way many Chinese behave, which manifests itself daily in a host of different ways. A driver's total and (probably) unthinking lack of consideration for other road users for example, or a cyclist's complete obliviousness of what is happening around him – which really has to be seen to be believed. Disagreements about any mortal thing generally lead to shouting and wild gesticulation in one fell swoop, with the first to lash out invariably being the one in the wrong, while a crowd of curious onlookers will gather at the first signs of a confrontation. I thus have more than a little sympathy with the official approach to security issues. Furthermore, the Chinese have an old saying that goes: 'The mountains are high, and the emperor is far away' and, on the whole, this is the view I have adopted as well, however naïve it may be. For even if all is far from well with the world, I at least continue to feel secure here in Tianjin, the merest drop in the ocean, one amongst a population of well over 1.3 thousand million people, in a country of around 9.5 million square kilometres. China is a big, big place.

Returning to Xinjiang for a moment though, I read with sadness a letter in the Guardian Weekly the other day from pre-earthquake Kashgar where the writer described an all too familiar tale of destruction-in-the-name-of-progress. The railway line from the provincial capital Urumqi to Kashgar was opened about eighteen months ago if my memory serves me right. Nominally, of course, it was to link this remote area of the Province with the rest of China whilst, in fact, it has proved equally, if not more, useful in bringing in hundreds of Han Chinese every week all hoping to make a new life. In a region that was, previously and presumably, relatively safe from the marginalisation of ethnic groups, when it probably took three days along potholed roads to reach the place, the Guardian writer speaks of an unrelenting assault on the place. 'Across the province *unsafe* ethnic housing is being ripped apart, ancient minarets are being prettied up and surrounded by plastic walls, wooden vine trellises torn down and replaced by marble-effect Roman pillars and lakeside paths drowned in concrete'. I look out of my apartment window here in Tianjin – it all looks and sounds horribly familiar. In just under one week's time I am off to Tibet with friends from UK, a Province which, I suspect, will suffer much the same fate once the Lhasa railway opens. Perhaps China's new president, former deputy Hu Jintao, will see things a little differently from his predecessors, but I confess I'm not really too optimistic on that front. I can't help but feel that with departing president Jiang Jemin still very much in the wings – he is remaining as head of the party's military commission after all – his outgoing remarks that 'all people's interests are basically identical' do not bode well, and that we can all look forward to yet more concrete and neon, ceramic tiling and electric palm trees. Conformity will remain the only safe strategy for survival with little offered in the way of political change, public accountability or individual identity.

Over the past few weeks, my cultural life, if I have the cheek to call it that, has focussed on the *gu zheng*. Keen to know something about traditional Chinese music before returning to England, a friend and I signed up for lessons at the Tianjin Conservatoire. Rather like a zither, it has twenty-one strings and produces a hauntingly beautiful sound. (For the musicians among you, the strings are tuned to a pentatonic scale, so it's difficult to produce anything really terrible, although, by altering the tension of the strings with your left hand, you can play all the notes in between – intentionally or otherwise.) I have to say that I am pleased with my progress, and if my playing lacks something in its subtlety at the moment, at least none of my neighbours have complained – yet. As a pianist, I am particularly attracted to those musical effects that could never be produced on a piano – the vibrato one can achieve by waggling the string with your left hand as you pluck it with your right, or, better still, the bending of the notes when either you pluck a string and increase its tension as it as it is still vibrating or the reverse, when you pluck the already taught string and release it. I'd never been particularly enthusiastic about microtonal music before, but the *gu zheng* produces some very special sounds in this area and is proving to be great fun.

A couple of weeks ago I attended a concert up the road in Beijing given by the China Philharmonic Orchestra and featuring two concertos for traditional instruments and orchestra. The first of these, by one John Sharpley, was, of course, for *gu zheng*. Called 'When Cranes Fly Home', it was a first performance, and given by Chinese-Canadian Han Mei. Although the programme notes were singularly unhelpful, I can at least assure readers that it was an atmospheric and attractive work, the sound of the orchestra and the *gu zheng* intertwining to produce something eminently listenable without being over sentimental. However the piece and the performance were as nothing when compared with what was to follow – the Pipa Concerto by Japanese composer Minoru Miki, played by the phenomenal Yang Jing, to whom it was dedicated. I was utterly mesmerised as I sat bolt upright in my seat, listening and watching her every phrase and every move. Rarely have I come out of a concert feeling so alive. The composer, the piece itself (the *pipa* is an ethnic Chinese guitar by the way) and the young Miss Yang are worth scouring the CD catalogues for.

I was moved most certainly, but I am obliged to add, angry too at the thought of the ticket prices. I paid over two hundred *yuan*, just short of twenty pounds, for my mid-priced seat. What a pity, therefore, that such magnificent music and such a truly great performance was accessible only by the tiniest of minority of the population. Is the majority in some way unworthy? When our Chinese classroom assistants here in Tianjin earn around one and a half thousand *yuan* a month – regarded as a good wage – that anyone can charge two hundred and twenty *yuan* or more for a ticket beggars belief. Yet this is simply another example of China's disturbingly polarised society. My Chinese friends could never in a month of Sundays afford to pay for such concerts themselves. And, of course, it is not just classical concerts that are priced to be beyond the reach of the average man in the street. A sort of 'Blues Brothers' tribute band is playing in Tianjin towards the end of April with ticket prices ranging from one hundred to an obscene four hundred *yuan* – far more than a week's wages. So much for socialism. 'It will be unimaginably wonderful scene of that evening ... no one will give up this precious opportunity,' says the poster in its customary Chinglish. I can tell you some one who will – along with 99.9% of the rest of Tianjin of course – although in their case, probably not through choice.

On a lighter note, and whilst on the subject of Chinglish, I dare not repeat what the packaging on the bar of 'exquisite article chocolate' I was given on Valentines Day exhorted me to do, and thus you will have to content yourself with a few quotes from a circular placed in my pigeon hole at school by one of my Chinese colleagues and marked for the attention of 'Members of the Rear Service Department'! Calvin, the author of the document, is a great guy and really keen to help us expats, so he produced a little leaflet to help us on our merry way. I quote: 'These forms should be created according to the actual repairing status, registered in time order and monthly refreshed. The date should be the code prefix added with an two-digit repairing item number 01-XX when the month is changed. The serial number of the remedy project is composed by the prefix of coding that is set by date. The number will be another 01 with the X of months. In order to save time, the forms, (the File of Repairing Management the File of the Foreign Teachers' Apartment and the Monthly Repairing Management Report Form of Rear Service Department) will share the same date and mode.' I shall miss this sort of word soup when I return to UK believe you me – he and his prose are so well intentioned. And, of course, it is not only Calvin who plays with the English language. Where else but in China (or to be more precise, Tianjin railway station) would you see the delightful, precautionary warning 'No skipping' for example? But maybe similar gibberish is to be found elsewhere in the world. Indeed, a friend of mine recently e-mailed me the text of a notice they had spotted just outside Dublin which read quite simply 'Fine to park here!' I can't make that one out either.

As anyone who has been to Tianjin will confirm, the immediate area is singularly lacking in what one might call 'beauty spots'. Nevertheless, there are one or two such places marked on the map, and as a result, a month or so ago, I planned a grand day out to 'Tuanbo Lake Scenic Area' – officially designated a 'tourism area for one's holidays'. Quite an experience it turned out to be too – I was grateful for my hip flask on more than one occasion. We decided to go by bus, as Simon, one of my Chinese friends, had discovered that a certain route passed relatively close to the lake, although it has to be said at the outset that our driver was rather less than certain. Nevertheless, the conductor seemed eager to oblige and so we paid the five *yuan* and headed out of the city. A pity therefore that forty-five or so minutes later she advised us to get off her bus at a point (I am sure) rather further from the lake than was strictly necessary. But to give her her due, she pointed out another bus which she said was the connecting service to Tuanbo (or words to that effect) and which, following protracted farewells and exhortations to *man zou* (literally 'go slow') we boarded.

This time, our driver (and the other passengers for that matter) were pretty sure they knew where we should go – indeed quite an enthusiastic crowd of well-wishers gathered around my much mended map as I pointed out where I thought we were and what our intended destination was to be. But, alas, I was wrong on the first count and as a consequence not altogether surprised when it tran-spired that, once again, the bus driver really had no idea where we were headed. In the end, and, I suppose, inevitably, he and his friends waved us goodbye in the middle of a nameless and godforsaken little place that didn't exist on my map at all, or at least if it did, was lost under a bit of Sellotape. But, in fact, all was not lost, for we were met by a driver of a motorbike taxi who offered to take us to the lake in his sidecar. 'No, it wasn't far' he said. 'Maybe it is just over the hori-zon' he added. In fact, we were in the sidecar for well over an hour while he himself raced hell for leather along rutted tracks, through fields, across wooden bridges and around derelict buildings and fac-tories strewn with the ubiquitous litter. But, give him his due, he did at least know the whereabouts of the lake and, after a few enquiries managed to find the so-called scenic spot too.

Well, 'odd' was hardly the word for it. It was a place of maybe one hundred and fifty newish toy-town style houses, completely empty – no-one lived there at all; a holiday complex looking rather like a stage set for some eerie sci-fi film where the world has been sent into a deep sleep. We wandered down one of the streets and were disturbed only by a chain clanking in the wind and the occasional plastic bag. There was a hotel though, and, somewhat to our surprise, it appeared to be open although it is doubtful whether it had seen a guest for many a long day. Simon and I went up to it and spied two sleepy but immaculately dressed girls in the foyer. They were, no doubt, instructed to greet visitors, but were so surprised to see us

*Wei's kites, made in
Tianjin, are famous
throughout China.*

they really hadn't a clue what to do. Nevertheless, after a little hesitation and a nervous giggle or two, they sheepishly opened the dining room door, only to reveal three or four people asleep (dead?) on the floor. Another hesitation and another nervous giggle and they closed it again and decided to try the private dining rooms. Oh dear! Number One was firmly locked, while Number Two had the remnants of meal still on the table – as it had probably been for a week or more – looking for all the world like Miss Haversham's wedding breakfast. They approached the final room rather gingerly. Relief! It was empty and tolerably clean. And so after a few desultory wipes of the plastic tablecloth, we were offered a seat.

The meal was surprisingly good all things considered and our walk around the lake afterwards very refreshing. A pity therefore that there was very little water to be seen – despite its evident size. The

Listening to the expert. An early lesson on the gu zheng. Tianjin.

circumference was in the order of seventy kilometres and in the centre was a man-made island complete with pagoda and, we were told, a leisure complex. We thought we could just see it through the mist, but, of course, there was no access. It was not that we were out of season or anything like that, it was simply that there was insufficient water for a boat, whilst the ground was far too marshy to permit a walk across, and, with spring in the air, the ice had just about disappeared so skating there was out of the question. Poor Tuanbo – I don't think things had quite worked out the way they were planned. One wonders how many hundreds of thousands of pounds and man-hours had gone into the construction of the whole place. Maybe, in the future, some enterprising soul will start to clear up the litter and maybe lay on a bit of transport in some shape or form. Maybe, but probably not.

199

Being predominantly a non-Christian country, the Chinese as a whole do not celebrate Easter. However, last weekend we enjoyed something which, if not totally dissimilar in purpose was markedly different in practice. *Qing Ming Jie* – the 'Clear and Bright Festival' has been celebrated in China for hundreds of years. Although, on the surface, it simply comes across as a day for paying respects to one's ancestors – westerners generally refer to it as the tomb cleaning festival – it is very much a celebration of the coming spring, new life and family values too. As well as sweeping the graves, one of the more important ceremonies is the offering of food and goods to the dear departed. If the food is very real, the goods are not and far more likely to be made from tissue paper, taking the form of anything from a shirt and tie to a TV set. These are then 'transferred' to the dead by burning them. More often than not, so-called 'paper money' ('Bank of Hell' money) is burnt at the same time too – this money distracts the evil spirits who would, given half a chance, intercept the goods and have them for themselves. Thus, while the evil spirits are chasing the money, the valuable goods pass safely to the dead.

Qing Ming is, most definitely, a social event, and there is still an expectation that the whole family will make the trip to the ancestral tombs. The festival is thus associated with get-togethers and outings of all sorts, particularly to the countryside, and from this a number of other customs have emerged. In Tianjin, as elsewhere in China for example, where people go kite-flying at the drop of a hat, *Qing Ming* is often the occasion for kite competitions, with individuals and groups vying to create the most stunning and imaginative kites. Such activity is not confined to the children either; like karaoke, it is a serious business – emphatically not something to be trifled with. Consequently, although it is wonderful to watch, it takes none of us by surprise to see, literally, hundreds of adults, young and old, enjoying a spot of kite-flying on the clear, sunny afternoons we have enjoyed recently.

So on that cheerful note I will sign off. I am meeting up with Catrina Lambert, an old friend whom I have not seen for twenty years, in Beijing this weekend, and have five more friends coming to stay for Easter itself. Although we will not be together all the time, we are joining up for the aforementioned week in Tibet which I am looking forward to immensely. Kate, Janice and John will be amongst the last tourists to be able to 'do' the Three Gorges now that the dam on the Yangtse is virtually completed and the waters are already rising fast, while David, Denise and I may well be amongst the first western tourists to travel to remote nature reserve of Jiu Zhai Gou in northern Sichuan Province. We are joining a Chinese tour group for the duration which will, no doubt, furnish me with a ton of material for my next newsletter.

CHAPTER 20

One-way Ticket to Lhasa

May 2003   2003年 五月

With the number of SARS cases in northern China increasing dramatically at the moment, a lot of sensible and, of course, some rather more eccentric health precautions are currently in place – both here in Tianjin and in Beijing. For a start, many public events are being postponed or abandoned altogether. I think the Rolling Stones' far eastern tour is off, (as a colleague of mine said in the staffroom the other day, things must be really bad if, despite the Stones' years of contact with most substances known to man, they decide to cancel because of SARS) but whether or not a forthcoming production of 'Cats' goes ahead remains to be seen. I would be particularly sad to see this one bite the dust, as the show is tailor-made for China – the Chinese for 'cat' (singular or plural) being *'mao'*. Coincidence or what? Sadly, though, many of my Chinese friends and a fair proportion of the Asian community generally seem to be in panic mode much of the time. But some good might have come out of it and I am pleased to report that the amount of spitting that goes on has been significantly reduced in recent weeks. Long may it last. However, although most of my western friends and colleagues remain level-headed about it all, it is a sorry fact that we have lost about one quarter of our pupils in the past week – temporarily I hope. But life goes on. I wear a gauze face mask in crowded or enclosed places, wash my apartment floor with Dettol every other day or so, and my temperature is taken before I am allowed into the school buildings; if I have reason to go across to the Sheraton next door for the supermarket or the ATM or whatever, it is taken a second or a third time as well. But more about SARS a little later. Meanwhile, read on.

With the spring term finishing at lunchtime on the day before Good Friday, there was just time to collect my luggage before boarding the train to Beijing. Here I was to meet up with Denise and David, friends from England with whom I was travelling to Chengdu in Sichuan Province, and where, in turn, I was due to meet three further friends, Kate, Janice and John, hopefully fresh from a Three Gorges experience, before setting off on our all too brief expedition to the Roof of the World. Timing was of the essence, and I am pleased to say China Railways was running true to form – the trains really do run on time over here. The Beijing SARS scare was just beginning over the Easter period, so although Tianjin was crammed as normal, the streets of the capital were significantly less busy – so much so that the usual crowds around the 'fried pimple', 'goat cock' and 'slurry' stalls just off Wangfujing were nowhere to be found. Although Denise, David and I gave these particular delicacies a miss, we did eat 'spicy' in readiness for our journey to the lands of the utmost west.

The T7 Express from Beijing West to Chengdu left precisely at 4.00 p.m., and we quickly settled down in our pricey but comfy soft berths for the twenty-seven hour journey. With the restaurant car right next door, the train was made up of about twenty coaches so we counted ourselves very lucky in this respect, and a convenient station stop at Shijiazhuang a couple of hours or so after departure enabling us to buy some '999 Beer' (for emergency use obviously) we were more than well set up for the first day of our holiday together. During our night's sleep, the train's route followed the course of the Yellow River – a pity that I could not show my friends just how aptly named it is – and we surfaced at around 8.30 the following morning shortly before Qin Ling – a grubby country town maybe, but set amongst some truly wonderful mountains. Although quite a number of the more worthy passengers got off the train to do a little keep fit on the station platform, the majority stayed on board and did their bit to instructions being broadcast on the train's loudspeakers.

I am ashamed to say I neither exercised on the platform nor on the train itself, but spent the next ten minutes or so reading a disconcerting little leaflet about Acute Mountain Sickness and the pros and cons of taking 'Diamox', whilst, perhaps inevitably, feeling worse and worse by the second. If Acute Mountain Sickness sounded horrendous, with its 'constellation' of symptoms including severe headache, nausea, rapid heart beat, periodic breathing, dehydration, etc. etc., then its possible progression to high-altitude pulmonary oedema sounded even worse. This condition, I read, was more likely to occur in men than women (that word 'likely' seemed ominous) especially if they had a bit of a cold (was that a sore-throat I had coming on?) whilst the symptoms of the potentially life-threatening high-altitude cerebral oedema, the accumulation of fluid on the brain (and yes, I could sense I was about to develop a headache too), do not even bear repetition. As well as the aforementioned 'Diamox', I also examined the instructions for the emergency supply of 'Prednisolone' I had with me – something to be taken in a crisis situation only. I looked for it anxiously in my first aid kit. I was beginning to sweat. What height was Qin Ling? Surely this would be the perfect place to spend the next two weeks. How much higher was Lhasa? Would my health insurance cover an air ambulance? I pulled myself together. I was a middle-aged man simply going on holiday, not in training for the Royal Marines or working for my Duke of Edinburgh's Bronze Award. I re-read the bit about the undesirable side-effects of 'Diamox', tingling of the fingers and around the mouth and some variation to one's sense of taste, and they sounded almost fun. I took my half tablet and hoped for the best. It worked too. Three hearty cheers for Tianjin SOS Clinic!

After Qin Ling, we followed the valley of one of the north-flowing tributaries of the Yellow River for much of the morning, aware of the scenery becoming increasingly mountainous as we went. We noticed the earth too. Far from being thin and stony as one might have expected it to be in such an area, it looked rich and fertile – a refreshing change to the lifeless, polluted stuff we get around Tianjin. And although, like Tianjin, many of the larger towns we passed through seemed to have their fair share of filthy chimneys belching who knows what into the atmosphere, we also whizzed through many attractive villages where the station master would salute our express from his painted square on the platform. Snaking through southern Shaanxi Province, across bridges and through cuttings and tunnels, much of the route was on a single track, and in many passing places, slow trains to wondrous, unpronounceable destinations would often be waiting to let us through.

Almost twenty-four hours after setting off, we reached Guangyuan in Sichuan Province – the Heavenly Kingdom as it is referred to by the Chinese – where, to our delight, our train's arrival was accompanied by some appropriately socialist-sounding anthem from the station's hoary old PA system. From here, as we travelled deeper into the Province, the vegetation became ever more lush, and, with the odd temple or two thrown in for good measure, including a particularly fine-looking complex just outside Sichuan's second city, Mianyang, things were beginning to get quite exotic. Arriving at Chengdu at the appointed hour, the rather plush Amara Hotel was our destination, and, just as planned, our three friends were waiting for us in the bar. Things were going like clockwork. It was to be a quick drink though, as hunger got the better of us, and so after downing a quick Tsingtao beer we went straight out for a meal – spicy Sichuan food was the order of the day of course. We found the perfect place too, just a few hundred yards from our base, and using that well tried jumble of phrasebook and spoken Chinese with a fair bit of pointing thrown in, managed to order something fairly decent if not quite what we had intended. What looked as though it was spicy squid turned out to be spicy chickens' feet instead. I don't think we would have ordered them if we had known, but they were pretty tasty nonetheless.

Easter Day, and we rose none too bright but very early for our two-hour flight to Lhasa. If we had hoped to see the dawn rise over the foothills of the Tibetan Plateau we were to be disappointed, although, in actual fact, I had no complaints as I was fortunate enough to have a window seat which afforded some spectacular views of snow clad peaks poking up through masses of cloud. Lhasa airport is well over two hours from the city, but we had no grumbles on that score either, as we made ourselves comfortable on the bus, proudly wearing our welcoming *ha-da* scarves of course, and thoroughly looking forward to the adventures that lay ahead. Our journey took us through some dramatic terrain with the deep blue Yarling Tsangpo on one side (which flows into the Brahmaputra I was surprised to learn) and of course, towering mountains all around. What a pity we weren't able to see the Tsangpo Gorge some way to the east of the airport though – the deepest gorge in the world, and, unbelievably, three times the depth of the Grand Canyon.

Although there were a lot of people out and about, dressed for the most part in what we might call national costume (plus cowboy hats – China, as readers will have gathered by now, is not short a few cowboys) there was surprisingly little traffic – certainly far fewer motorbikes than in other rural areas of China I have visited. What vehicles we saw were either army convoys or fantastic belt-driven engines attached to carts laden with people or produce. The people we saw, men and women alike, were re-doing the roads, digging and clearing irrigation ditches, washing clothes in the river, repairing their houses (at one point we saw two young men filling a wicker basket which was strapped onto some poor woman's back with heaps of earth and rocks) or attending to their crops in the fields, each with their little mounds of sacred stones to guard against evil spirits. There was, not unexpectedly, a lot of other evidence of Tibetan religion all around us too, chiefly in the form of onion shaped incense burners and hundreds of coloured flags (red for fire, white for clouds, blue for sky, yellow for earth and green for water) these latter adorning the corners of virtually every building. There were also many trees, especially as we got closer to Lhasa itself, which softened the landscape considerably, and made the place seem friendly and welcoming. It would have been nice to have joined some of the dozens of labourers asleep or picnicking under the trees, and maybe even shared a cup of tea with them; in front of several houses we saw kettles of boiling water suspended over what looked like small TV satellite dishes but were, in fact, reflectors designed to focus the sun's rays and heat the water.

Although we were advised to have an 'adaptive rest' that first afternoon, I had taken my half 'Diamox' and was anxious to do a bit of exploring. So, following a brief siesta and dodging some of the more professional-looking beggars, we headed first for Barkhor Square where all manner of Tibetan and pseudo-Tibetan trinketry was for sale and thence to the Jokhang Temple where we loitered expecting all the while to be evicted as a service was about to take place. But we had misread the vibes, and. instead of being summarily dismissed, were escorted to the front of the queue of worshippers and ushered in, to have the temple entirely to ourselves for ten or more precious minutes. Later we were to rejoin a queue for a while, the purpose of which we had no idea, (it was in fact to kiss the Golden Buddha – a bit of a production line that one) but thereafter we just soaked up the atmosphere of the place – which with the *Shakti* Brand yak butter lamps and candles, the constantly changing light and the repetitive chanting of the monks was quite unlike anything I had experienced before. And outside, too, things were overwhelming, with dozens upon dozens of people at prayer, some with wooden mittens strapped to their hands, falling to their knees, throwing their hands out in front of them, and then pulling their body along a few feet before repeating the entire process. What, of course, we were in fact witnessing was an age-old expression of religious belief that even the Chinese had failed to secularise. True, the gates of the temple were opened by the (secular) police and we were allowed to queue jump because the guards wanted us to witness a show rather than an act of worship, but I came away profoundly moved by the experience nonetheless. Moved, yes, but also quite disturbed for reasons that encapsulate completely the dilemma most western visitors face when visiting Tibet. It is a fact that in order to maximise tourist revenue the Chinese are quite happy to allow the religious rituals to take place. Were we, therefore, as visitors, showing our support for the Tibetans or for China's dubious 'liberation' of what had been a sovereign state? Were we, by our very presence, tacitly approving of what amounts to the subjugation of the Tibetan people?

The presence of the Dalai Lama in India, too, has meant that China has felt compelled to maintain its grip over the Tibetan people where, as regards other minorities, that same grip has been steadily relaxed. And as Patrick French in his book 'Tibet, Tibet' argues, by remaining faithful to their inherited cultural values, however idiosyncratic they may seem to outsiders, Tibetans do in fact make life much harder for themselves in a world where no foreign power dare intervene for fear of upsetting the mighty People's Republic or its own trade relations. Even after one day, we were all only too aware of the extraordinarily heavy police and army presence around us, while the amount of bureaucracy was excessive even by Chinese standards – an effective way of emphasising who is in control of course. Despite the fact that Tibetan script tended to precede the Chinese on shop fronts and hoardings, the latter was always several sizes bigger and several shades bolder. And despite, or perhaps because of, the huge, bronze yaks adorning the roundabouts, there was no mistaking the architecture of the new town at least. With tour guides and hotels almost entirely run by and largely for the Han Chinese, and the inevitable boy-meets-tractor sculptures in the parks, it would be a remarkably blinkered person indeed who was not able to see beneath the surface veneer.

On our second day we made the six-hour road journey to Shigatse, Tibet's second city, where we were to stay in the Shandong Mansion – a hotel that is apparently featured in the Guinness Book of Records. Its claim to fame – the tallest building in the highest city in the world (two of our rooms even had oxygen machines), the place was nothing special, but then neither was Shigatse City. Our road followed the valley of the Yarling Tsangpo for much of its route, where the trees in the early green of spring that had made Lhasa seem so pleasant soon gave way to increasingly wild and inhospitable terrain, and where the only splashes of colour were provided by the coloured flags and other hangings, the picturesque Tibetan houses with their ornately decorated windows and doors and, of course, the river itself. Although the journey was not particularly comfortable, it was made worthwhile if only for our lunch stop roughly half way there, when we clambered down towards the river to discover an astonishing series of little water wheels driving primitive grinding mills. There is something immensely satisfying about looking at something that has remained unchanged for possibly thousands of years and where you can actually understand its underlying technology. Not a nail or a screw in sight either, the whole mechanism was operated by wooden pegs and pinions. But it was not so much the sight of all this that made the experience so memorable as the smell, which was quite wonderful. For the mills were grinding sandalwood, and, of course, the resulting fragrance scented the air quite beautifully. We were discovering that religion pervades just about every aspect of Tibetan life, and our guide explained that the ground sandalwood would be used later in the manufacture of incense sticks.

Our first port of call in Shigatse was the massive monastery of Tashilhunpo, the official seat of the Panshen Lama, second only to the Dalai Lama, and almost a city in its own right, with its temples and halls and living accommodation for over seven hundred monks. It was as lovely as the rest of Shigatse was ugly in fact, and, as well as escaping some of the more extreme vandalism of the Mao era, had also benefited from some reconstruction in the '80s and '90s, surprisingly tasteful, and some considerable investment too – from the Government in Beijing no less. The tomb or *stupa* of the fifth to the ninth Panshen Lamas was particularly memorable and, in fact, only completed in 1988. Although these five lamas originally had separate tombs, these were destroyed in the Cultural Revolution, and whilst

Right: En route to Shigatse, Tibet.

Below: Travellers on the Khamba La high pass, Tibet.

Bottom: The debating monks at the Sera Monastery, Lhasa, Tibet.

the bodies themselves were hidden by the good monks, their respective identities became so confused that when things were rebuilt they were simply bundled together.

Moving on from Shigatse wasn't quite as straightforward as it might have been, and the Shandong Mansion was certainly not in the Guinness Book of Records for its quality of customer care. Although the Room Service Directory made it very clear that 'the mulberry takes' ('why shouldn't it?' I ask), and that the management were quite prepared to 'accept the silver' for this, and whilst our 6.00 a.m. morning call arrived bang on time (without us having to 'beat the outside line' let alone 'stir the telephone number') there was no sign of that all important 6.20 breakfast our tour guide had booked. *'Meiyou'* The girl at the desk had simply failed to pass the message on to the kitchens, which remained padlocked. Who said Tibet isn't really part of China? Sharp words were exchanged and we were bussed to a nearby hotel and breakfasted very well indeed.

Our journey along the quiet road-cum-dirt track to Gyantse was a revelation both in terms of the scenery we saw and the people we met. There was the water-powered barley mill with its predictable dusty miller who offered me my first ever pinch of snuff that I narrowly avoided sneezing back into his face. To sneeze after taking snuff is a sign of Buddha's blessing. Then there was the rambling family home with the aged grandma spinning her prayer wheel with its mantra to the god *Avalokiteschvara* as she went about her daily chores, her fresh, handmade yak pats drying in the sun, with yet more yak pats stacked in the kitchen, ready to fuel the stove. There were the soaring snow-clad peaks, the high passes of Karo La and Khamba La (both around five thousand metres), the skylarks (if that really is what they were) and Yamdrok Lake – a 'turquoise classic' as one of my guidebooks describes it. And, of course, there was the monastery complex at Gyantse itself with its photogenic *kumbum* containing, we were informed, ten thousand images of Buddha. We saw it from the outside only. If ever I have cause to compile a list of 'good chopstick days', then this will be on it. Gyantse itself, as one of the least Chinese influenced towns in Tibet, was refreshingly devoid of neon lights, white ceramic tiles and concrete pillars and, instead, full of an old world atmosphere. It is also closely associated with the great King Gesar of Ling whose legendary, heroic deeds are contained in the ancient Tibetan poem of the same name – one of the great epic poems of the world and at over one million lines long, easily the world's longest single work of literature. This has been handed down by word of mouth in an unbroken tradition among the Tibetan nomads for more than a millennium, and to this day, so-called divine bards, many of whom are illiterate, sing the heroic story, often in a state of trance. According to the recent BBC radio programme David and Denise kindly taped for me, the bards, who believe their ability to recite the epic is a divine gift from King Gesar himself, are still generating new episodes, among which is one where Gesar tackles Adolf Hitler.

Talking of legends, our hotel in Lhasa was named after the myth-ical Tibetan valley of *Sham Ba La*, the tale of which gave James Hilton the idea of Shangri-La in his novel Lost Horizon. Not the most luxurious of places, and with a wildly idiosyncratic floor and room numbering system (the floors were numbered UK style – ie ground floor, 1st floor etc, the lift controls numbered US style – ie 1st floor, 2nd floor etc, and to cap it all, the actual room numbers were pre-ceded by a lucky '8' – Tibetan style) it was at least conveniently placed for the local restaurants (I can recommend both 'yak sizzlers' and the fantastic cheesecake made from yaks' milk), the pilgrims and monks outside the Jokhang Temple, the market traders spilling off Barkhor Square and, of course, the nightlife. The *Mad Yak* restaurant and cabaret bar is not recommended though. Our evening of traditional Tibetan music and dance was a decidedly lacklustre affair. Most importantly however, it was only a ten-minute or so walk away from the Potala Palace – something I wanted to see above all else. Although Tibet as a whole was far from the idyll painted by James Hilton, the Potala was very special. Thirteen storeys high with over one thousand rooms, it is/was the official residence of the leader of Tibet, the Dalai Lama – although, of course, the present Dalai Lama (the fourteenth re-incarnation of Buddha), and a sort of king/high priest/emperor/pope rolled into one – has been in exile in Dharamsala in India since 1959. The building dominates Lhasa, and despite the fact the Chinese have tried to secularise it by turning it into more of a museum than any thing else, when we went, the place was full of believers completing the pilgrim circuit. And although the interior was truly amazing, for me one of the highlights was simply standing on the palace roof – probably as high as I will ever get on the face of the Earth. A pity therefore that the view was, for the most part, that of the new city, which is an extraordinarily tasteless affair. Being a bit short sighted it looked far better with my glasses off. From the ground, the best view of the Potala is almost certainly from the huge square that has been created in front of it. Looking very like Tian'anmen Square in Beijing, a large area of ramshackle housing was demolished to provide a show ground for military parades, trade fairs and the like for which the Potala forms a suitably imposing backcloth. When we were there, there was obviously a promotion for JCBs going on, with the ubiquitous red inflatable arch and a series of over powered loudspeakers churning out Kenny G.

The clear blue skies we got every morning afforded some wonderful photo opportunities, and as our breakfasts in Lhasa weren't up to much, most of us spent at least a couple of mornings doing our own photo shoots, so we got to know our particular area of the city several days before Tom, our excellent guide, formally introduced it to us. But we were indebted to his expertise when it came to visiting those places slightly further afield – the Sera Monastery for example, some four kilometres to the north of the city, where the five hundred or so debating monks must count as one of the most remarkable religious discussions I have ever witnessed – and the Norbulingka – three kilometres to the west, which used to be the Dalai Lama's summer residence. This latter contains the only picture of the fourteenth Dalai Lama on public display in China, and even that is tucked away around the back, as well as a picture of a car given to one of his predecessors by the Brits in the 1930s. A pity there were no roads in Tibet at the time and the thing had to be transported in little bits on mules and yaks before being reassembled *in situ*. Still it's the thought that counts.

I have not led a life completely devoid of incident, but hitherto, my main claim to fame was being in Prague in August 1968 when the Russians invaded. Well, from now on, the events that began at five minutes to midnight on Wednesday 23rd April 2003 will rank a close second. It all started with a phone call from Tom our guide. To my surprise he said he was in the hotel foyer. Apparently, amongst the passengers on Kate, Janice and John's Three Gorges cruise was a suspected SARS case. All the passengers plus anyone they had been in close contact with over the previous five days had to go for immediate screening. And he meant immediate. The six of us, plus Tom and his wife (whom we had not hitherto met) were whisked off to the

The Potala Palace, Lhasa, Tibet, as it appears (impossibly) in many official guidebooks.

Left: The Potala in reality with its huge parade ground in the foreground.

Below: The Roof of the World.

Lhasa Friendly Hospital, a misnomer that one, for temperature checks, blood tests, questioning and x-rays. Fifteen minutes you might think. How wrong can you be? For the best part of three hours we were to remain largely outside the hospital buildings in masks and hair caps, looking for all the world like the forlorn runners-up in a Thora Hird look alike competition. Patience gave way to amusement, despair and anger as the hospital drives, corridors and dirty, cold rooms were spattered with what I presume was disinfectant from an insecticide spray, and while a dozen or more doctors, nurses and paramedics played some officious looking version of Chinese whispers. And things got worse. When eventually the tests were complete, we were summarily informed that we were all to be placed in quarantine in the hospital for ten days observation.

Pandemonium ensued but to Tom's eternal credit he eventually managed to get our incarceration transferred to the hotel, but not before there had been a stream of phone calls to this authority or that. Why, in China, does no-one ever want to take responsibility themselves? But still we were to be in quarantine and were instructed to phone our temperatures through on a regular basis. So, shortly after 3.00 a.m. we returned to the *Sham Ba La*, cold, miserable, and probably more than a little anxious. At the time, it was difficult to imagine a place one would less like to be than Tibet and we were beginning to think that the one-way tickets to Lhasa issued to us before our departure from Chengdu were more than a little ominous.

The phone rang again early-ish the following morning – our travel agent from Tianjin, who had passed on our whereabouts to the authorities, wanted to know the outcome. He commiserated with us, of course, and following his advice I got straight onto to British Embassy in Beijing. The result, no doubt after a lot of behind the scene activity, was that we were not only allowed to leave Tibet that same day, but that we had to go. Hasty packing ensued and, after some wearisome delays at the hospital, we headed for Lhasa airport, one hundred or so kilometres away. 'A pity the Embassy had not been able to arrange a police escort,' I thought to myself as we drove at breakneck speed through roadworks, dodging assorted livestock and overtaking slow moving vehicles at every available opportunity.

But to no avail. In the end, and despite all we had gone through, we missed the plane; and that was an odd business if ever there was one. After the event I was to discover that the airline had actually been instructed to delay the flight until we were aboard. No doubt someone, somewhere, had got cold feet. So back to Lhasa we lumbered, thoroughly fed up, only to be told that the *Sham Ba La* was full – there was to be no room at the inn. Believe that one if you will – we certainly didn't – we were beginning to feel like lepers. Tom, of course, put on a brave, professional face and more phone calls ensued, until finally we were put up in another and rather smarter place, the *Da Ji* (which I translate as 'big chicken' – although I have probably got the tones wrong), to prepare ourselves for a re-run the following day. And this time we made it.Never have I been more relieved to be on a plane – doubly so when we were told the Tibetan border was to be officially closed the following day. If nothing else, the whole affair brought home just how reliant you are in life on forces and resources beyond your control. To quote a little bit of Chinese philosophy: 'Men honour what lies within the sphere of their knowledge, but do not realise how dependent they are on what lies beyond it.' How true.

And on that wise note I must leave it for today. Although our departure from Tibet marked only the halfway stage in our holidays, the rest will have to wait until next time. My term is due to finish in early July, after which I'll be returning to the UK after what has been three extraordinary and wonderful years. But, all being well, there'll be one last letter from me sometime in mid June. Watch this space.

CHAPTER 21

Home-time

June 2003　2003年 六月

So here we have it … the final instalment … the last lap. Three years in China and, I believe, twenty-one newsletters. Not a bad record. Three pretty amazing years too, with many highlights, although, inevitably, a number of rather more downbeat experiences as well. In fact, as I contemplate packing up my belongings and shipping them back to England I am feeling just a bit down at the moment. Before I set out, well-meaning friends advised me to give China two years – anything less would be a disservice to myself and to my new country. Now that three years have passed, a different crowd have told me that the reverse culture shock, when you excitedly bring your experiences back home with you, can be much harder than the initial move abroad and, furthermore, that once you've been in China for three years you will never really get it out of your system again. Oh dear. I wonder what I am in for? Will people be muttering behind my back 'Ah well, he's been abroad you know!' in an effort to account for my social inadequacies?

Sadly, it is inevitable that SARS has clouded my last few months here, and not just as a result of my unfortunate experiences in Tibet. You will be reassured to know, however, that despite the highly publicised civet cat connection over the origins of the disease, this has not necessitated any alteration in my personal eating habits. Although the news has possibly resulted in many a Cantonese changing his diet, I have never come across this particular delicacy in the north. Dog and horse are fairly standard menu items of course, but cats, rats, bats and suchlike are strictly southern specialities I'm pleased to say. On a more solemn note though, while all my western friends seemed to have taken the presence of SARS in their stride –

adopting reasonable health precautions, wearing face masks for a while (until we heard that they were more likely to harbour the virus than offer protection) and keeping our apartments clean and permanently smelling like clinics, the same, alas, cannot be said for a fair number of my Chinese friends who promptly went into panic mode, spreading and over-reacting to scare stories in equal measure.

Although daily temperature checks are still done very seriously at my School, and at most other western-ish establishments too, coming back from Beijing the other day, the bored paramedic at the motorway checkpoint gave us only the most cursory of glances. Good, but really not good at the same time I think. And although, nationally, the Chinese government did/are doing a tolerably efficient job in containing the spread of the disease, it was little short of a miracle that it never really spread into the countryside. Luckily here in Tianjin, there have been no new cases for three or more weeks and so I expect the WHO will take us off the list of undesirable places to visit in a little bit. One of the reasons for China's so-called success story is, of course, that the authorities can still gloss over anything 'undesirable' with little fear of redress. They can also do things that could never be countenanced in the west. At least two of the universities in Tianjin, for example, are actually closed at the moment – not only are outsiders turned away, but the student population cannot leave the campus either. This has been so for over seven weeks now.

Apart from some bizarre restrictions placed on the various entrances to my apartment block, SARS' most significant impact on me personally has simply been the closure of a number of my favourite bars and restaurants and a reduction in travel opportunities. Only last weekend, for example, I received a phone call from my Chinese friend in Chengde to the north east of Beijing suggesting that I did not visit his family before returning to UK. Nothing personal I hope, but, Jerry said, people from Tianjin and Beijing were still not welcome. Hardly surprising when the rural population learned a month or so ago that outsiders possibly exposed to the virus were to be quarantined in their hometown without the locals' consent or knowledge. When the news was leaked, the almost inevitable result was that a number of hospitals, schools and other large buildings in the region were deliberately wrecked to prevent them being used as isolation centres. So much for China's much touted new era of openness. Whether the makeshift roadblocks are still there I don't know, but what almost certainly remains will be the mistrust of outsiders. So I will probably be better off staying at home which is a pity as I would have liked to have gone back to see Jerry's family. I think it is probably true to say that there is a growing mistrust of central government in China at the moment and, if this is the case, the situation won't have been helped by incidents such as this. Perhaps a hitherto largely pliant rural population may just be starting to doubt their government's wooden propaganda machine and whether or not Beijing really has their best interests at heart. That will be interesting.

As a bit of an aside, I gather that the rising waters of the Yangtse River behind the Three Gorges Dam took thousands of people by surprise earlier this month. As the steadily rising reservoir lapped at their fields, villagers apparently rushed to uproot vegetables planted just weeks ago. Although site engineers had posted markers months earlier showing where the high water level would be, in a sign of the confusion surrounding the project, and by sheer force of rural tradition as well no doubt, many planted in fields they had been told were doomed. Clearly some farmers didn't believe the signs and didn't believe what the government said here either.

Despite travel restrictions, I have managed a few short trips, including a wonderful day out by the sea at Cai Jia Pu with friends from the UK. Just under two-hours from Tianjin and surrounded by desolate salt flats, the little village and in particular its crowded pier was a hive of activity. Dozens of ancient fishing boats were moored in the little harbour, and while the day's catch was off-loaded, the ships' crews seemed delighted to have us aboard, and allowed us to wander around and take photographs as though there was no tomorrow. The seafood restaurants too were working flat out, as were a team of fashionably and somewhat inappropriately dressed Chinese photographers with the most expensive looking paraphernalia I have ever seen.

A second short trip took place a few weeks ago. On this occasion, I was supposed to be going camping on the Great Wall with a dozen or so friends only to be turned away about five miles from our destination. This section of the Wall was apparently closed because of SARS, although I can't help but feel the word is now being used as justification for all manner of petty restriction and restraint that go to make China the place I know and, I suppose, love. But all was not lost. We followed a track up a little river valley, argued with the local farmer, and, after two *yuan* per head had been coughed up, camped in the foothills of the mountains to the north west of Beijing. Forget about the giant ants, it was glorious – my first camping experience in China, and one of only a handful of experiences sleeping under the stars.

My last major bit of travelling was shortly after Easter though, when, following our return from Tibet, David, Denise and I set off for JiuZhaiGou in northern Sichuan Province, accompanied by a young lady who can really only be described as the tour guide from hell. She was doing her job, she had the itinerary, and like it or not we were going to adhere to it. Well, of course, we didn't like it, and in retrospect, I am, perhaps, just a little ashamed to say that we made our feelings known – on more than one occasion too. But, in fact she was utterly heedless of our wishes at the best of times and little short of a liability at the worst.

The journey to JiuZhaiGou never promised to be anything more than tiresome, but in the end it actually turned out to be fairly awful. Things started off well enough though as we took the long, winding road that followed the Min River, a tributary of the Yangtse, north from Chengdu, but began to deteriorate when it was apparent that our van was not going to make it. The result was a stop-over in the little town of WenChuan to await the arrival of a replacement vehicle. Still it was pleasantly warm outside as we ate cherries and drank our chrysanthemum tea. If the truth be known it could have been idyllic were it not for the fact that we were sat in the forecourt of the bus depot and were to be subject to a four-hour delay. Seeking to relieve the monotony I wandered off as I had read about the minority Qian women who live in this part of Sichuan, and the charms of their fancy footwear. 'Never accept a gift of brocade slippers from a Qian maiden unless you are sure you want her for life!' I had been warned. Let's just say I wasn't inundated with offers.

The outcome of our prolonged break was that it was some fifteen hours or so after departure before we eventually arrived at our destination. Although beyond WenChuan the scenery became increasingly lovely, not least the architecture – rather less evidence of cement block dreariness here and instead quite a number of beautiful timber-framed stone houses with slate roofs – it has to be said that the Han Chinese aesthetic pervaded even in this remote area, and many of these otherwise lovely buildings were faced with trashy white lavatory tiles. The last four hours of the journey was in complete and utter darkness though, with heavy rain, a small avalanche and more roadworks than I had thought possible thrown in for good measure. And at journey's end – the grim *HuaYuan* Hotel, horrendously over-priced, virtually empty, and the sort of place that sets out to provide you with what they say you want. Our guide's justification that they were not used to western visitors was an understatement if ever there was one. With its erratic plumbing and a chef who had clearly not found his niche in life, it is not a place I long to revisit. Although it had only opened its doors in 2000, it was already in a fairly advanced state of decay, with no sign of the 'luxious musement' facilities so glowingly advertised in their brochure. I was in a bad mood all right, as you might just have guessed, a state of mind not enhanced by the fact that I ripped my bedding as I tried to squeeze in between the sheets and woke up to be offered a breakfast in a dingy, deserted dining room where there was actually nothing I could possibly eat. Even my trusty jar of Marmite was to no avail. Though the hotel boasted a 'generating set' whatever that might be, it seemingly couldn't run to any bread in the kitchen. But the mountains beyond the acre or so of cement rubble that girdled the place looked wonderful.

Indeed, JiuZhaiGou was/is a very, very pretty place – there can be no doubt about that. But, it could also be almost anywhere else in the world. Parts of Scotland, or the Alps, for example. Indeed anywhere where soaring mountain peaks capped in snow, woodland, waterfalls and lakes come together. Undeniably lovely, but apart from the colour of the lakes – the water was a dazzling turquoise – I'd seen it all before. The JiuZhaiGou experience was an extraordinarily sanitised affair too – I even wondered at one point whether they switched off the waterfalls at night. Certainly one or two particularly beautiful cascades had been enhanced by the odd boulder or bit of wood surreptitiously cemented in place, while the water-driven prayer wheels looked just a little too chocolate-boxy to have any genuine spiritual significance. Decking was clearly in vogue as well, as the paths through the woods were on newish wooden walkways – nicely done and affording only the occasional glimpse of some rather less eco-friendly-looking concrete paths underneath. However, the set-up,

Above: Jiuzhaigou, Sichuan Province.

Left: CaiJiaPu near Tianjin

The School Photo, Tianjin.

tasteful though it was, left you with no option but to follow the people in front. Wandering off the beaten track was clearly not something that was encouraged. We were bussed from one beauty spot to another too – again no room for the free thinker – while the opportunity just to sit and gaze was rudely interrupted by alternate blaring music and some inane tour guide commentary. We liked the place well enough, but the Chinese we met absolutely loved it, and in their inimitable noisy way, posed for wish-you-were-here photographs, just possibly wishing too that the shallow veneer such things presented were more real than they possibly were.

Apart from the many travel opportunities and remarkable cultural experiences I have been privileged to enjoy, even ordinary daily life provides so many eccentric riches that I can honestly say the past three years have been second to none. The pupils I teach and my colleagues at school have all been great and, for the most part, stimulating company. I have enjoyed many friendships out of school too and the ordinary man or woman in the street is invariably a real pleasure to meet. The fact that so many friends were able to join me for my birthday boat trip a few weeks ago was really quite touching. Not that everything has been wonderful. The petty bureaucracy and laughable hierarchy of officialdom and officiousness continually

222

grate, as does the almost endemic unhelpfulness of so many of those who are in a position of a little importance and just like to flex their muscles in their sullen and sulky way. But then I sometimes wonder if the very fact their activities assume such proportions in my mind might merely be one of the inescapable side effects of the quality of life I enjoy. For never again am I likely to be able to afford the five-star luxury of such places as the Sheraton with such unerring regularity. Equally though, neither will I have the opportunity to enjoy kebabs, naan bread and 'summer beer' at the plethora of little open air cafes you find in the back streets, and where you can eat and drink your fill for little over one pound. Although the brusqueness in the way tables are set and cleared and bills presented and paid still jars a little, such places are undeniably genuine, with not the slightest hint of gloss or pretence.

But these areas, like so much of traditional China, are destined for demolition, to be replaced by yet more desolate shopping malls, soulless blocks of flats and gated communities – another of the more dismal trends here. The fact that my home for the last three years is also home to the most wonderful cultural and architectural mix is something which seems to go unheeded by the city planners, who are either ignorant or unprincipled or both. Tianjin's street life is disappearing fast as the stall holders and café proprietors are uprooted and, with pitiful compensation, transported to the more distant suburbs where they are presumably just left to pick up the pieces. So much of modern China seems to be mere window dressing in this respect – truth taking a backseat to image. China's leaders may exalt these developments as a sign of the country's high-tech prowess, but hidden behind the glossy hoardings advertising everything from phones to fashionable footwear, the demolition is carried out by brute force, with hammers and pickaxes, while the bricks and other salvaged materials are carried away in tricycle carts or in baskets slung across the backs of donkeys.

It is of course a truism to say that the more you know about something the more aware you are of just how much more there is to know. Well, I think I am probably reaching saturation point. Right now I can just about hold my three years in China in my mind without feeling too overwhelmed by the weight of it all. But if surface cracks are already appearing in the Three Gorges Dam, then perhaps this is a sign. Maybe it really is time to come home.

猴年

THE YEAR OF
THE MONKEY

hou nian

CHAPTER 22

Last Tango in Shenzhen

September 2004 　2004年 九月

When I left China in the summer of last year, one or two friends, possibly knowing me a little better than I knew myself, warned that withdrawal might well set in after a few months back home. Well, having initially dismissed the idea as complete nonsense, I now have to admit that they were, to an extent, right, and as a result this letter comes from Shenzhen in south east China – a city of some seven or eight million, just over the border from Hong Kong.

Shenzhen was, fifteen or twenty years ago, little more than a fishing village, and probably destined to remain a rural backwater if its location had not caught the eye of Deng Xiaoping – China's late, but highly revered leader. Two decades later it is a seething, sprawling metropolis, with BaoAn, the district where I live, at least ninety minutes bus ride away from the city centre. Hardly surprising then that I've only been there the once and, in fact, most Chinese need a special permit to allow them past the NanTou Checkpoint. Shenzhen was China's first special economic zone for free trade and foreign investment, opened by Deng in 1980, not long after he had inherited a country wrecked by the excesses of the Cultural Revolution. Since then, so I am told, reforms have meant that the country as a whole has achieved an economic growth of around 9% a year, while some three hundred million people have been lifted out of poverty. The particularly spectacular development of Shenzhen, now apparently China's richest city, is regarded by many as the jewel in Deng's crown. We shall see.

Although, to date, I have only been to Shenzhen City Centre once, I am a fairly regular visitor to SheKou – a district of Shenzhen where quite a lot of westerners congregate to sample the delights of its two

Irish bars, western supermarkets, stylish international restaurants and of course, the Starbucks coffee shop. It was here that I met up with Robert – a former student of mine from Dorset who is now living in Shenzhen and hoping to make a name for himself as an interior designer – and where I took my first visitor – one of my godsons, Jonny, who arrived fresh from Hanoi, *en route* to Shanghai. Both Robert and Jonny were excellent company, and I am fairly sure I impressed the latter at least with my command of Chinese when I succeeded both in getting him a 'rigidity seat' on the express train from Guangzhou (Canton) to Yichang (on the Yangtse) and, the following day, putting him onto the bus from the busy crossroads outside my school to Guangzhou itself.

Zheigge gonggongquiche qu Guangzhou ma? (Does this bus go to Guangzhou?)

Dui. (Yes)

Zheigge ren shi wode erzi. Ta yao qu Guangzhou huochezhan. Qing bangmang ta. (This person is my son [I couldn't say Godson]. He wants to go to Guangzhou railway station. Please look after him.)

I think Jonny was impressed and I was certainly feeling extremely self-satisfied. It wasn't until a few days later though that I got the e-mail:

'To the godfather... thank you for a really nice couple of days, it was nice to see you, and thanks for the help with the tickets and everything. Just one thing. The bus from the end of the road probably isn't the best way to Guangzhou. Let's just say the driver stopped every five hundred metres, they made me change bus and that I got dropped off way out of the centre... No biggie but it took a long time... had nine minutes before the train left! Ha ha that's what I call doing it by the skin of ya teeth!'

Home, now, for me, is a small, and very shabby ground floor flat with its fair share of tropical insects, in BaoAn Education City – a huge and seriously impressive collection of modern buildings housing upwards of three thousand students from all over Shenzhen and the surrounding area. Because of the sheer scale of things, all board during the week, with the site divided into a number of different schools catering for either different age groups or for different curriculum models. Mine, Shenzhen College of International Education (SCIE), was only one year old, when, for reasons which may or may not become clear later, it was relocated to Education City two months

228

ago, much to the chagrin of one of the other schools here who, I believe, promptly lost the use of some of their premises. However, although I suspect relations are not too good at present, there does seem to be enough space for all, and classrooms are bright and spacious. But there the pluses stop. Mine was completely empty when I arrived – and I mean *completely* – bar a broken overhead projector and a small old fashioned melodica – the sort that I can last remember seeing in the early sixties – a mini keyboard with an unsanitary tube to blow down. And even this I rescued from a dusty corner of the library along with a small glass plaque that reads (in English and Chinese) *'Best Behaved Class'*. I intend hanging this little gem in a suitably prominent position and I may well keep it as a souvenir. Sadly though, there is little sign of the comprehensive order I placed last May ('We have much money to spend, Mr. David') and which would have had me up and running by the end of Day 1. Complete chaos and more than a little disappointment, however, have been partially redeemed by the fact that my colleagues and students are sheer delight. I met Booboo, Pepsi and Loco on my first day – three charming fifteen year olds who were seriously considering signing up for IGCSE music along with their decidedly plump friend whom I was sure called herself 'Ample'. I was wrong – she was/is actually called 'Apple'. Pity. With them, too, came a young man called Zoe. 'It is a strange name for a boy I know. Maybe you can call me Mr. Zee.'

Unlike my school in Tianjin, which was an international school, SCIE is a Chinese school that has developed in a fairly unique way in that it offers the International Baccalaureate Diploma, A-levels and the International (I)GCSE, with tuition in Year 10 upwards almost entirely in English. It will be interesting to see whether it has a long term future in the wake of the so called 'elite' British schools that are setting up in China at the moment. Dulwich College International opened in Shanghai earlier this month, and according to an ex-Tianjin friend of mine who is on the staff there, pupils will wear a formal uniform of shirt, tie and jacket with grey slacks, raising the prospect of blazers and school ties on the Bund for the first time in something over fifty years. Dulwich is also hoping to open schools in Suzhou and Beijing shortly, while one is planned for Shenzhen itself in a year or two. This will be interesting competition. No uniforms here, the students dress very informally and call me by my Christian name.

Left: My music room at School, Shenzhen, Guangdong Province.

Below: My shabby bed-sit at School, Shenzhen, Guangdong Province.

It's probably early days to make any other valid comparisons between my new home and Tianjin (itself an economic development area), but, on the surface, and in BaoAn at least, much is the same. The same tall tenement buildings, those more than a few years old decidedly shabby in appearance, whilst the most recent are garishly lit on the outside contrasting markedly with low wattage steely blue lighting emanating from within. But here in Shenzhen, there are neither the older concession buildings nor much in the way of traditional housing to soften the overall effect. It was these old streets, and particularly those that had escaped being 'restored to their original look' as the Chinese say, that made Tianjin such a fascinating place to wander around. Back street cafes still abound though, and my favourites, so far, are a number of cheap and cheerful little places in the village of XingWei – roughly five minutes away by bus. No trouble if you miss the last bus back either, there is a regular 'patrol' of canny motorcyclists who will, for three or four *yuan* happily whisk you back home. Not for me the curving glass skyscrapers and Corinthian columns that characterise much of downtown Shenzhen. Give me XingWei any day although I must confess I could do without the patriotic slogans that adorn the sides of some of the walls. One, somewhat disturbingly proclaiming, in English, *'Client is God'*, assails the unsuspecting passenger on the 776 bus. One can't help but think that the Chinese have taken the maxim 'The customer is always right' just that bit too far.

At the time of writing I can hear the school tannoy playing soporific music across the campus as it will do for the next couple of hours. It's too hot and humid in the middle of the day so we are all supposed to take a two-hour siesta. ('Lunch and nap time' as it is called on my daily programme.) How lovely to be able to do this to a constant beat and some sugary harmony. Equally appealing are the martial strains at 7.30 a.m. as the children, roughly three and a half thousand of them, do their morning keep fit, or the even louder and fatuously jolly tunes that accompany the kindergarten's morning work out. For some unaccountable reason, they were doing this to What a Friend We Have in Jesus the other day. Although I can rarely escape from the primary school teacher who regularly addresses her class through a reverberating megaphone, I can, by gazing from my office window (I have a designated work space with phone, computer etc. in a fairly pleasant communal office) shake off some of the excesses of twenty-first century China from time to time, and just make out a piece of well-tended topiary that exhorts us to speak English all the time.

Not many people, I suspect, can earn their living whilst having such an adventure, and I county myself very lucky. Education City is certainly a grand place to behold and will, I am sure, prove to be an adventurous place in which to work. The whole set-up is typically Chinese though; grand conceptions – a whole city devoted to schooling with a fleet of huge coaches to take them home and back at the weekends, contrasting sharply with the bungling and bureaucratic nonsense of one's everyday life.

In fact, I had my fare share of Chinese nonsense when I went to collect my shipping from Shenzhen airport a week or so ago. I had three large boxes of stuff, called tea chests but actually made of thickish cardboard, which I had sent on ahead, and which, amazingly, arrived after only two weeks. That my belongings were at the airport was confirmed by written notification from the shipping company, while, to make absolutely sure, one of my Chinese colleagues telephoned to verify that the boxes really had arrived. Take a tip from me though. If ever you have the misfortune to have to collect a package from Chinese Customs, avoid Shenzhen Customs Officer Number 5323800. After being sent from one office to another and then to a third and a fourth before returning to the place from whence we came, I finally encountered this aforementioned individual. A smug, officious piece of work if ever there was one. Yes, he acknowledged that the boxes were in the store but no I couldn't have them because the man with authority to sign the paperwork was at a meeting. How long would this meeting last? I do not know. Roughly. One hour … more? Maybe all day. What is this meeting about? It is confidential. Where is the meeting? In the office. Where is the office? I do not know. What do you mean you do not know? I cannot say. Cannot or will not? It is a very important meeting. Can you show us where the meeting is taking place and maybe we can interrupt. It is not possible. Do you mean to say that I cannot collect my belongings at all today? He is at a meeting. Yes, so you said, but why has not someone else been given the authority to sign on his behalf? Why am I wasting my time? And so it went on. The Chinese frequently have run-ins with petty officials who like to exercise their muscle on those lower down the pecking order, but I wasn't in the mood. Eventually though, through a process of gradual attrition, he was persuaded to make a telephone call on my behalf (I have just enough Chinese to make myself assertive but insufficient to understand the replies when need be) and two armed guards arrived and escorted me to yet another office. They looked about fourteen years old so I wasn't too perturbed. Here some rapid and consequently, unintelligible conversation in Chinese took place and I was sent to a remote warehouse where I found my boxes. Hooray? Not quite. Officer 5323800 decided to have his revenge. I was to open the cartons and let him rifle through my stuff. Fortunately I had made a very detailed inventory back home in England and although I cannot claim to have had the last laugh, I was determined to give as good as I got, as I slowly and very methodically ticked off each item of clothing and each individual book, CD, tape, jar of Marmite or whatever from my packing list. I thought (hoped) he might give up, but no, he allowed me to complete the task before marching off in a peevish fashion. I then went into yet another office where the whole incident appeared to have caused quite a stir. Amidst smiles and laughter, I got my papers stamped and, as my stuff was being taped up, once more returned to Officer 5323800 who by this time was sick of the sight of me but who by now clearly felt he had the authority to countersign. Three hours it took.

Equally shambolic, but considerably less stressful was the 'Welcome to New Teachers' extravaganza that was held in our honour. Apparently 'planned' for weeks, but hastily rearranged from 7.00 p.m. to 4.30 p.m. shortly after lunch, it took place in a huge cavern of a room, rather like an economy class entertainments lounge on a cross-channel ferry, bedecked with disco lights, projectors, karaoke equipment and all the rest. We were captured on camera as we arrived and projected around the room for a few seconds before being welcomed in stereophonic surround sound and asked to take a seat. Well, the place could have sat six hundred easily I should think, but on this occasion there were only two small huddles of people, maybe fifty in all, one exclusively western the other exclusively Chinese. Had I been at the school more than as few days I would have broken the mould, but to my everlasting shame I sat with my English speaking colleagues and sampled one of the nibbles (a pepper and Germolene flavoured boiled sweet – shrink wrapped to keep all the flavour in) before washing the taste away with a glass of warm beer.

The entertainment mainly consisted of karaoke, which the Chinese treat *very* seriously, even if they do sound awful, as indeed Mr. Zhu our deputy president did, and a few lack lustre games the purpose of which I, as a bystander, had not the slightest inkling. The grand finale was to be a fashion show though, and as I had been asked, quite understandably of course, to take part, I was looking forward to it. Well there were no fashions to be seen anywhere. All we did was walk to the centre of the room 'mirroring' our partner, hold hands and walk to the edge of the room where we would re-group and then do it all over again. The Chinese went wild with enthusiasm. We went through the whole rigmarole maybe four or five times without any hint of a let-up in the adulation we received. I simply cannot understand it. Remaining on the dance floor while the karaoke struck up some sort of Latin rhythm, we then made, or at least I made, a feeble attempt to tango with Tina. We have two Tina's on the staff – I alas, drew the short straw. I made to leave and proffered my apologies. 'But David, you cannot go yet. You have not been released!'

Well that just about sums up this, my first instalment of 'Grierson's Bumpy Guide to China (Second Edition)' and you are hereby released you from your reading. I'm off to catch the bus to FuYong where there is a curious little place called the 'Dying Coffee Shop'. I'll report back next time.

CHAPTER 23

Welcome To Dying

November 2004   2004年 十一月

I was so disappointed to hear a few weeks ago that an eagerly antic-
ipated colleague was not going to be joining us after all. When the
School opened in September we were told that this particular gentleman was receiving hospital treatment in Australia and would be
with us after half-term. Well half-term came and went but there was
still no sign; the truth, as it turned out, was that he was looking for
another job and this he evidently found. Thus Aladdin, and yes, that
was his real name, will not be sharing an office with me this year.
What a pity – I was so looking forward to meeting him – and his
mum too. I have long been a devotee of Widow Twankey. Oh yes I
have! A feisty, warm-hearted soul if ever there was one.

Clearly our erstwhile colleague's lesson had to be covered and
thus the head of English scrutinised his department's teaching com-
mitments to see if a bit of re-arrangement might provide a short to
medium term solution. Towards the bottom of his pile of timetables
he came across a blank sheet headed 'Miss Liu'. Strangely, he had not
heard of her before, so set out to investigate. Sure enough she
existed, had a small desk in one of the staff offices, was drawing a
salary but actually had no teaching commitment at all. Curious. On
being asked why, the aforementioned Miss Liu shrugged her shoulders and when being asked, one assumes reasonably politely, to take
on a portion of Aladdin's work she refused point blank and went back
to her book. The situation is not yet resolved, but Miss Liu remains
and, as far as I am aware is just as busy as she was before.

It will not take the astute reader long to have realised that good
organisation/leadership/management, call it what you will, is not
what might be called a strength of the school. Take some of our

235

meetings for example. These are convened so hastily that preparation is rarely possible – although this, of course, might just be deliberate strategy. Bosses over here are far more used to people who placidly turn up rather than contribute to discussion or debate. Furthermore, assuming they had arranged anything to do in the first place (sadly, more often than not, rather unlikely) the Chinese teachers are well used to cancelling any plans they might have at the drop of a hat when someone higher up a chain of command clicks their fingers. This sort of passive acceptance places the western staff in a difficult position. It may be Chinese culture to kowtow in this manner, but it goes very much against the grain for the expatriate teachers, who want to use their expertise to play a part in the overall development of the School, and who use their free time in what seems to me to be a far more productive and lively way than most of the Chinese. While none of us wants to be seen to undermine authority, and while we acknowledge the need to respect the traditions of our host country, there is, I feel, a growing divide between the foreign and the Chinese teaching staff over what might be considered acceptable of which this is merely an example.

A further recent instance of cultural differences in acceptability is over the vexed issue of the school photocopiers. We have just three in our School and none is working at the moment. (Actually, neither are our washing machines, but that's neither here nor there.) The copiers weren't working just before half term either. 'Why' I asked Frances, one of our more switched on administrative staff, 'were the photocopiers not repaired over the half term break?' She seemed almost surprised by the question and proceeded to give me a long diatribe over the need for us all to hold a meeting about it. The meeting is needed, I was told, in order to get the authority to instruct someone to make a phone call to get the service engineer to come in. Frances, of course, does not have the authority to call such a meeting and thus start the ball rolling. People with the power to act are extraordinarily reluctant to let anything go and those without it are fearful of summary dismissal should they act beyond their authority.

Which leads me nicely on to my next observation. One disturbing similarity between Shenzhen and my previous school in Tianjin is the general indifference shown to our Chinese colleagues in particular. Take Martin Zang for example. He was appointed some twelve months ago to look after expatriate affairs – by which I mean visas, work permits, etc. rather than anything of a more licentious nature. True, he wasn't brilliant at his job, but he was certainly more than adequate. While we were still in the UK he was the main source of information about the School, whereas now, and especially for those who speak no Chinese, he is/was an absolute lifeline. Well, I heard yesterday that he had been offered an increased workload and a 15% reduction in salary. The reason? His boss has a 'nephew' or something like that who needs a job, and Martin's position seems to fit the bill. *Guanxi*, the name given to this openly corrupt network of *connections* is rife throughout China, and Shenzhen is clearly no exception. The slippery are just as crafty down south as they are in Beijing. Martin goes on Friday and will be sadly missed. Western staff, it has to be said, are treated with considerably more respect, but even then it appears that our well-being and job satisfaction take second place to stock checks, not that I have resources anyway, signing for things in triplicate and the other minutiae over which the Chinese are truly obsessed.

But, enough of the moans. I am actually in a very positive frame of mind. Life is good, and now that I have my resident's permit, opportunities for travel and for doing more or less what I want present themselves once more.

The first time I celebrated the October Festival was in Tianjin in the autumn of 2000, and I remember getting into a little bit of hot water, confusing, as I did, the Chinese National Day, always on October 1st and celebrating the anniversary of the founding of the Peoples' Republic in 1949, with the much older Moon Festival – a variable feast dependent upon the phases of the moon. This latter was something the Chinese authorities tried to suppress in the Mao years, although, in true Chinese style, it never really disappeared and now seems that it is far more of a celebration than National Day itself. At Festival time it is traditional to offer gifts of moon cakes to one's family and friends, and, as an honoured guest, I have been offered a great many in my time, some nice, some appalling. The ones that look – and taste – a bit like super rich treacle tarts are particularly deceptive – that bit of boiled egg and/or dollop of spicy shrimp paste always comes as a nasty shock. Families also get together to enjoy the full moon with evening picnics, lanterns and a spot of karaoke or whatever. We celebrated with a school concert which was greatly enjoyed by pupils, staff and parents alike. Not too long and with plenty of variety it contained some truly excellent

The Astor Hotel, Tianjin, then and now.

moments – one of my A-level students played the *pipa* (Chinese lute) quite beautifully, most of Year 10 took part in a wonderfully colourful dancing display, while the school choir made its debut to sustained and well-deserved applause.

Despite the jollities, however, there seemed to be a degree of unfairness about the half term holidays which took place a couple of days later. Called 'Golden Week', this is the official state holiday to celebrate National Day rather than the Moon Festival, when schools close, most businesses and factories shut down, and the public transport infrastructure reaches breaking point as folk get together for reunions. Why am I complaining? Well it sounds a nice enough idea until, that is, you read the small print. Golden Week actual reduces down to three less than shiny days – we had to *make up* the other two days by working the following Saturday and Sunday. The Chinese see nothing inherently unfair about being given something with one hand only to have much of it taken away with the other. I'm afraid I do although, of course, I can do absolutely nothing about it. As the 'Warm Notice' in the staff office informed us in its garbled Chinglish: 'With two weekends add on to it (the previous and the following weekend), total day off up to seven days, that is so call golden week. This is to be making up of the three days statutory holiday and four days of weekend. Timetable for Oct. 9 and 10 will follow those for Thursday and Friday.'

Even with the shortness of the holiday, the proximity of Shenzhen airport to my School (a mere ten minutes by motorbike and bus) meant that I was able to take advantage of every minute of it. Needless to say my chosen destination was Tianjin. I decided to do things in a bit of style too and thus I booked into the Astor Hotel, built, as far as I can remember, by a British missionary in the second half of the nineteenth century. Quite an enterprising guy too by all accounts – he used the profits from the hotel to fund his evangelical work. When I was living in Tianjin, the Astor seemed to be one of the very few places appropriately preserving and celebrating the city's heritage. On returning therefore, I was pleased to see new plaques on many of my favourite buildings; at last an acknowledgement of their historic importance. Furthermore, some of the crumbling '60s monstrosities had been demolished to reveal a number of previously hidden gems. As I wandered through the former British Concession along roads once called The Bund, Racecourse Road, Victoria Road, Meadows

Road and the rest, I felt a great sense of nostalgia for the place. Tianjin has a heart, in marked contrast to what, at the moment, I consider to be the soulless sterility of Shenzhen. Not everything was rosy though – the Tianjin Metro remains resolutely shut (despite truly appalling traffic problems – but then Tianjin is not alone here) and the airport has avoided all attempts at a facelift and still looks like something straight out of the Cold War. Some of my favourite eating and drinking haunts have been demolished too. Still, you can't have everything.

Whilst on the subject of eating and drinking, I am becoming a bit of a regular at the Dying Coffee Shop in FuYong – the perfect place for leafing through back numbers of 'Promulgate' magazine. If you can put up with the hammer drill in the kitchen and the variety of TV screens curiously tuned to different stations, you will find that they serve quite a decent pot of coffee. As I normally just pop in for a short while after swimming or a quick shop, for some reason you can never get enough of the aptly named 'Vinda' loo rolls in FuYong, I have not yet tried their menu. But I have come to terms with the flickering computer monitor in the foyer ('Welcome to Dying') so am likely to settle down pretty soon and tuck into a 'fat boiler', maybe sample the 'hot poisons' or try something served 'push aside' style. House specials include the enchanting prospect of 'sweet acerbic short nibs', 'iron club' spaghetti, 'grue cake' and a 'honey and lemon bellywash'.

In addition to my little jaunt to Tianjin, I've been fortunate to be able to manage a few more short trips away including a weekend in Hangzhou, south west of Shanghai, which I last visited a couple of summers ago and where, if I remember rightly, it poured with rain for the duration of our stay. This time though, the weather was perfect. As well as enjoying the pavilions, pagodas, bridges and glorious mountain scenery around the famous West Lake (one of China's oldest tourist blurbs reads: 'In heaven there is paradise, on earth … Hangzhou') I also managed an easy trek along the picturesque 'Nine Creeks and Eighteen Gullies Road' to the village of Longjing – the tea capital of China. There, in a very ordinary little teahouse, a little old lady gazed at me. *'Yingguoren!'* ('Englishman!') she murmured wistfully after I had introduced myself. Not being accustomed to such veneration, I looked around and, amazingly, spotted a picture of our own dear queen sitting in just about the same spot as me. She too, it seemed, was partial to a cup of Longjing *cha*.

The taxi ride to Hangzhou from the airport, and I was well and truly ripped off there – I never learn, takes you through suburbs that looks like some giant Legoland – enormous, brightly coloured detached houses, four or five stories high, made of shiny bricks and complete with turrets and either chromium spires or miniature Eiffel towers. These edifices are the palatial homes of China's *nouveau riche* – and there are a lot of them around – especially in Zhejiang Province. One guy I met told me of a friend of his who had built a replica of the White House about one hundred kilometres from the city at a cost of many million pounds. Even the interiors, he said, were faithful reproductions of the Washington original. Not my taste exactly, but then little of what is 'new' in China is I'm afraid.

Much more to my liking was the little town of AnJi which we passed through on the way to Moganshan, sixty kilometres north of the city – an idyllic mountainous area which was developed as a summer resort by the Europeans living in Shanghai and Hangzhou in the first part of the twentieth century. In AnJi, the road is lined with hundreds of little workshops all selling bamboo or turning out bamboo furniture and other artefacts. The road's central reservation was also a genuine sight for sore eyes – beautifully planted shrubs and plants, tended by a great gang of gardeners that our taxi only narrowly avoided hitting.

Having driven through well tended tea plantations on the lower slopes of Moganshan itself, (one complete with its own graveyard), once we reached the village proper we were free to ramble. Partially hidden in the forests of bamboo with their occasional fir trees, we came across dilapidated yet still impressive colonial style houses built by the rich Brits and others some seventy or eighty years go. Of particular interest was an old chapel (of the Primitive Methodist variety if my understanding of church architecture is anything to go by) that now served as a store room for the local water company, and the former Queen's Hotel, now simply known as 'No.126 Moganshan'. Later converted into a bank before being requisitioned by Mao for his own personal use in the '50s, it now houses a museum dedicated to his glory, but as we had to pay to get in, on top of the hefty entrance fee to the village itself, I gave it a miss.

A fantastic foot massage – why have I waited fifty-four years for one of those, it was absolutely glorious, and 'awaydays' to 'Happy Valley' (a surprisingly well run theme park), DaMeiSha (aka

Shenzhen-on-Sea, which boasts some absolutely enormous coloured 'angels' on the beach that look like something out of a Spielberg film), and White Cloud Mountain in Guangzhou where some of my braver friends enjoyed a spot of bungee jumping while I listened, rapt, to the massed voices of innumerable Chinese as they sang about the insignificance of one blade of grass but how a field of grass can serve as pasture and how fat cattle can bring prosperity (you know the sort of thing – and no prizes for guessing who wrote the words) just about complete the story of my adventures so far. But there'll be many more ahead, of that I'm certain.

So, until next time
Duo duo baozhong (Take care)

CHAPTER 24

An Undiscovered Treasure

December 2004   2004年 十二月

'Shenzhen is an undiscovered treasure for tourists' states the opening sentence in 'Destination Shenzhen' – a magazine I picked up the other day. Well, 'undiscovered' it most certainly is; I have yet to unearth its elusive charms although, an optimist by nature, I shall continue to try. However, for sheer awfulness, there can be few places on earth able to compete with XingWei Lukou, where the concrete road that leads to my school joins National Highway 107. If there is ever a competition to find hell on earth, then this most surely be a front runner in the 'urban hell' category. Five solid, horn-blaring lanes in either direction, plus additional vehicles on the pavements, slip roads, and rutted tracks that have been driven through on the verges. The traffic, which is just about unbroken twenty-four hours a day, consists mainly of gigantic container lorries and long distance coaches plying their way between Shenzhen/Hong Kong and the Chinese interior. Although I rarely choose to linger, getting across the road is always a time consuming exercise, an understatement if ever there was one, and so I frequently find my mind wandering. Just what can possibly be inside all those containers? … look where they're from (Mexico, France, Indonesia, Germany, Felixstowe) … I wonder where they are going now… what sort of lives do these people lead?… why have so few of the truck drivers any road sense? As Susan, one of my friends at School so rightly observes though, this is what modern China is all about. It no longer the country of tank parades in Tian'anmen Square – China's new leaders aim to make China the twenty-first century's superpower by a rather different route. Whether they will succeed of course, nobody knows. One thing is abundantly clear however – this mad dash for growth has

243

resulted in China having sixteen of the world's twenty most polluted cities, (although it has to be said Shenzhen has more greenery per citizen than any other major city in China), a rapidly falling water table, appalling river pollution, extensive desertification and a steady loss of agricultural land.

On a lighter note, Susan also believes that all the hoicking and gobbing that goes on in the vicinity of XingWei Lukou is some sort of religious ritual. But she is new to China and I think she might just be a little misguided here. Her theory is that the road traffic authorities have attached timers to the traffic lights so that the lorry drivers know exactly how long they will be stationary, thus indicating how much time they have to perform their rites. Knowing that Buddhists must carry out ablutions before prayer, she maintains that the amount of 'ablute' coming from the drivers' mouths and nostrils is abundant proof that there is an important Buddhist temple somewhere on National Highway 107. There is probably a flaw in her logic, but she at least is convinced of its veracity, and regards the whole business as an impressive example of China's new religious freedom.

Despite the fact that China's population is still increasing by some ten million a year, a terrifying statistic, here in Guangdong Province the road traffic infrastructure is already close to breaking point – particularly at times of national holidays. The same is true for our water and electricity supplies, TV reception, computers, (I completely lost the first draft of this letter at the end of November) washing machines (oh how I wish Aladdin's mum had joined us earlier in the term), plumbing, you name it. If Shenzhen City is the jewel in China's crown, it is a pity that some of its sparkle hasn't reached the suburbs where any twinkle is more likely to be the result of an erratic power supply, and where you stand less than a 50/50 chance of the internet working at any given moment. I wouldn't mind this at all, of course, if I were teaching in a small rural community, but knowing how Shenzhen's magnificence is proclaimed to the wider world, (I heard it described as China's coolest city the other day) I do find the current situation extraordinarily tiresome if not utterly fraudulent.

If the internet is up and running though, I sometimes make time to peruse the 'Shenzhen Daily' – www.sznews.com/szdaily if you are interested. Although there has been virtually nothing in the press or indeed in any of the Chinese media about the US elections, and I am sure at least one or two people back home will envy me there, among one of the genuinely fascinating stories carried in recent weeks was that of China's last woman proficient in the mysterious *Nushu* tongue, probably the world's only 'official' female-specific language. She died at her home in Hunan Province a month or so ago. Ninety year old Yang Huanyi, who was illiterate in Mandarin Chinese, learned to read and write the language as a little girl. (Nushu characters are apparently made up from four kinds of strokes, including dots, horizontals, verticals and arcs.) Chinese linguists say her death put an end to an age old tradition in which Nushu women shared their innermost feelings with female friends through a set of codes incomprehensible to men. I can remember my sisters devising something similar when I was a little boy although I don't remember if anything was actually put on paper. I must ask. However, the letters, poems and prose Mrs. Yang wrote were written down and have been collected into a book published early this year so this might be the ideal Christmas gift for them.

As if to counter the sad demise of Nushu, one of China's current 'great leaps forward' is for the urban population at least to develop proficiency in the English language. The government aims to have not only those of school age, but the majority of citizens of Beijing, Guangzhou and Shanghai bilingual within a generation. Whilst such an aim might appear quite laudable on the surface, a little reflection has lead me to the conclusion that such an ideal is as unjust as it is unrealistic in that it can only serve to further widen the divide between the east and the west , or, put another way, between the urban rich and the rural poor.

Although objective information is always hard to come by, a surprisingly frank item on China Central Television (CCTV) a few weeks ago reported on the shocking state of some schools in some of the poorer provinces of the rural west where a teacher earns around three hundred *yuan* a month (less than twenty-five pounds) and where parents, even if they can afford to send their children to school, often choose not to do so because of unsafe or even collapsed buildings. What chance do these have of even the most basic education let alone the 'luxury' of being proficient in a foreign tongue I wonder? Yet it is migrant peasant workers from such places that have been the bedrock of the China boom. All the more shameful then that they should be so poorly rewarded for their efforts. What chance do they have of 'bettering themselves' for want of a better expression when even counter staff at the local Starbucks, they call them 'baristas', are required to be fluent in three languages – Mandarin, Cantonese and English? Yet, in the cities, even this life is only for the lucky few.

However hard hitting the television item was, this can only be the tip of the iceberg as CCTV is firmly controlled by the central government. You might hear rumours, for example, of mass civil unrest in Sichuan Province, where up to one hundred thousand already disadvantaged peasants are protesting about the construction of a huge dam which will destroy their livelihoods, but such stories are impossible to verify. CCTV remains strangely silent. For the wider picture, I occasionally turn to the one other English TV channel I can get, but, I am afraid, little of any worth is broadcast on 'Pearl', which comes out of Hong Kong (I found myself half-watching a two hour prime-time documentary called 'Adorable Kittens' the other week – the aural equivalent of comfort eating I suppose), and whilst I enjoy the BBC World Service on my little short wave radio, I can rarely stay tuned in for more than a few minutes at a stretch before the signal gets lost in the ether.

But to return to the drive to improve English, some of the classrooms at my school are doing their bit and now have posters proclaiming 'Let English Come to our Daily Life', 'English is the Bridge to the World' and similar worthy sentiments. And at a less parochial level, the local governments in Shanghai and Beijing have recently stepped up their campaigns to rid the cities of Chinglish by setting up panels of experts. But as one of these so-called experts was more than likely responsible for giving ex-president's Jiang Jemin's blueprint for modern China the utterly daft designation 'The Three Represents', I for one think, hope, their efforts are doomed to failure. Indeed, only next door to the classrooms displaying the admirable posters, one of my colleagues has awarded form prizes to the '6th Optimal Cadre' and the '15th Ascensive Star'. So, long live our 'frog free' days, may the 'Rise in the East the Inside the West Tea the Restaurant' continue to prosper, and may the supermarket shelves continue to sell a certain brand of shampoo the name of which I dare not mention – suffice to say it is clearly intended for the more hirsute woman.

I have often thought that if I could have my time all over again I would like to be a specialist or up-market travel agent. Thus it was

Left: A moment of tranquillity at Xingwei Lukou, Shenzhen, Guangdong Province.

Below: Zhaoqing – picture postcard China, Guangdong Province.

with some enthusiasm that I planned a staff weekend away to Zhaoqing, to the east of Guangzhou, a few weeks ago. Although not as spectacular as some other places I have been to in China, the scenery was still lovely and, most importantly, the air was clean and fresh. Modern Zhaoqing itself was unremarkable, but the old city, contained within partially intact city walls and guarded by the curiously named 'Glamour Looking Tower', was very atmospheric, and I enjoyed wandering around the little streets, watching people relaxing with friends, maybe playing dominoes or mahjong, or simply sleeping in the warm autumn sunshine. These city walls seemed to

Left: Paddy fields near Changsha, Hunan Province.

Below: Enjoying afternoon tea in Changsha, Hunan Province.

enclose a world where time had stood still for several hundred years – KFCs and mobile phones would have seemed as out of place here now as they would have done during the time of the emperors. Not far away from Zhaoqing, at Dinghushan, we also enjoyed a good long walk, actually it was quite a steep climb most of the way. following streams, discovering pools and waterfalls, exploring little paths, and generally living the good life in this unspoilt UNESCO protected area. The highlight of Zhaoqing however were the Seven Star Crags – seven stars that supposedly fell from the sky to form a pattern of mountains resembling the Big Dipper. These limestone peaks, whilst

248

not on the same scale as those in Guilin and Yangshuo closely resemble the pictures you see in Chinese restaurants the world over and can be explored by boat, rickshaw as well as on foot. Needless to say I did all three.

A second break took me to Changsha – about an hour away by air. Shenzhen Airport is, incidentally, a very civilized place, despite its rather shady sounding 'publice area' – which at best sounds as if you would be lucky to escape from it without picking up some nasty condition. Although I had travelled through this city before – on the long train ride between Beijing and Yunnan Province in the far south of China – I had not had the opportunity of exploring. Its chief claim to fame is its proximity to the birthplace of Chairman Mao, and, in fact, the huge statue of him in the city centre is one of only two I have seen in China. Not that this was a particular attraction for me. My two highlights were just about as far away from that as you could possibly get. The first was a wonderful (if enormously expensive) museum housing the mummified remains of the Han Dynasty 'Marquess of Dai' who lived around two thousand years ago. I have only recently been aware that mummies existed outside ancient Egypt and it was with considerable fascination that I was able to look around the exhibits which included a huge triple sarcophagus – two delicate and richly decorated inner caskets with an outer one (which was about the size of one of the container lorries on the aforementioned National Highway 107) looking as if it could withstand just about anything. As well as the mummy itself, the sarcophagus, and the usual collection of artefacts, silks, shoes and the like, the marquess's internal organs were all on display in a series of grisly bell jars. Such was the state of the preservation that forensic scientists were able to ascertain that the poor soul was suffering from TB, bilharzia, gallstones and arteriosclerosis and that her last meal was a few slices of watermelon.

My last meal (in Changsha that is) was just as simple. At the outset, I had mentioned to my host that it was the old China I liked, and thus, on the Sunday afternoon, he took me to a very rural area about one hour's drive from the city centre. After chatting to a few locals in a café, sitting around a little table with a built-in charcoal stove and a thick blanket-cum-tablecloth on our laps – very cosy, we set off, on foot, down a small track that led us to a single storey cottage belonging to a pig farmer and his wife. Here, sitting around

an open fire on a baked earth floor, no fireplace, I was offered betel-
nuts, boiled peanuts and green tea, and found myself feeling considerably more relaxed and 'at home' than I would have done if we had
gone to yet another glitzy, expensive restaurant. Not that I would
want to live there all the time of course. The rural idyll is fine for an
afternoon but I for one would want a chimney at least – as it was the
smoke just got lost in the rafters. But there was no doubting the
warmth of the welcome I received.

The short flight back to Shenzhen was an interesting experience
but one I don't care to repeat too often. As a result of having perhaps
toasted my friends' good health just once (or maybe twice) too often,
or maybe because beetle nuts contain some mysterious (illegal?) substance, I must have dozed off, for all of a sudden I was startled by a
sudden movement in the aircraft. I opened my eyes and to my horror
saw my fellow passengers with their arms in the air. My heart missed
a beat. I panicked and tried to get to my feet which I only half succeeded in doing, whamming my knee on the seat in front with some
considerable force. As I slumped down again I became aware that the
other passengers' arms were now by their sides, that some were con-
torting their shoulders and that one of the stewardesses was issuing
repetitive commands on the tannoy. Although my Chinese is OK for
everyday situations, I could make no sense of what I assumed were
evacuation instructions. I turned to the person next to me. She was
absorbed in her own preparations. I frantically looked across the
aisle, but again no-one was aware of my predicament. Then people's
heads slumped forwards as though there had been a sudden jolt. I
shot a glance across the aisle once more. No sign of fear – just a passive acceptance of what was to come. I looked at the person next to
me. She smiled sweetly. And then, just as soon as it had all begun,
people were sitting still once more. What I had witnessed so disturbingly was an exercise routine designed to keep the blood flowing.
'Hallelujah for that!' I cheered inwardly, and in doing so was immediately reminded of my dad many years ago who had fallen asleep
during a performance of Handel's 'Messiah' only to be awoken by
people jumping to their feet for the 'Hallelujah Chorus'. Startled, he
too got up in a hurry, and in doing so bashed his knee loudly and
painfully on the seat in front. 'I hope your parents enjoyed the concert,' a friend had said afterwards. 'A pity your dad wasn't well!' It
must run in the family.

Back at School we have just had a plethora of sports days. It was the turn of the senior school this week – two solid days devoted to race after race, event after event with the same four minute quasi Sousa march played throughout, non-stop. I joke not. But don't get me wrong, I enjoyed being out in the warm winter sunshine, shirt sleeves in mid December can't be too bad, although I could not help but feel that with a little more organisation the time could have been cut down considerably. Although some of the younger forms had been practising for days, weeks, months even for their events, (particularly marching around the campus in regimented crocodiles – shades of Tian'anmen Squire I thought) and the frenzied activity of the staff in my communal office (as they made banners, flags, sashes, a giant polystyrene chicken and jolly bits of this and that) resembled a sweat shop, (in the UK of course the pupils would have done all this) the senior school's attitude was just a little bit more laid-back and the majority shambled up rather later than we teachers who had a photo-call at eight o'clock. When eventually staff and students were assembled, all the teachers were issued with regulation baseball caps (I donned mine most reluctantly) and marched onto the sports field to listen to four or five speeches of the healthy body/healthy mind/great country variety. Somewhat incongruous really as race number one was the staff sack race. As the 'Inform' on my desk the previous day told me: 'All staff are require to join in the game where the teachers are divided into four groups then each will run in a gunnysack along a track of 200 metres'. Although I had never heard of a gunnysack before, one of my Chinese friends explained all. 'It is the game of racing in bags. The English often do this'. Maybe we do. I suppose I'd just not thought about it before.

With temperatures around nineteen or twenty degrees Celsius and brilliant blue skies, it hardly seems as though Christmas is just around the corner. But I have been opening the windows of my advent calendar for some time now and rationing myself to one mince pie a day too – I was delighted to be able to find these when I left England in August and they seem to have frozen quite well. We have a carol evening planned for next week and a couple of parties for staff and students too which should be nice, although some of our Chinese teachers cannot really understand the concept of 'Secret Santa' whereby you buy, anonymously, a present for a colleague whose name you have drawn out of a hat. Several male staff have refused point blank to buy a present for another male regarding it as an affront to their manhood, and one even went so far as to suggest that we ought to pin up a notice showing who is buying for whom. Jean, our young biology teacher and mistress of ceremonies for the occasion, is going slowly insane. And as for Christmas itself – well for the first time in my life I shall not be at home with my family. This year, Christmas and New Year will take me to Shanghai, Nanjing, Xi'an and Yangshuo (near Guilin) where I will be meeting up with old friends, rediscovering some familiar places and finding some new ones too I hope. But more of that anon.

252

CHAPTER 25

Merry Christmas! Mr Grillson

January 2005   2005年 一月

Schools in China operate for two semesters a year – September to January (with a short break for the National Holiday in early October) and from a week or so after the Chinese New Year (which this year falls on February 9th) to the end of June/early July with a few days off for May Day celebrations. Long terms for both teachers and pupils. One advantage of being a westerner though is that we can also claim a bit of holiday for Christmas and New Year too, so this year, we lucky ones enjoyed an additional week's break. But more of that later.

Students in Chinese schools traditionally work hard – very hard indeed – and this is due, in part at least, to the effects of the one child policy. Chinese parents also invest very heavily in their children, particularly, perhaps, the generation of parents whose prospects were stolen by the Cultural Revolution. And with only one child to carry the burden of expectation, the pressure on that child to succeed is often very great indeed. In what I think is probably a complete opposite to the position in the UK, educationalists in China are now trying to persuade children to work less hard at their studies. But that's as may be. The children themselves know that their hopes of a better life for themselves and their families depend to a greater or lesser extent on their academic achievements, and in a country where pensions are even more of an uncertainty than they are back home in the UK, the pressure on young people to succeed and, in the future, to look after their aged relatives, for family ties are also very strong in the far east, is considerable.

Consequently, our school days are very long (8.10 a.m. to 4.20 p.m.) with an hour's break for lunch. Activities run from 4.20 to 5.50

p.m. – most students opt for extra study sessions and tutorials rather than more creative or sporty pursuits – and self study is from 7.00 to 9.20 p.m. All the students board, but most go home on Friday afternoons, when lessons finish at 12.10, or more usually 11.25. Although the children put in long hours, the teachers get off very lightly by any standard. There are simply too many of us and Miss Liu, of whom I wrote a month or so ago, is far from being the only one without any perceptible function. Out of a possible forty periods, I have the heaviest teaching load of any member of staff with a mere twenty-two lessons. 'It is too many!' claimed one of my Chinese colleagues who teaches nine or ten lessons a week and spends most of her 'working' day asleep in front of her computer. She evidently doesn't do mornings. The concept of going to work is simple. Turn up in the morning and go back home at night.

A few years ago, when I was in Tianjin, I had to look really quite hard for any of the familiar trappings of Christmas. Few decorations, no carols anywhere, absolutely no frenzied spending spree, and very much a 'business as usual' attitude from the average man or woman in the street. All this made Christmas shopping in 'Ancient Culture Street' a real pleasure. Furthermore, my returns to the UK just before Christmas Eve were, I am sure, all the better for it; I experienced none of the jadedness that overtakes most people beyond their early teens at this time. This year though, in Shenzhen, things were very different; for a start, I wasn't going home. But this apart, Christmas paraphernalia was everywhere, endless carols and pseudo-carols were pumped out from countless tannoy systems, shop attendants wore little Santa hats, while market stalls sold trees, tinsel, spray snow, and everything else you can imagine (although, strangely, no wrapping paper). It was mostly pretty garish too – nothing like the wonderful stuff I saw at the Christmas Market in Salzburg a few years ago. The usual greeting 'Hello, you speak English?' was extended to 'Hello, you speak English? Merry Craze-mass!' How apt.

At school, a very jolly entertainment was organised by the students just before the holiday. Now I used the term 'organised' in its loosest sense, for although there was degree of structure about it, there was also a pervading shambolicness about it too. It must be said that organisation is not really a strength of the majority of Chinese I have come across, and this was manifest in the performance. Some items, of course, were excellent, and as is the case with schools the world over, one or two students really held the show together. Kevin the MC for the evening, for example, spoke effort-lessly in English and Chinese and also accompanied the final singer on the piano with a real sense of showmanship. A pity that much of the effect was lost in the blizzard of artificial snow that suddenly erupted from hidden canisters all around the room. So violent was the snowstorm in fact that several members of the audience left screaming which seemed to be the signal for most of the rest of the assembled throng to take part in a mass exodus lest they should be in the firing line for the next burst. Not even at the Edinburgh Festival have I witnessed so many clamouring for the doors. Other items were equally odd – a Christmas show with a aggressive display of *tae kwondo* was a first for me (and I reckon I've been to more Christmas concerts of one sort or another than anyone else I know), Lan (a rather large and rather idle A-level student of mine) proved he was an expert at that weapon that consists of two bits of wood joined together with a bit of chain – I'm inclined to mark his mock exams generously next term just in case …while Flora sang 'Chestnuts Roasting On An Open Fire' at least an octave higher than anyone else I've ever heard. So spectacular was her singing that Santa, who made a, presumably, scheduled appearance during the piano interlude, was moved to throw his sweets into the audience over-arm. Amazing that no-one was hospitalised. My barbershop group told me that they had slightly altered the version of 'Rudolf the Red-nosed Reindeer' that I had so painstakingly rehearsed with them but omitted to explain they'd turned it into a rap with a bit of break dancing thrown in, while the school's 'Westlife' look-alikes never really lived up to their earlier promise and failed to synchronise with either the pitch or the tempo of the backing track I had done for them. 'Is it like a Christmas concert back in England?' I was asked at the end, as I was rubbing spray snow out of my eyes whilst trying to ensure that the two elec-tric pianos borrowed from the music room (on the eighth floor of a building several hundred yards distant) really were going to be returned before the students went to bed. 'No, not really' I was bound to reply. 'What was different?' 'Hard to say, just like that' I answered. 'But it was a great evening. Honestly, it was!'

Slightly more traditionally, we also held a carol evening around the Christmas tree. With KFCs and Pepsi Cola instead of mulled wine and mince pies, it may not have been quite authentic but it was much appreciated all the same. I particularly enjoyed seeing a group of staff and students singing lustily about peace on earth, a Jew and a Moslem sharing a carol sheet, Buddhists and Christians standing side by side, and those of no fixed abode joining in with just as much gusto as the rest. It was very moving – and if this camaraderie is something that international schools can help bring about, then let's have a few more of them.

The short Christmas break which followed took me and a couple of friends, Dennis and Jim, on a whirlwind tour of Shanghai for Christmas itself, and thence to Nanjing, Xi'an and Yangshuo, near Guilin for New Year. Three of the places I was visiting for the second or even third time, but Nanjing was new to me. Spending Christmas away from my family and my home for the first time in my life was strange, but the company was good and Christmas Day itself, if lacking a little in spirituality, was a gastronomic treat. Lunch was at the rooftop restaurant of the Shanghai Art Museum which was formerly the British Racecourse Club, whilst our evening meal was at a very up market Renaissance Hotel. 'Merry Christmas! Mr. Grillson' read the name card on our table for Christmas dinner. Although we may not have 'danced trippingly' on that particular evening, we certainly enjoyed our 'delicious dainties' as we relaxed to the sweet sounds of a very beautiful Chinese girl playing the violin. That she should have been dressed as Santa Claus with a red fur-trimmed miniskirt was just one of those Chinese idiosyncrasies I have come to accept without question and indeed often love.

Shanghai is China's biggest city and of course it would be nonsense to say that I know it well. However I do know of lots of things to do and I was, I like to think, Dennis and Jim's perfect tour guide. Although we didn't make it to the factory recently discovered by a friend of mine where they still make shoes for women with bound feet, our few days there were action packed if nothing else. From the hi tech *maglev* magnetic train at the airport, four hundred and thirty kilometres an hour, or the amazing Jin Mao Building overlooking The Bund, where we enjoyed a very nice bottle of Chilean red wine from 'Cloud Nine Bar' on the eighty-something floor, to the *shikumen* (traditional Chinese housing) some of which has been tastefully restored and transformed into stylish restaurants and boutiques for the rich Shanghainese, we enjoyed some of the best things in life that the city could offer. The prosperity that the media project to the outside world was at our feet – all lovely, true, but all providing an even starker contrast between China's haves and have-nots than is comfortable at Christmas time. Put kindly, one could simply say that the Chinese government hasn't yet worked out how to extract money from the newly thriving businesses and to put it into the system for the general good. More cynically, my feeling is that China, one of the most unequal societies in the world, is one where the ordinary citizen never will have a voice against petty tyranny and official corruption, and that the government never will succeed in doing what it should. Incidentally, it was over the holiday period that I read that China's one hundred richest men increased their personal fortunes by 25% over the previous twelve months while an additional eight hundred thousand people had joined those living on incomes below the poverty line. There is clearly something wrong somewhere.

Nanjing, the former capital of China, and about four hours by train from Shanghai, is an attractive and prosperous city and made for a most satisfying couple of days. Tina, one of my colleagues from school was from the city and she gave us a small itinerary of 'must sees'. One such place was *XuanWu Hu* – a pleasant park and lake in the centre and just the place to walk off some of the excesses of the previous weekend. Although it was very cold, our discomfort must have been as nothing compared with the young bride and groom waiting for their winter wedding photographs. The Chinese attach great importance to the wedding albums and in order to get things just right, these pictures are frequently taken several weeks, months maybe, before the actual event. Well, this young bride was obviously perishing cold – and not just because she was hugging her anorak and snuggling up to her husband/husband-to-be. An icy wind was blowing too, snow was in the air, and her flimsy wedding dress can have done little to protect her. I asked, in my best Chinese, if I could take her photograph. She was delighted and began to take the anorak off. I stopped her as quickly as I could. No! I said – the anorak was just perfect. It made her look very, very beautiful. I don't think she quite understood my sense of humour. I also think the cold might have affected our brains, as, mistaking it for a taxi, we flagged down a passing police car and almost climbed in to get back to our hotel.

The anniversary of the Nanking (as it was then called) Massacre last month received a little coverage on CCTV but not as much as I would have expected as the Chinese remain openly incensed at

Japan's lack of apology for what has since been called 'The Rape of Nanking', when, in 1937, the invading force slaughtered three hundred thousand men, women and children in the city. There is, of course, a permanent memorial and exhibition commemorating this atrocity but I am afraid I lacked the guts to go, preferring instead to visit the mausoleum built to Sun Yat-Sen. This huge edifice, constructed in the mid twenties, was built to honour the man whom both the communists and the Taiwanese nationalists regard as their founding father. We explored on foot – a pity that 'Dr Suny Af-Sen's Marsoleum Sightseeing Couch' was not operating. I like to think that 'marsoleum' rhymes with 'linoleum' by the way – it has a certain ring to it.

Impressive though it was, it was not quite on the scale of the mausoleum near Xi'an dedicated to Emperor Qin Shi Huang and to the famous army of terracotta soldiers nearby. The warriors themselves need no further description from me of course – fantastic, marvellous, incredible ... are all adjectives that really fail to do justice to what has been dubbed the eighth wonder of the world. But what sort of man was this first Qin emperor who lived two thousand years or so ago? Do the ever-so-sweet strains of the alto sax playing 'I'd rather be a sparrow than a snail' on the summit of the mausoleum provide a clue? Probably not. Instead, perhaps the knowledge that those of his three thousand concubines who had not given birth were buried alive with him, or that the workforce who built the mausoleum were all executed so as to preserve the secret of its whereabouts might give you more of an inkling as to his nature. One reads that wealth and riches as well as more utilitarian objects were buried with their owners so as to provide the necessities of a comfortable time in the afterlife. I'm not sure I would fancy reaching the Chinese equivalent of the Pearly Gates facing a mob of concubines and goodness knows how many thousands/tens of thousands of ex-workers.

For me, the highlights of the exhibition are not the warriors themselves but two exquisite half-size bronze chariots each drawn by a team of four bronze horses. A further seventy such chariots are believed to be still buried in the sixty-five square kilometre site by the way. Why were they built half size I asked? Our knowledgeable Chinese guide explained that the ancient Chinese believed that their souls shrunk to half-size after death. Perhaps Emperor Qin was banking on being able to sneak away unseen. Qin Shi Huang was apparently Chairman Mao's 'favourite' emperor by the way and it's perhaps not too hard to see why. Both were unifiers; it was Qin Shi Huang, in fact, who first established China as one nation and brought to an end the so called 'warring states' period. But at what cost? I warm to neither man.

Our final destination was Yangshuo, surely one of the most beautiful places on earth. Although this was my third visit I was still astonished by the extraordinary loveliness of the scenery. It's an easy place for a westerner too. The hotel was comfortable (we stayed at the aptly named 'Paradise Resort' rather than the 'Internationalised Human Living Villa') and, as I believe, the town boasts more English speakers per head of population than even Beijing or Shanghai, it was easy to get around and do what we wanted to do. On the look out for something excitingly different for New Year's Eve, I was drawn by the somewhat incongruous sounds of what I can only describe as Chino-Jewish *klezmer* music being played on an electric violin by a very odd eastern-European looking guy outside one of the bars. The perfect destination I thought. Good klezmer, I was once told, demands that one dance, so maybe I would be dancing the New Year in. That would be a first. In the end, though, I remained glued to my seat – perhaps it wasn't such good klezmer after all.

Getting back from our whistlestop tour, I was surprised how cold Shenzhen had become. Still dry though; a mere 1.1 milimetres of rain since October 1st. Not only did I have to don my jumper for the first time, but I was also forced to spend some of my hard-earned money on an electric fire for my little flat. But whilst I might be snug and warm at home, at school we freeze. There is no heating anywhere – offices or classrooms. Staff teach in coats and pupils sit huddled in hats and scarves. As I write, Frances, one of our administrative staff, is typing slightly clumsily with mittens on. Nights are cold too which makes eating in the little restaurants in XingWei rather less fun than they were before, and rather than lingering over my beer and noodles and indulging in a spot of people watching, I dash back home as soon as I have finished. I've been tempted to risk the school canteen from time to time, but literally don't have the stomach for much of what is on offer. It was goose heads and tofu again last week and I doubt whether one can ever have enough of either 'Old Friend' or 'Vinda' loo roll to cope with a helping of that.

Back home, although I watch DVDs from time to time, broadcast films on TV are virtually impossible because of the frequency of the advertisements. Alongside such puerile inanities as the one for chewing gum 'Just how wild can candy get?' or my own particular '*bete noire*', the vacuous woman who simpers over her pillowcases and takes what is surely an unfeasible delight in the action of press studs ('I am a fashion conscious girl and I like a duvet cover for all seasons ...') the rest are almost all for beauty products – skin whiteners, freckle removers, endless hair products (I suppose I'm just jealous – I have virtually no need for these anymore), anti-ageing creams, and goodness knows what else. Hardly surprising therefore that China should have hosted the world's first 'Miss Plastic Surgery' competition, reported on CCTV by one Anita Lim – a highly appropriate name I thought, especially when shortened to A. Lim. 'China will soon host the finals of the country's first beauty contest in which every contestant has gone under the knife' announced Ms Lim a few weeks ago. 'I want to convey a message to society – that the pursuit of beauty is ageless,' added sixty-two year-old Liu Yulan, the oldest contestant who turned to plastic surgery to smooth facial wrinkles and fill out her drawn cheeks. I switched off.

The Year of the Rooster will soon be here as will David and Denise, a couple of friends from UK who will be spending the Chinese New Year holidays with me for what will be their third visit to the PRC. Yet more travelling in store for us all. I am also greatly looking forward to the arrival of Jane Gibson, another good friend from home who will be joining the teaching staff at my School for a few months which is very exciting for all concerned. Less exciting, and, in fact, the cause for some unease, is that we heard a few weeks ago that the school's financial backers have had a bit of a bust up with each other and that at least one of the parties have withdrawn their financial support, throwing the school's management into even more chaos than it was before, and believe you me I am working in a mighty chaotic institution. There are rumours that the School will move, some of my friends believe this to be a good thing although personally I am not convinced, and that we will possibly/probably amalgamate with an already established Chinese school in central Shenzhen. It's all in the melting pot. Of course one thing is certain, and that is that our contracts will have become invalid overnight. Put in a nutshell, it seems that here, in China, a contract is with an individual person rather than any institution he/she might represent and if the two part company for any reason, neither the individual nor the organization accept any responsibility and as a result you are left in limbo. A gross oversimplification, true, but the outcome is inevitable. Personally I am not too worried – at least I *had* a contract initially which gives me a little clout which I suppose is something to be grateful for. My Chinese colleagues were not so fortunate. '*You yige haoda jiaqi*' they wish me. Have a good holiday. I will I know – and I hope they do too.

鸡年

THE YEAR OF
THE ROOSTER

ji nian

CHAPTER 26

A Tale of Two Systems

March 2005   2005年 三月

A few weeks ago I remember writing that my School's financial backers had had a bit of a bust up. This, in fact, proved to be rather an understatement, and behind the scenes, there has clearly been little short of out-and-out war between the various parties involved in the School's monetary affairs. It has been a bit of a dirty war too, driven, to some extent, by greed and ego, in which the single most important thing has at times been forgotten – the pupils' education. It's about time that someone somewhere had a discreet word with a couple of these shysters – education is hardly the most honourable venture to go into if your motive is quick profit.

To cut a long story short, we were informed that the School was moving some four working days before the Chinese New Year holiday. New premises had been found with an already established Chinese school in central Shenzhen and it was to be all systems go. Fortunately, with the help of Alison, one of our Chinese admin staff, most of us found new apartments on the Sunday, I taught my final classes at the old BaoAn campus on the Monday and Tuesday, packed up my classroom and apartment on Tuesday night, one advantage of having so few resources was that this task at least was easy, and left with the lorry on the Wednesday morning. On a personal level, it was very straight forward – I only found out very much later than Alison herself had spent so much time helping the foreign staff that she had no time to find a place herself. She is still commuting to her aunt's house each day – some ninety minutes each way.

Although plain sailing for me, educationally, I fear, the move has been a bit of a shambles, particularly as many students along with a couple of the teaching staff decided to stay put. Despite our best efforts, the inevitable result was that both here and on the old campus, several classes are/were without teachers – not a particularly satisfactory situation to find yourself in when you are in the final term of your IGCSE or A-level courses. In my own case, almost half my students were left behind, and I now have a mere ten or twelve classes a week. I can almost hear some of my UK teacher friends calling me a 'jammy so-and-so' or more likely something a bit stronger, but I'm actually feeling more than a little uncomfortable about the whole thing.

To add to our problems, there is also some doubt as to whether our new host school really wants us on their site. True there are/were lots of empty rooms and spare items of equipment and suchlike, but when you are used to a lot of space as well as doing things your own way, to find yourself having to accommodate others is tough for all concerned. Still, co-existence, comfortable or otherwise, seems to be a hallmark of much of what is happening in China today. Hong Kong and Macau have been embraced by the mainland under the slogan 'One China, Two Systems' for several years now, and if the PRC gets its way, Taiwan will follow in the not too distant future. A curious slogan really, for if one compares the impoverished west with the developed east one quickly comes to the conclusion that the slogan should more properly read 'Two Chinas, Two Systems' – one China for the urban elite and one for the masses. Even more irreverently though, if one spends more than ten minutes with any form of Chinese officialdom one becomes aware that it should be 'Two Chinas, No Systems Whatsoever'.

Several friends have commented on the mounting cynicism in my letters and I suppose I am aware of this. Much as I enjoy being over here, I am increasingly aware that I will never manage to do more than scratch the surface of the culture and society in which I have chosen to spend most of the past few years. What were, hitherto, charming idiosyncracies are now turning into irritations which in turn are slowly growing into annoyances. Whereas once I could laugh at the petty bureaucracy I now become angry at just the thought of it. But rather like a promising relationship that has passed its infatuation stage, I'm still hopeful that a firm and lasting friendship will remain at the end of the day.

As I write, it is proving to be a real pleasure to have an old friend from Dorset on our teaching staff. I have enjoyed helping Jane get

My new apartment, Shenzhen, Guangdong Province.

her bearings, although this didn't take very long at all, and she already knows far more about the immediate locality than I do. Give her a map and she'll sort out your bus journey or best walking route in the twinkling of an eye. Our new School is fortunately very conveniently situated for shopping and Shenzhen's leisure facilities, and although the airport is no longer on my doorstep, the railway station is only a short bus trip away, while for those who feel so inclined, Hong Kong is within spitting distance. My new apartment, too, is lovely by any standards, but especially when compared with the dank little box I was obliged to call home before. Views over the city, spectacular at night, with Shenzhen Reservoir in the middle distance and views of Hong Kong on the horizon make for a very pleasant outlook indeed, and once I've sorted out my tiny balcony and got rid of the surplus junk left behind by the previous tenant, things will definitely be looking up.

The only insoluble drawback would seem to be the noise of the traffic, which is solid twenty-four hours a day, seven days a week. Being so close to the Hong Kong border I suppose this is only to be expected, and I am sure I will get used to it before too long. However, it would appear that a fair percentage of China's growing export of manufactured goods passes my door daily. And the returning container lorries are far from empty either. I learned only the other day that Britain alone sends fifteen thousand tonnes of waste plastic to the PRC for reprocessing into raw materials for manufactured products. Furthermore, China pays so well for this raw material that local authorities back home now have a viable economic product from their household plastic recycling schemes. So it seems that everyone is a winner. Well perhaps not quite everyone – I have yet to get a really good night's sleep.

I had only been 'in residence' for a couple of days though, hardly time to get truly acclimatised, before the arrival of a couple of friends from the UK (old China hands – this was David and Denise's third visit) and another whirlwind tour. This time our itinerary took us to Lijiang and Guangzhou before my friends flew up north to Harbin for the annual ice festival and I went back to my old stamping ground, Tianjin, for a few days. We met up again in Shanghai from whence my friends left for Hong Kong and I returned to Shenzhen. As ever, it was an exhausting itinerary but great fun. And, as ever, although there were spectacular sites galore, it was the little things that made the trip so memorable; the tiny girls feeding each other sticky rice with their chopsticks, the carts driven by ingenious Heath Robinson-inspired engines, crammed with people, or livestock or, more often than not, a mixture of the two, the charcoal engine pulverizing the dried chilies, the farmer walking his pig on a leash, the van with a sofa on its roof-rack, complete with occupants … There was certainly no shortage of experiences to delight the eye. The food too; the delicious sliced ginger, the chewy twigs that tasted like raisins, the regional specialty with its texture of long dead, dark grey jellyfish, the durian fruit that stank to high heaven … And all this was on the first day.

I had been to Lijiang once before, with one of my sisters and her family, so I knew that my friends would be well and truly captivated; the Old Town is quite exquisite both in terms of architecture and location – lying as it does at the foot of the poetically named 'Jade Dragon Snow Mountain'. However, this time it was the excursions from Lijiang itself that proved to be the highlights – and in particular our minibus trip to the First Bend on the Yangtse, where the mighty river, the colour of Chinese jade, does a complete U-turn, and Tiger Leaping Gorge where even with the water level at only ten per cent, the sheer power of the river was breathtaking. And if the little diversion to Lashi Wildlife Park on the way home was a disappointment (had it passed its best or was it yet to peak, who knows?) this was more than compensated for by the magnificence of the natural scenery *en route*. With Lijiang County one side of the Yangtse and Shangri-La on the other, as the little town of Zhongdian is now officially known, the area was close to my idea of paradise.

The First Bend on the Yangtse, Yunnan Province. Original painting by Carmen Lee.

The first time I visited Lijiang I was doubtful as to the authenticity of the place. It was almost too good to be true – from the beautiful girl washing her long dark hair in the stream – did she do it on the hour every hour? to the funeral procession along the main street – did this take place at 3.30 p.m. every afternoon? And as for the quaint wicker panniers carried by men and women alike or the old ladies in their charming blue and white Naxi dresses – how much of this was real and how much was laid on? Were we visitors to little more than a live-in theme park? Well, although I am still not certain about Lijiang itself, in the nearby villages I am sure things are quite genuine. The funeral procession we drove past – the men of the village cheerfully carrying the coffin with its huge floral tribute along the road, leaving the grieving women in the village itself – was completely authentic. And if the traditional dresses and wicker baskets were not quite so pristine, being much worn and well patched, they were eminently practical, as likely to contain a fat hen as a small child, and undoubtedly the real McCoy. The daily markets

269

Above: Denise enjoys a spot of shopping in Lijiang, Yunnan Province.

Left: Tiger Leaping Gorge, Yangtse River, Yunnan Province.

we saw also did a roaring trade – even in China I have rarely seen so many people crammed into such small spaces; the only way to get through was to keep close behind the most heavily laden baskets being carried by the oldest, frailest looking members of the community. These people have the knack of parting the crowds in much the same way as Moses had of parting the waves.

Whether or not the traditional way of life can withstand China's phenomenal rate of progress without being artificially preserved remains to be seen however – already new roads are in place (how else did we manage to get to Tiger Leaping Gorge and back in a day?) and already the signs of crude commercialisation are sprouting up – the 'Shangri-La Health Resort' only just beyond its foundations stage in late February is probably doing a roaring trade already. But there is hope too. The local Dongba language, which Beijing tried for so long to eradicate, is being taught in Lijiang's schools once more, which I hope guarantees at least some future for its script as well – the world's only extant hieroglyphic language. And devotees of Michael Palin will be pleased to hear that Dr. Ho is alive and well and still holding his regular surgeries in the nearby village of BaiSha. At eighty plus he is just as lively as he was when I first saw him three or four years ago. His special tea may not be to everyone's taste, but I drink some at least once a week and feel none the worse for it.

We celebrated the start of the Year of the Rooster in Guangzhou on board a boat in the Pearl River. Although we had expected a fabulous show of fireworks the night before, which would have been New Year's Eve, we were sadly disappointed by the total lack of anything celebratory – a feeling only made worse by the TV news which showed what fun there was to be had downstream in Hong Kong. True, Guangzhou was overflowing with giant roosters – many powered by electricity, some made of paper others of fur fabric, some tasteful, others startling but most just a bit too cutesy for my taste – but there were no signs of real merriment anywhere. The following morning we witnessed a rather lame Dragon Dance too in a vast restaurant-cum-supermarket so had rather given up on the idea of seeing the New Year in with any sort of style when, by chance, we heard that there was going to be a firework extravaganza that very evening. We immediately headed for a pier on the banks of the river where I, entirely in Chinese I might add, booked a boat plus meal, established the cost and time of departure and ascertained that there

would be no karaoke on board. You quickly learn the absolute necessity of establishing this last fact. The result was thirty minutes or so
of quite the most spectacular fireworks I have ever seen. And of
course, not only was our view uninterrupted, but we got double the
spectacle as the whole show was reflected in the water. It was very
slick and quite wonderful.

After it was over, our boat joined a convoy of similar craft making
their way through the floating debris back to the jetty. In true
Chinese style though, the details of disembarkation had not been
thought through and we witnessed quite a heated exchange between
the boat crew and the jetty officials before we were allowed off the
pier. We had visions of spending the night there which in retrospect
might have been interesting as we had a bird's eye view of what
seemed like the entire population of Guangzhou crossing the bridge
in order to get home. Hundreds upon hundreds of soldiers were mar-
shalling the vast crowds as we squeezed past and made our way back
to our hotel. This latter was located on Shamian Island – an area
colonised by the Europeans at the start of the twentieth century.
Walking down the leafy streets and surveying the crumbling concession buildings which have been rescued in the nick of time, one
could easily imagine one was in Paris or the genteel quarter of some
other European city. I have earmarked the area as a definite retreat
when I am having a 'bad chopsticks day'.

One of the more interesting places I have visited in China has
undoubtedly been the old village of Daqitou, about ninety minutes by
bus from Guangzhou. As with the chance remark letting us know
about the firework display, the very existence of Daqitou would have
remained unknown to us were it not for a fascinating article I came
across in the free magazine I picked up in a local branch of
Starbucks. Such magazines in China are not generally known for
their erudition, Chinglish normally prevails, but this article was so
well and so enthusiastically written that my friends and I were determined to discover the place for ourselves. So it was that the three of
us found ourselves first battling against the crowds at Guangzhou
Central Bus Station and then, some forty-five minutes later, providing the main attraction on Local Boneshaker Number 13 from
Sanshui Bus Depot. The journey itself was as uninspiring as any in
this neck of the woods, and having passed through Nanbian and
Leping, two singularly grubby little towns, we were not expecting too

*Daqitou near
Guangzhou (Canton),
Guangdong Province.*

much. But just how wrong can you be? As the bus turned a corner, an ugly building moved aside to reveal a cluster of strange hump-backed buildings sitting all forlorn amongst the wasteland, maize fields and duck farms. We had found the lost village of Daqitou – not exactly lost of course, and if not really ancient, it was only built in the late 1890s, certainly old enough to provide us with a glimpse of Guangdong's past.

The person responsible for its construction was one Zheng Shao Zhong – a military commander during the Qing dynasty, and a favourite of the infamous Empress Dowager Cixi. When he retired from the army, the Empress gave him a handsome gratuity, large enough to construct homes for the families of all the Zhengs in the area. Zheng's military mark is still very much in evidence too, for Daqitou is laid out with military precision, the two hundred houses

273

in the central complex standing solemnly in strict ranks. In addition to a number of features to help in its defence, further characteristics were incorporated to protect against Guangdong's notorious climate; narrow passageways and a sea of roofs would have provided ample shade while the whole compound was built on a slight incline to prevent flooding in even the worst summer downpours.

Although virtually all the houses were empty, there were still signs of recent activity. Probably because of the proximity of the Chinese New Year, several rooms contained the remains of candles or incense sticks which had been placed in front of formal portrait photographs presumably of the ancestors. Furthermore, almost all the houses had an eerie 'Marie Celeste' or maybe 'Flannan Isle' sort of feeling about them – the odd pot and pan left on the draining board, piles of crockery, even a tear-off calendar bearing the date 13th January 1992. Some had gracefully crumbling altars too or maybe sturdy staircases while, in others, beautifully carved if somewhat tattered wooden doors and beds lurked in the darkness, silently recalling Daqitou's past. It is, of course, tempting to ascribe a ghostly explanation to the disappearance of Daqitou's residents, but the truth is, alas, rather more mundane. The crumbling houses were deemed unsuitable for modern living and the entire community was rehoused just down the road by the provincial government. The former residents, it would appear, now return only to pay their respects to the dead and so Daqitou's old houses exist in a fascinating state of limbo; not exactly alive, but not dead either.

Our holiday together finished in Shanghai, fast becoming a real home from home for me and my various travelling companions. Unfortunately the weather was grim this time, but this did not cramp our style. On the plus side we enjoyed our awayday, courtesy of China Railways, to Suzhou and two of its many gardens although some other places we visited were a disappointment. On the recommendation of one of our guidebooks for example, we decided to take a trip to *Xiangyang Market* close to the old French concession area. Never again. Gone were the market stalls – instead the whole place was a warren of bland retail outlets some even displaying the notice 'no bargaining'. How un-Chinese can you get? Fortunately though, things were better nearby, for whilst, generally speaking, Shanghai's old alleys or *shikumen* are being demolished, many remain, and in one gap between the downpours we enjoyed getting lost in a maze of

Left: The Bund in Shanghai is just as busy as it ever was. The Chinese character on the side of the boat 'ji' means skill. Perhaps it could be more appropriately applied to the cyclist.

Below: Pudong viewed from The Bund, Shanghai.

275

Enjoying a bit of ballroom dancing on a street corner in down town Shanghai.

them. Although ramshackle, these alleys are completely beguiling. I was specially taken with all the paraphernalia hanging out of literally every window (usually a combination of meat, mops and birds in cages with, invariably, one or more pairs of giant knickers as a bonus) and by one particular house which was almost completely hidden by shrubs and potted plants. The owner, a man well into his eighties I should imagine, was clearly pleased with his horticultural skills and needed no cajoling to pose benignly beside his kitchen door which he surreptitiously opened allowing us a glimpse of the botanical miracles within.

I cannot finish this letter without at least some mention of the late Zhao Ziyang who died in January this year. 'Who?' I hear you ask, for it appears we westerners have as short a memory as the Chinese. Zhao was in fact a former Premier and General Secretary of the Communist party, and it was he who tried, and failed, to prevent the massacre in Tian'anmen Square in June 1989. In so doing, he condemned himself to years of political and social oblivion, living under virtual house arrest in Beijing in a small *hutong* style house, reportedly guarded around the clock and shut from the outside world with a bicycle lock. John Gittings' obituary column in the 'Guardian

276

The old French Concession, Shanghai.

Weekly' puts the events surrounding Tian'anmen Square in a nutshell: 'In April 1989 ... the party newspaper the 'People's Daily' condemned the student (pro-democracy) movement as a 'planned
conspiracy'. That inflammatory editorial brought more students into
the square, paralysing Beijing. Zhao argued, unsuccessfully, that the
editorial should be withdrawn, and proposed to visit the square, but
was voted down. ... He withdrew from office, while his arch rival Li
Peng prepared to declare martial law. Only then did Zhao defy internal party discipline and make his pilgrimage to the students. When
he appeared at last ... his first words were a confession of failure: 'I
am sorry I have come too late.' He urged the students to stop their
hunger strike, saying that the government would talk with them (a
commitment he no longer was qualified to make) 'we all used to be
young' he said. ... Zhao's apology, sincerity and tears moved the
students, but also told them that he was politically finished. Honesty
was only possible when it was irrelevant. Zhao was dismissed from
all posts in the Communist party, accused of having committed serious political errors by supporting the turmoil. Party diehards wanted
to see him put on trial. Instead he was prohibited from public utter-
ance.' The rest, as they say, is history.

Unsurprisingly, news of Zhao's death was minimal, for, in China, the Party still gives the orders and strives to ensure a monopoly over the reporting and recording of events. It was given a brief mention on Hong Kong TV, but I heard nothing on CCTV 9 (mainland China's English broadcasting channel) and, although one could apparently read a few terse lines buried on the inside pages of a handful of newspapers, there has, as far as I know, been no official recognition of the life and work of one of the most important Chinese leaders of the post Mao years. Things may yet change of course, and it may well be that the past is re-written (it often is) to include a politically acceptable version of his contribution to modern China, but we will have to wait and see.

Alas, this being a Chinese school, we have no Easter holiday ahead of us so it will be business as usual until our short mid-term break in early May. However, the fact that I will be at work for much of the time has not deterred Kate, another of my intrepid UK friends, from joining me for a couple of weeks' holiday. Actually, the fact that I will be at School was possibly a bonus – I must ask. Needless to say I'm looking forward to her arrival very much and will, of course, report back on our adventures next time.

CHAPTER 27

Go West Young Han or Along the Old Silk Road

May 2005   2005年 五月

Several friends, possibly just a little concerned, have written to let me know that China's troubled relationship with Japan has been making international news of late. I gather Shenzhen itself got a bit of a mention too, when the recent wave of anti-Japanese sentiment swept the country. Mostly expressed in the form of protests and a bit of petty vandalism, the unrest was, I'm pretty sure, encouraged if not actually orchestrated by the government here or in Beijing. What the actual trigger was is not terribly clear though. Maybe it was the newly published Japanese history book describing the murder of three hundred thousand civilians in Nanjing in the 1930s as an 'incident', or perhaps the repeated whitewashing of the atrocities carried out at the Germ Warfare Experimental Base in Harbin during the Second World War. Others argue it was more likely Japan's recently announced plans for oil and natural gas exploration off the coast of some disputed islands in the East China Sea, or President Koizumi's regular visits to Japan's National Cemetery which honours (amongst others) several Class A war criminals, or even a strategy to prevent Japan getting a permanent seat on the UN Security Council. All these, no doubt, have had some part to play, although it is widely believed amongst my friends that the real reason is rather more to do with a more general but definitely growing political restlessness. Put simply, I suspect what we saw in Shenzhen and in some of the other big cities too, was the young Chinese being encouraged to deflect their current frustration with Beijing onto Japan and in so doing express a little nationalism – always a winning sentiment over here.

279

By releasing the valve on the pressure cooker just a little, the government will be hoping to have allowed sufficient steam to escape to enable them to keep a nice tight lid on things back home.

In Shenzhen, most of the action was centred on the large and very up-market 'Jusco' store where I usually do my weekend shopping. Mainly Japanese owned, it is definitely a cut above most of the local Chinese shops, and one can buy butter, a limited variety of cheese, decent bread, jam (no Marmite though) and even a few different sorts of breakfast cereal – all items that are hard to get in the average Chinese supermarket. Shopping there is a remarkably pleasant experience too, and these days I barely notice the aroma of the ripe durian fruit as I wander the aisles in search of this and that. Some forty thousand people, mainly in their twenties, gathered there a few weekends ago, according to Patrick, one of my American friends, who went to see what was happening. With a massive police presence just to make sure the crowd didn't overstep the mark, it was, I believe, the largest such gathering in China. There was a bit of bottle slinging (plastic I hasten to add) – bottled water is an absolute necessity rather than a fashion accessory over here so there was no shortage of ammunition – and a few Japanese cars were kicked; but while there was a fair bit of banner waving and chanting, it was the covering of a huge 'Panasonic' advertising hording with a tarpaulin that caused the most frenzied excitement. In reality, the internet headline I read: 'Chinese Boom City Descends into Anti-Japanese Fury' seems just slightly excessive.

Despite these recent events, my overriding experience of China is that it is a remarkably placid and trouble free place to be. True, I did have my wallet nicked earlier this year, but so far as I can remember, this has been the only incident of an 'unlawful' nature that I have encountered in almost four years. Yet Shenzhen in particular gets such a bad press. 'Take care, David! It is dangerous! Do not go out alone!' I was advised by well-meaning Chinese friends before I left, while some longstanding western friends of mine, visiting Hong Kong as music examiners a month or so ago, were actually warned by the examinations board about crossing over into the mainland to visit me. Shenzhen clearly isn't doing a very good job on its public relations front.

Returning to the business with Japan though, whilst there are strong, indeed strengthening, economic ties between the two countries, politically one is aware that Japan and China are barely on speaking terms. Apart from talks in third countries, I gather that China's and Japan's leaders have not met since 1999. Without the 'lubricant of multi-lateral diplomacy', as I have heard it so eloquently described, it is little wonder that the region has more than its fair share of long-standing tensions: between Japan and China, between China and Taiwan, between the Chinese mainland and Hong Kong, and between North Korea and just about everyone else. The present climate of silence, sulking and suspicion is, in part at least, due to the face-saving culture that is so much a part of every life here, and no doubt much of the rest of south east Asia too, where saving face is far more important than resolving issues. On the surface, internally as well as internationally, everything is proclaimed to be hunky dory, a reflection and confirmation of government policy. Beneath the gloss though, it is painfully obvious that all is not as it should be. Rather than address niggles before they become confrontational issues though, it is customary to pretend that problems simply don't exist or, if they do, that they will somehow just go away. I suppose it might be human nature to act as though things are better, or in some circumstances worse, than they really are, but in China, one becomes increasingly aware that one is living in almost total fantasy.

At much the same time as the anti-Japanese troubles at 'Jusco', Jane and I got embroiled in our own little international incident at nearby ZhongYing Street. Otherwise known as 'China-England Street', this is easily the most unique of Hong Kong and Shenzhen's border crossings. Located in the east of Shenzhen, and *en route* to the seaside, the street boasts access to Hong Kong on one side and the Chinese mainland on the other – the two sides separated by stone markers placed there at the end of the nineteenth century. Well, despite our residence permits, foreign experts certificates, multiple entry work visas and British passports we failed to get so much as a glimpse. Armed border control guards with many stripes on their sleeves, in their mid-teens too, so they were obviously fast-trackers, made it abundantly clear that we did not have the necessary documentation – although quite what this constituted was less well explained. In true British style we stood our ground and argued in very broken Chinese for a good twenty minutes, building up quite a crowd of sightseers and a lengthy tailback of would-be visitors too, but it was clearly a losing battle from the word go as no-one had the authority to do anything.

If our attempt to explore ZhongYing Street was a failure though, the same afternoon was a spectacular triumph, succeeding, as we did, to get to another of Shenzhen's few historic sites. Dapeng Fortress was built over 600 years ago and is a fine example of a Ming Dynasty (1368 – 1644) military encampment that has not only weathered foreign invasion and two dynastic changes more or less intact, but, most impressively, has somehow escaped the ravages of the zealous Red Guards during the Cultural Revolution. According to my invaluable copy of 'Destination Shenzhen', the fortress was built to resist Japanese pirates who had been harassing the southern coastal areas of Guangdong Province. Although I knew there had been no love lost between the Chinese and the Japanese for many a day, clearly Japan and China's troubled relationship has gone on for a very long time indeed.

Weekends have been really quite eventful recently, for as well as wining and dining, shopping and sightseeing, I've also been to a couple of excellent concerts. The first of these was held in the aptly named 'Shenzhen Children's Palace'. Palatial it certainly was and gratifying too to see the place nearly full with an extraordinarily large number of young people. Not a mobile phone in sight either – Shenzhen is clearly a far more cultured place than Tianjin, where not only would the audience answer their mobiles during a performance, but would actually make phone calls too. Not that all was peace and tranquility – the man in the seat behind me with acute symptoms of goodness knows what provided the obligatory background noise for the authentic Chinese experience of Mahler's over-long Fourth Symphony. Maybe he should have stayed at home with his TV set and some 'Fisherman's Friends'. He could have watched the latest episode of 'Sex and the City', discreetly beamed in from Hong Kong, whilst rejoicing in the bizarre knowledge that it was actually being sponsored by his chosen medication.

I'm also getting quite adventurous when it comes to eating out. Risking condemnation from my Chinese friends, I went to my first Japanese *sushi* restaurant the other week, while one of the concert evenings was delightfully rounded off with *dim sum* – the traditional fare for either a slap-up breakfast or late night snack here in southern China. Looking back on it I must be turning native too, for just

Cards in Dapeng near Shenzhen, Guangdong Province.

as the Chinese make no distinction between sweet and savoury, I
found myself almost alternating mouthfuls of shrimp dumpling,
durian fruit, steamed sweet doughnuts and chickens feet. Actually I
lie – I let Carmen, one of my Chinese friends, chew on these last dainties and I made do with a couple of extra spring rolls. Talking of
which, I got just a little confused the other weekend whilst trying to
request a window seat on the short flight between Xiamen and
Wuyishan, and instead of asking for a *chuang hu* (window) I asked
for a *chuan juan* (spring roll) instead. An easy mistake to make I'm
sure you'll agree. The intriguing outcome though was that we got neither and instead the two of us were placed several rows apart – something I couldn't have asked for even if I had wanted to.

The flight in question took place over the short Easter holiday
when, somewhat divisively I thought, the school's western staff were
given a long weekend. But as I had a friend from England staying
with me for a couple of weeks, rather than make a stand, I cast my
principles to the wind and took advantage of the extra day to do a bit
of travelling together. Our destination was Xiamen and the delightful
Gulangyu Island – an area developed by the Europeans at the start of

Left: An old gateway on Gulangyu Island, Xiamen, Fujian Province.

Below: Wuyishan, Fujian Province.

the twentieth century. It still retains a lot of its faded charm although I was surprised and saddened to see just how many of the old villas and mansions had been allowed to decay – the vast majority in fact. Those that have not been rescued are, I fear, already past the point of no return. Some were accessible by clambouring over the remains of formal gardens which had degenerated into waste ground, but others could only be glimpsed through huge, well-rusted ornamental gates which framed views of what had clearly been splendid houses in days gone by. I had hoped our hotel might have been a converted mansion but instead it was a new and surprisingly tastefully designed villa-style complex, close to the beach, with its various rooms and suites linked by long passageways and staircases. After a few drinks though, and with signs only in Chinese, it became very confusing; it seemed as if the architect had been inspired by Harry Potter's 'Hogwarts', where the staircases and landings shift position from time to time. And if the footsteps and sounds of riotous living that punctuated the night were anything to go by, clearly something very odd if not actually magical was taking place outside our bedroom door that first evening. All the more curious considering our room was at the end of the corridor.

Saturday dawned bright and fair though, and with the sun glinting on the waves, we decided to shun the electric buggies that whisked people around the island's ring road and go for a morning stroll. People, as ever, seemed so friendly and pleased to see us – especially the group of young nurses who begged us to pose with them for photos and gave us little pennant flags by way of saying thankyou. It was only afterwards, over a couple of aged 'Magnum' bars that we realised we had become walking advertisements for the outpatients department of the local hospital, the 'Gulangyu Frantic Clinic', situated on the remote northernmost tip of the island. Whether or not the nurses thought we were likely clients, or why the clinic chose to advertise itself with flags are two mysteries that will, I fear, remain for all time. One possible patient though, a handsome young man, was lying on the beach close by – looking for all the world as though he had been washed up by the tide. Maybe the nurses were part of a search party. Kate was particularly concerned and extraordinarily anxious to leap off the promenade and attempt some resuscitation. Being a little older I warned her against such a dramatic action although we did have a good look to see if he was still there on our return trip. He wasn't – which was possibly a good sign – unless, of course, the nurses had simply whisked him off.

Following the aforementioned evening flight to Wuyishan, and having negotiated airport security ('Have No to Hand Over the Movement the Lee the Cabinet') and the eclectically stocked gift shop, precious few souvenirs unless one fancied a ten-foot high golden eagle carved in solid mahogany, we stayed in another spectacularly located hotel – this one surrounded by subtropical forest and built right at the foot of the Wuyi Mountains. Eschewing the idea of a walk the following day – the rain was persistent and we would have got drenched – we opted instead for a taxi ride to some of the more scenic spots. A bit unfortunate as it turned out – not only did the mist prevent us from getting the full panoramic spectacle, but the fact that thy taxi had blacked out windows further limited our view. But what we did see was magnificent and, in particular, our lazy ninety-minute boat trip, bamboo raft trip to be more precise, along the Nine Bends River, skippered by a delightfully rotund round-the-world rafts-woman, was an unforgettable experience. The rain had eased off a little by then too, and there were photo opportunities galore. Strange that our companions on the boat, Taiwanese I think, were more interested in photographing Kate and me (well Kate to be more precise) than they were the surrounding mountains. 'You are very much woman!' she was confidentially informed by one admirer. Alongside the general spectacle of the landscape, one of the more curious sights were the ancient Yue coffins which we managed to glimpse although we didn't really get much of an opportunity to look at carefully. Some four thousand years ago, members of one of China's ethnic minorities, the Yue people, placed their dead in wooden coffins positioned in niches high above the river, where they were left to dry in the wind. That there were, until fairly recent times, many more coffins than there are today is due to the fact that a certain and one assumes/hopes obscure, branch of Chinese medicine believes that an infusion of coffin wood is highly efficacious.

For what is likely to be one of my last bits of more extended travelling in China, Jane and Dennis, two of my western colleagues, and I went to Xinjiang Province in the far north west for nine days in the early part of May. We were due for another of those bizarre Chinese holidays where one is promised a week, but in fact is expected to work for part of the weekend either side to compensate for the

Wuyishan, Fujian Province. Original painting by Carmen Lee.

privilege. Fortunately though we had got our flight tickets before being advised of this (we were flying out on the Friday afternoon, and notification of the weekend working arrived on the Tuesday) so needless to say we excused ourselves with a clear conscience. As if in retribution though, our flight was nine hours late. If ever I have felt that China was grinding to a halt then this was it, and the airport poster advertising some product or other under the slogan 'All is Charming' did little to placate us. When the delayed incoming flight eventually arrived, six hours late, we built up our hopes only to have them dashed when we discovered that forty or so angry passengers were refusing to budge from the aircraft and were demanding compensation. I have spoken about the lack of systems for dealing with even the most mundane of matters on many occasions before, and here before us was just the sort of example I wasn't looking for. No-one at the airport knew what to do. Or more accurately, no-one at the airport had the authority to do anything – especially not at nine o'clock at night on the eve of a national holiday. By 11.20 p.m.

things were getting fractious to say the least, and our complimentary bottles of water did little to relieve the tension. I was fast losing interest/patience/sanity when, all of a sudden, the boarding light was switched on and there followed the customary stampede for seats. We were in the air shortly after midnight, given an oversized gherkin and sweet bread roll to keep us quiet, very prettily packaged in pink boxes with little white snowflakes dotted on them I might add, and eventually touched down in Urumqi at 5.00 a.m. in the morning – an hour when I am afraid I am not at my best. Strange to think that the distance between two points in the same country is more or less equal to the distance between London and Nigeria or Saudi Arabia. And strange, too, to rub my eyes and see Jeanne Peloquin before me, a Canadian friend from my Tianjin days. In a country of more than 1.3 billion people, the odds against meeting someone you know are, I suspect, pretty remote. She too was spending her May holiday in Xinjiang, and it was with real delight we teamed up for a few days.

If Urumqi itself, or Wulumuqi as the Chinese call it, is rather less exotic than its name might suggest, few places on this earth can surely equal two thousand year old Kashgar, one of the towns on the Imperial Silk Road, some thousand miles to the west, where we were to spend the first part of the holiday. With its glorious location between the Taklamakan Desert and the foothills of the Karakoram (we didn't notice the mountains until the third day though, when a small sandstorm left the air crystal clear), fabulous mix of cultures from those curious '...stan' countries you have heard of but cannot quite place on the map, (Kazakhstan, Kyrgyzstan, Tajikistan, Uzbekistan – yes and Afghanistan and Pakistan too) together with the charming Uighur people and a sprinkling (although an ever increasing sprinkling) of Han Chinese, the place has shot up to become my number one destination in China – and that takes some doing I can tell you. Our hotel, formerly the Russian Consulate, was overflowing with eastern promise, the fabulous Sunday Market – the 'mother of all bazaars' as our guide book called it, exceeded even our wildest expectations, our preferred mode of transport, donkey carts, took us to places far off the beaten track, while the food was a real treat for the palate – freshly squeezed pomegranate juice, *shiliuzhi*, became a firm favourite, along with warm naan bread and delicious pyramid-shaped lamb pies – straight from the oven and eaten hot as we walked down the crowded streets.

Above: One of the many carpet emporia, Kashgar, Xinjiang Province.

Left: Kashgar's population take good care of their teeth.

The hospitality we received was generous to a fault too, and nowhere more so than in one of the many carpet shops we visited, where, having bought five or six carpets between the four of us, we were invited not only for a cup of tea, but to share kebabs, pasties, dried fruit … you name it. Lounging on bales of carpet or sitting on the floor, the experience was as far from a lunchtime meal in Dorset, or Shenzhen for that matter, as one could imagine. Breaking bread with our new found friends, and having our cups of tea constantly refilled by our hosts was an extraordinarily moving experience too.

Not that all was so life affirming. I found the posters of Mao, Deng Xiaoping and Jiang Jemin looking patronisingly upon crowds

Left: Not everyone appreciates Uighur music, Kashgar, Xinjiang Province.

Below: No shortage of something good to eat when FengLei does the ordering. Urumqi, Xinjiang Province.

of indigenous people dressed in their national costume particularly obnoxious. The splendid Id Kah Mosque too, provided us with a further reminder that for the majority of the population of Kashgar, this was tantamount to being an occupied land. For it is a sad fact that the steady influx of generally young Han Chinese into these lands of the utmost west has not only changed the look of the place, but also done much to change the traditional way of life too. While a lot of the old city still remains, a great deal more has been destroyed and replaced with huge open squares, totally inappropriate shopping malls, monstrous chromium and glass government buildings and hideous ceramic tiled apartment blocks. At the same time, what local culture remains is either being bulldozed or bubble wrapped for the hordes of visitors who will no doubt visit when Kashgar is high-lighted as a 'must see' in the next edition of the 'Rough Guide' or 'Lonely Planet'. But what brought this 'occupation' into sharp focus was the simple conversation we had with a young Uighur boy just outside the mosque. 'Are you a Muslim?' we asked. 'Of course!' he replied. 'And do you worship in the mosque?' we inquired. His face fell. 'It is not possible,' he said, 'students and government workers are not permitted to do this. We can visit but we cannot pray.'

But the Uighurs are nothing if not tough, and nowhere was this more cleverly and subtly demonstrated than in the way they set their clocks. Despite the vastness of the country, Beijing time is the official time everywhere. Sensible, possibly, but a fact the Uighurs simply choose to ignore. They operate their own unofficial Xinjiang time – some two hours later than Beijing time and far more in keep-ing with the position of the sun in the sky. We changed our watches then and there.

Whilst my friends chose to return to Urumqi by plane, I opted for the 16.49 'Eastern Orient Express' which runs on a recently opened single track line and follows the northern Silk Road for much of the way. I was looking forward to my twenty-four hours in the relative luxury of a soft berth compartment only to discover that I had been downgraded. In true Chinese style, and with no notice, it transpired that local government officials had requisitioned all the soft berths for themselves – no doubt they too were off to Urumqi for a few days holiday. Hard class wasn't too bad though – after all it was only for one night. An open carriage (no doors) with top, middle and bottom bunks, loud muzak (the Chinese believe that when the noise stops the ghosts come in), endless announcements, no air-con, and lights out at ten o'clock sharp. Not the ideal ingredients for a sound nights sleep perhaps, but I rested well enough and didn't really surface until 8.00 a.m. the following morning.

Although I dozed for a good bit of the way, the journey itself was through some seriously wild terrain. A mere fifteen minutes out of Kashgar and we were travelling through strange weathered forms that could have been the remains of a ruined city but which were more likely the result of temperature change and wind erosion. And although there was clearly a lack of water, where there were lakes and rivers, the desert was lush with vegetation. For me, the only disappointment was missing out on the ruined city of Qiuci, just out-side the oasis of Kuqa, where the train stopped for a short time. But as it was around four in the morning, this will just have to wait for another day.

Back in Urumqi for just one night, we were thrilled to be invited to a traditional Uighur wedding. Tony Hawkins, a friend of ours back home in Dorset, had made close acquaintance with a family from Urumqi some nine or ten years ago, and so it was with some excite-ment that we arranged to meet up with FengLei, her son, parents and young niece for an evening together. They had booked a table for us at the local Uighur restaurant only to discover that most of the rest of the patrons were at a wedding reception. Of course we were invited to join in. And what an evening it was. Course after course – mostly delicious, all just that little bit different, and, Chinese friends please note, all without bones. FengLei herself had made mulberry wine and smuggled a bottle in and several 'gan bei's later we had made peace with the world. And then there was the dancing. After a few truly spectacular professional dances to get the party going, we were up there with the best of them and really getting into the wild rhythms of the Uighur band.

The following day, feeling just the tiniest bit fragile, we made the three hour bus trip to Turpan, a place I had visited before and which I was anxious to introduce to my friends. It was good to go back and explore the Flaming Mountains, Kerez Irrigation Channels, and Grape Valley once more, and in particular to re-visit the ruined city of Jiaohe which for me and a couple of my Tianjin friends, is still one of the most wonderful places in all China. But, I must confess, after Kashgar, Turpan itself seemed just a little ordinary. Perhaps I have been spoilt. Maybe I should have just lived on the memory of that first time, three or four years ago.

CHAPTER 28

Leaving on a Jet Plane

July 2005　2005年 七月

With most students at Shenzhen College of International Education having just finished their exams, this seems as good a time as any to put pen to paper for what will be my last letter from China. Our students have all been working towards their International GCSEs and A-levels and many of the older ones hope to be taking up places at western universities in the autumn. Whether they will or not depends on their final results of course, but most are working hard – some frantically so. A-levels in particular are demanding enough as it is without having to sit them in a foreign language. The run-up to these exams is rather different from what I am used to, with teaching here going on until the very last minute – including quite a few extra classes in the evenings and at weekends. I have mixed feelings about this, but it does seem to be very much the Chinese way. Whereas, in the UK, students will generally have a period of exam leave to consolidate their knowledge and prepare themselves generally – that's the theory anyway – this concept seems alien to both students and most of staff. Quite what our present batch of sixth formers will make of college life in the UK remains to be seen. Time will be far less structured than they are used to; I hope they can use their free time wisely and don't simply fall at the first hurdle.

Whatever happens in the future though, there's no denying that the majority of youngsters here are used to hard work; and used to it from a very early age too. When at least one of them has been doing two hours of piano practice plus one hour of calligraphy a day for the best part of the last ten years, it's hardly surprising that she's good. And I wouldn't care, the student in question isn't even doing music … or art for that matter!

What constitutes *good* teaching in the average Chinese teacher's eyes is well illustrated by Chopin, (pronounced 'choppin') one of my colleagues, who has been doing some photographs for the new SCIE prospectus. He came into one of my lessons a week or so ago and was snapping away as I was coaching individuals and small groups with their instrumental music making – keyboards, pianos, guitars, that sort of thing. It was a productive lesson and I was on very good form. Following an impromptu concert, I was about to call it a day and get the class to clear up when Chopin asked me if he could have some photos of me actually teaching! I knew what he meant of course, but despite what I had been up to, this clearly didn't count as *proper* teaching in his eyes.

But enough of school. To celebrate my birthday early last month, a group of eighteen of us spent the weekend on Shamian Island in nearby Guangzhou – an area colonised by the Europeans in the Victorian era and developed as an imitation of life at home. Sipping a café latte at the 'Darling Coffee Fort', grabbing a quick bite at 'The Village of Gruel' or walking down the leafy streets and surveying the crumbling concession buildings which have been rescued in the nick of time, one could easily imagine one was in the genteel quarter of some great European city. All this of course in marked contrast to the infamous 'Qingping Market', little more than a stone's throw away, and, likely as not, the origin of the saying: 'if you don't eat it some-body else will'. Definitely not for the squeamish that one. Although there were a fair number of westerners on the island, what was particularly noticeable were the large numbers of prams and pushchairs about. For Shamian Island is a base, maybe *the* base, for international adoption. Here, well-heeled western couples, usually American, who want a Chinese child come to do the necessaries. It is, of course, completely above board, the scheme itself managed by the 'China Centre for Adoption Affairs'. With the one-child policy still very much in force, boys are considered to be of greater value, particularly in rural areas, and so, on reflection, perhaps it is not so strange that the vast majority of the children put up for adoption, as many as 95% in fact, are girls. Most of the babies will have been living in orphanages since birth although there are some, no doubt, who will have come from foster homes instead. Generally though, the mother is not known and the unwanted baby is simply left in an area where she knows he/she will be found and taken in. Although

Left: Engaged in some 'proper' teaching, Shenzhen, Guangdong Province.

Below: Students at work. Resources for A-level music were somewhat limited in the early days. Shenzhen, Guangdong Province.

the preparatory work, including, one sincerely hopes, rigorous vetting, takes two or three months, the would-be parents' actual trip to China lasts a mere twelve to fifteen days during which they will visit the region and orphanage from which their prospective child comes before coming to Guangzhou itself to deal with the legalities. They are also required to make a $3,000 orphanage donation and pay $1,200-$1,500 in what are probably euphemistically called 'provincial legal fees'. An interesting business; let us hope it brings happiness to all concerned and that these undeniably beautiful little

Students at play. End of year festivities in Shenzhen, Guangdong Province.

children are not just fashion accessories. My first impressions were decidedly mixed on that count.

While on the subject of fashion accessories, and without wishing to sound too sceptical, I was reading about the 'Make Poverty History' campaign's wristbands on the internet last week. I have not actually seen these things myself, and no doubt many are worn for all the right reasons, but I do wonder how many wearers are aware that the majority of them are made in China – in Shenzhen and surrounding cities in fact – and in conditions that fall far below what can be considered morally acceptable? Shenzhen's 'Ta Xing Rubber Manufacturing Company' for example requires all its employees to provide a deposit against future possible breakages of machinery while in Fuzhou, capital of neigbouring Fujian Province, workers are paid well below the locally agreed minimum wage of 2.39 *yuan* an hour to as low as 1.39 *yuan*. When a medium sized café latte will cost you twenty-two or twenty-three *yuan* (about one pound fifty) then I am left feeling slightly uneasy. Is this an inevitable result of ultra-capitalist economics and unrepresentative communist politics I wonder?

Even so, these workers are arguably luckier than some, and to stay with my old hobby horse of the ever widening gap between the rich and the poor a while longer, I learned, from a surprisingly frank Chinese TV documentary incidentally, that the average income in some rural areas is often as little as one thousand five hundred *yuan* (£100) a year, while in some hilly regions populated by the minority ethnic groups, the situation is often even worse. Although such people are not totally forgotten by the international development agencies – Britain's Department for International Development (DfID) for example is investing fourteen million pounds in a rural education programme in Gansu Province – one longs to see far more in the way of humanity from China's own and growing urban elite. Yet I do not exaggerate when I say that, by and large, those from the wealthy east are not only unwilling but seemingly incapable of facing the reality of the situation. Instead of re-assessing their position maturely and objectively, the preferred choice of action seems to be to cocoon themselves in relative or, in many cases, absolute luxury. With the Chinese economy surging forward at the rate of 9% a year and the government able to afford to send a man into space and host the 2008 Olympics, international aid donors will, I am sure, be finding it increasingly difficult to justify financial support for China. Again I am left wondering if this is another inevitable result of capitalist economics and communist politics. Heaven help the people of rural Gansu if the DfID money dries up.

I have written of the wealth gap many times now, of course, and it is not often that one can laugh at some of the outcomes. But there are occasions and one or two stories in the local papers over the past couple of weeks have raised a few smiles in the staff office here at SCIE. Theft of manhole covers and power lines for scrap for example have apparently become rampant, according to 'China Daily' – the official English language newspaper – one particular cable cutting incident leaving eighty thousand people in the dark. But that was only the beginning. Apparently this particular cable fell onto the motorway below where, according to the papers, the fallen wire was caught on a passing tanker truck which proceeded to pull down seven pylons, brought traffic to a complete halt for nine hours and caused some 1.3 million *yuan* worth of economic loss. Not that such shenanigans are restricted to the less fortunate of course. Over the past few years, employees of the appalling China Construction Bank have syphoned off millions of pounds – branch officers either fleeing overseas with vast amounts of cash or squandering it in Macau's numerous casinos – easily accessible from Shenzhen. (I have had a couple of run-ins with staff at one of the local branches myself so was not at all surprised by this particular story.) Earlier this year, though, the bank apparently disciplined an astonishing forty thousand employees while its chairman resigned following allegations of cor-ruption – with a golden handshake too more than likely. Interestingly, his predecessor was fired and gaoled on identical charges a mere three years earlier.

But onto brighter things. At the end of June, what will amount my last weekend break from Shenzhen took me to rural Hunan Province where I and my young Chinese friends, DuBin and Happy Peach, enjoyed the wonders of the vast Zhangjiajie Mountain Park and the nearby town of Fenghuang – nearby by Chinese standards that is. Despite the massive two hundred and forty-five *yuan* admission charge, plus extras of course – the canny Chinese never miss a trick on that score, the area just inside the entrance gates to the National Park was a solid mass of cacophonous humanity. The area is huge though, and we soon lost most of the crowd, which, in true Chinese style, was almost entirely made up of tour groups, distinguishable from each other only by the colour of their baseball caps. The groups, of course, were each being led by tour guides, complete with megaphones, who were vying with each other as to who could speak loudest and/or with the most reverberation. Although we gave the cable car to the summit a miss and went up on foot, the ride back down on the open-air 'White Dragon Sky Lift' was a first for all of us. This open- air elevator is literally bolted onto the side of one of the mountains – quite extraordinary. Actually we would have missed it were it not for the fact that the free buses that ply the main routes in the scenic area stop at six o'clock sharp leaving unwary visitors to find their own way down. I don't know what I would have done if I had been on my own – there did not seem to be any contingency plans for the stranded Chinaman let alone a bewildered 'big nose'.

Zhangjiajie certainly gave the Chinese authorities the opportunity to indulge in their love affair with concrete (witness the number of half demolished mountains between Guangzhou and Shenzhen if you need proof that China adores the stuff) and I do not exaggerate when I say I must have climbed up and down close to ten thousand

Zhangjiajie, Hunan Province

steps that day. However, this barely detracted from the intoxicating loveliness of the place, the quartz sandstone peaks constantly appearing and dissolving in the mist, and looking, for the most part, like some colossal giant's fingers stretching up to the sky. As with the limestone scenery in Guilin, this is the stuff of Chinese paintings. The only down side was that we never really knew where we were; the Chinese are not great ones for maps. Neither, does it seem, are they particularly adept at manufacturing informative sign posts or plaques. We walked and climbed to literally dozens of viewpoints with fanciful if conjectural names, ('Huangshizhai' like a bride – shy and charming ... 'Monkey Marshall' commanding the soldiers [we totally disagreed as to which peak 'Monkey Marshall' was]... 'Yearning Couple Peak' ... 'Dragon Women Peak' ...) but never once did we see a map showing us the lay of the land or a sign post telling us how far it was to the next spot or, as evening approached, how to get out of the place. I was exhausted by the time we eventually escaped from the labyrinth and got back to our hotel. And although I woke up as right as rain the following day, I could barely move the day after that.

Although we succumbed to the luxuries of a taxi more than once, my Chinese friends preferred to take the bus most of the time, it being considerably cheaper, and inevitably much of the weekend was spent on the road. But as you will know by now, I enjoy travelling and our journeys took us through some of the most glorious scenery I have yet seen. Now I have long since been aware that the Chinese are, for the most part, a noisy lot, but hitherto I had not realised that those from Hunan Province were well ahead in the championship stakes. But who am I to complain? If the teenage girls in the back of one of the buses prevented me from dozing for an entire four-hour journey, I have much to thank them for. Cliches such as soaring peaks, verdant woodland and quaint villages spring aptly to mind to which I must add something along the lines of spangled paddy fields (with their attendant water buffalo and coolie-hatted peasants of course). As someone who was merely passing through, I was well pleased with what I saw, although the poverty beneath the rustic charm was all too obvious.

Somewhere between Zhangjiajie and Fenghuang is the rather drab university town of Jishou. Here we took a little time off from our sight-seeing to meet around a dozen of my friends' classmates who crowded into a small dormitory not only to see me but to be photographed with me as well. 'Enjoy it while you can!' I say; my celebrity status will surely evaporate the moment I take off from Hong Kong. These were lucky Chinese youngsters too, recent graduates, all happy to be with me for an hour or so, and all proud to be showing me their grimy college accommodation which they shared with five or six others. Some had fair English, but most, rather like me, had well rehearsed phrases which they delivered with a greater or lesser degree of nervousness. Few had spoken to a westerner before.

Fenghuang, Phoenix Town, is without doubt one of the loveliest places I have visited in all China – a truly picturesque riverside town yet to be discovered by most western tourists – it's not in my 'Lonely Planet' or 'Rough Guide' that's for certain. Even without publicity though, the tourist tack is slowly encroaching, although, while the

Above and left: Fenghuang (Phoenix Town) – as yet undiscovered by western tourists. Hunan Province

place remains as remote as it does, it may yet be safe for a few years. Apart from simply wandering the narrow, twisting streets lined with overhanging stone and timber houses, one of my most significant moments was joining dozens of other visitors lighting candles in memory of loved ones and placing them in paper lotus blossom boats to float down the river. Without telling my friends the reason, I lit one in memory of my dad whose anniversary occurred a couple of days later, I think it might have been Father's Day too, and placed it in the water with due solemnity only to see it caught by a wayward current and propelled towards the bank. I was initially a bit sad as I had hoped to watch it disappear into the far distance as opposed to see it inaccessibly marooned a couple of yards away. My Chinese friends, sensing my disappointment, were reassuring though and told me not to upset myself, and that, in time, the little lights would all make their own unique journeys towards the same end but that some would reach that end by a rather less conventional route than others. Unbeknownst, they had summed my father up to a T.

Good things cannot last forever though, and for me, Zhangjiajie airport marked the end of the line. The terminal building, what an apt name, with the acoustic perfection of a large gymnasium, was not only infested with mosquitoes, but jam packed with yelling passengers when I arrived for the 22.25 return flight to Shenzhen. Everyone bar me was seemingly on a group tour too, for, judging by the stares, I was almost certainly the only person travelling alone – as well as being the only western face of course. I initially felt quite smug about this and more than a little grateful not to be part of the unfortunately named 'Kolon Tours'. But nonetheless it was bedlam and, with a flight delay of two hours, my self satisfaction quickly evaporated; China Southern Airlines feeble attempt at customer service 'the flight will be delayed because of aircraft delay' did little to satisfy me I can assure you. Eventually I could stand it no longer and after an unfortunately angry rant in broken Chinese managed to persuade one of the airport staff to telephone my waiting taxi in Shenzhen; he was booked for midnight, I would not be landing until 2.00 a.m. and I did not want to be stranded some thirty odd miles from home. It was hardly the attendant's fault I know, but the concept of customer service just doesn't exist in China, and, of course, a humble employee cannot do anything that has not been detailed and authorised by his boss. In the end he used his own mobile phone to make the call and probably avoided a reprimand from his superiors as a result. At least I hope he did. Following on from this though, and much to my relief, he then ushered me into the VIP lounge where I was able to doze in relative comfort. In retrospect, I suspect this was as much to get me out of the way as anything else.

My contract runs out very soon now and many friends and family have asked me whether I'll be back in the future. Who can say? Even if I no longer bat an eyelid at the ranks of jaded school children doing their eye exercises and keep fit to 'Ride of the Valkyries' or Ravel's 'Bolero' (the music fades from one to the other a seemingly random basis), and no longer so much as smile at the 'Coping Log' next to the

Xerox machine, or the motto-cum-mission statement: 'cultivate world-leader quality in sync with the Times' (I still love the capital T though) there is, even after four years, so much that still fascinates and so much that I will miss. Alas, I have probably already received my last e-mail from Frances: 'I have informed the head of drivers to send a bus to pick you up tomorrow. Please inform me of any exceptional circumstances. You might not receive mails as we smile acquiescence on this arrangement.' It's not every day you receive a message as delightful as that.

Some things I won't miss though. My latest *betes noire* (or is it *bete noires*?) are the endlessly repetitive and extraordinarily badly edited adverts and public service announcements on English language TV. Prime offenders amongst these puerile little pieces are those for 'Zoar' skin whitening cream (say the word in as guttural a way as you can and you will have got the pronunciation just about right); surgical procedures to give you a bigger bust (actually this one is hilarious); dengue fever precautions – I just loath the simpering man and wife in this obnoxious bit of drivel; fatuously obvious road safety advice; exhortations to keep the streets clean and not sneeze all over the place (in fact these are two different adverts, but as they follow each other with such unerring regularity they have merged imperceptibly); inane information on being a blood donor; supercilious customer service directives; the one that starts 'There are many sorts of television programmes ...' (which really, really irritates me because I'm sure it is bad grammar); and some obscure guidance on so-called 'serving chopsticks' which I still cannot quite grasp. Most of this lengthy sequence recurs every ten minutes or so and takes almost as long as the programme you are watching. How I am looking forward to the BBC.

Other relatively hum-drum aspects of my daily life will leave a few holes though, as they are unlikely to have their counterparts in North Dorset: the octogenarians doing their keep-fit on the children's playground equipment; the *ad hoc* weekend music making in the parks; the endless parade of grotesque shoes worn by the fashion conscious twenty-somethings; the three guys who regularly take their lunchtime siesta in a conveniently positioned wheelbarrow just outside one of the local noodle shops .... And although I did manage to sneak a quick look at the new show flats on the way to the local supermarket – properties that intriguingly offer the discerning

Fenghuang, Hunan Province. Original painting by Carmen Lee.

would-be owner 'sea and pelican soul', I have, unfortunately, missed out on the opportunity of cruising the aisles of 'B and Q' which has opened nearby, (the Chinese call it *'bai an ju'* which translates literally as the 'one hundred peaceful getting-things-done-place') or of revisiting Qinhuangdao – a nondescript place if I remember rightly, but one which, less than one hundred years ago, used to be known as 'The Cardiff of China'. I wonder if any traces of its past glory remain. Only yesterday, too, I realised that I had forgotten to get my hair cut at 'NOLAS RIAH NOISSEFORP' (work that one out for yourself) or to photograph the nearby 'Auto Hairdressing Nurse'. Ah well – another day perhaps. The latter is a car wash by the way.

To conclude, and lest you should think I am slacking towards the end of term, I should tell you that during the post exam period I have been given the non-too-onerous task of organising a programme of events and so am busy with preparations and rehearsals for an end of term show, assuming I get my own way, karaoke will not, for once, feature on the line-up, and running a fairly light hearted 'culture course' for want of a better expression. The students are lapping it up too. There's no shortage of items for the former whilst the promise of a trip to Pizza Hut for the winning team in the latter has really got their enthusiasm bubbling. We have had drama games galore, and after a brief introduction to British politics, the teams were given the task of presenting a short 'infomercial' for or against the introduction of identity cards in Britain. The results were both hilarious and sharply perceptive. We've had them making pub signs, building bridges, matching artists and art works and finding out about a whole host of cultural icons from Camilla to jammy dodgers which they have been posing as 'statues' or 'photographs'. Great fun – if a little irreverent at times. So SCIE is a busy, happy place at present and although I am very much looking forward to coming home and belonging in the local community once more, I shall be sad to leave.

But in the meantime there is a frenzy of rehearsals to manage, including our newly penned staff song which, with apologies to John Denver, runs:

> So *zai jian* SCIE, it's end of term and I'll be free
> Hold the memories never let them go
> I'm leaving on a jet plane, don't know if I'll be back again
> Oh Shenzhen I must go.

And with that I must go as well.
Zai jian